ORD FOR T EUCHA

AND FOR
MORNING AND EVENING PRAYER
ACCORDING TO THE
ANGLICAN AND ROMAN RITES
2009

With seasonal notes,
information about recent
changes, and guidance from
the Orthodox tradition.

ORDO MISSAE CELEBRANDAE
ET DIVINI OFFICII PERSOLVENDI
PRO ANNO LITURGICO
2008–2009

☐   Roman provisions are given and are clearly distinguished   ☐

☐   where they do not coincide with Anglican usage.   ☐

© Tufton Books 2008
Faith House
7 Tufton Street
London SW1P 3QN

Tufton Books is a publishing imprint of the Church Union

First published in 2008

ISBN 978–1–85311–869–2

ACKNOWLEDGMENTS

The *Revised Common Lectionary* is © the Consultation on Common Texts, 1992 and is reproduced with permission. *The Christian Year: Calendar, Lectionary and Collects* (1997), which includes the Church of England's adapted form of the Revised Common Lectionary (published as the Principal Service Lectionary), the Second and Third Service Lectionaries and the *Common Worship* Calendar, and the Weekday Lectionary are © The Archbishops' Council 2002.

The Calendar and Lectionaries in *The Alternative Service Book 1980* are © The Archbishops' Council 1999; the Daily Eucharistic Lectionary derives, with adaptions, from the *Ordo Lectionum Missae* of the Roman Catholic Church.

The Lectionary authorised by the Convocations in 1961 and the Lectionaries from *Lent, Holy Week and Easter* (1986) and *The Promise of His Glory* are copyright © The Archbishops' Council 1999.

Material from these Lectionaries and Calendars is reproduced with permission.

Typeset by Rowland Phototypesetting Ltd, Bury St Edmunds, Suffolk
Printed in the UK by CPI William Clowes Beccles NR34 7TL

PRAENOTANDA

● PLEASE WRITE TO THE COMPILER with comments, questions, suggestions. (**Note that he has moved.**) He may to be able to supply new propers and other materials mentioned on various pages of the ORDO: but PLEASE say what you need and don't just say 'send everything'. Because of the exigencies resulting from early retirement he must insist on a stamped and addressed envelope and IN ADDITION *at least* one loose FIRST CLASS STAMP. Clergy who desire several items and who have discretionary funds . . .

Fr John Hunwicke SSC, John Coombes House, 28 St Thomas Street, OXFORD OX1 1JL

Visit the Compiler's Blog, 'Father Hunwicke's Liturgical Notes', at
http://liturgicalnotes.blogspot.com

THE FESTUM OF A SAINT ON SUNDAY

may not be observed even on a 'Green' Sunday according to the Roman Rite, unless, being of a patron, it becomes a Solemnity. Festa of Saints on 'Green' Sundays are suppressed by Rome; CW allows them EITHER to displace a 'Green' Sunday OR to be transferred to Monday OR 'at the discretion of the minister, to the next suitable weekday.' This year we also have S Barnabas colliding with Corpus Christi on the Thursday after Trinity Sunday. According to R:, if Corpus Christi is celebrated on the Thursday S Barnabas is suppressed (unless he is patron); if Corpus Christi is transferred to next Sunday, S Barnabas is observed. According to CW, Corpus Christi is observed on Thursday and S Barnabas is transferred to Friday.

Holy Innocents, Martyrs

R	MP	H: 34 (NEH 218)	Gen 37:13–20 or Baruch 4:21–27	◁
		Ps: 36, 146	Mt 18:1–10	◁
	Mass	*Gl; Pref of Christmas*		
		CW: Jer 31:15–17; Ps 124; I Cor 1:26–29; Mt 2:13–18		
		R: I Jn 1:5 – 2:2; Mt 2:13–18		

[EP of the Saints:
Ps 123, 128: Isa 49:14–25
Mk 10:13–16]

According to R:, the Holy Innocents are suppressed this year by Holy Family Sunday. According to CW, the Innocents are observed on the Sunday or transferred to the following Monday.

Conversion of S Paul, Apostle

W	MP	H: 226 vv4 & 6	Ezek 3:22–27	Isa 56:1–8
		Ps: 66, 147:13–21	Phil 3:1–14	Gal 1:11–end (=R:)
	Mass	*of the Saint; Gl; R; Pref of Apostles; CW, of Saints*		
		CW: from Jer 1:4–10; Ps 67; Acts 9:1–22; Gal 1:11–16a; Mt 19:27–30		
		R: Acts 22:3–16 or 9:1–22; Ps 117; Mk 16:15–18		
	EP	H: NEH 154	Ecclus 39:1–10	Jer 1: 4–10
		Ps: 119:41–56	Col 1:24 – 2:7	Phil 3:1–14

S Barnabas, Ap *(R: Memorial)*

R	MP	Ps: 100, 101, 117	Jer 9:23–24	◁
			Acts 4:32–37	◁
	Mass	*(Gl); R: Pref of Apostles, CW, of Saints*		
		CW: Job 29:11–16; Ps 112; Acts 11:19–30; Jn 15:12–17		
		R: Acts 11:21–26 & 13:1–3; Ps 98; Mt 10:7–13		
	EP		Eccles 12:9–14 or Tobit 4:5–11	◁
		Ps: 147	Acts 9:26–31	◁

S Luke, Evangelist

R	MP	Ps: 145, 146	Isa 55	Isa 61:1–6
			Lk 1:1–4	II Tim 3:10–end
	Mass	*Gl; R: Pref of the Apostles; CW, of Saints*		
		CW: Isa 35:3–6 or Acts 16:6–12a; Ps 147:1–7; II Tim 4:5–17; Lk 10:1–9		
		R: II Tim 4:10–17b; Ps 145; Lk 10:1–9		
	EP		Ecclus 38:1–14	Isa 55
		Ps: 103	Col 4:7–18	Col 4:7–end

For the two following festivals, see p. 69.

Visitation of the BVM

W	MP	H: 229	I Sam 2:1–10 [R: Song of S 2:8–14 & 8:6–7]	◁
		Ps: 85, 150	Mk 3:31–35	◁
	Mass	*of the Festival; Gl; R: Pref of the BVM; CW, of the Annunciation*		
		CW: Zeph 3:14–18; Ps 113; Rom 12:9–16; Lk 1:39–49 (50–56)		
		R: Zeph 3:14–18 or Rom 12:9–16b; Ps = Isa 12:2–6; Lk 1:39–56		
	EP		Zech 2:10–13	◁
		Ps: 122, 127, 128	Jn 3:25–30	◁

S Andrew Apostle (Scotland Solemnity)

R	MP	Ps: 47; 147:1–12	Ezek 47:1–12 or Ecclus 14:20–27	◁ or Isa 49:1–9a
			Jn 12:20–32	Jn 1:35–42
	Mass	*Gl; R: Pref of Apostles; CW, of Saints*		
		CW = R: (Isa 52:7–10; Ps 19:1–6); Rom 10: (9–11) 12–18; Mt 4:18–22		
	EP		Zech 8:20–23	Ezek 47:1–12
		Ps: 87, 96	Jn 1:35–42	Jn 12:20–32

STOP PRESS

I see in the bookshops 'Common Worship: Festivals'. Here is a warning:

This volume contains two categories of material:

(1) Material already authorised by General Synod which *you already have* if you possess the basic 'Common Worship' volume.

(2) Material *not* authorised by General Synod, but merely recommended by the bishops for the officiating minister to use under his *own* discretion. This material has *no greater legal standing* than what the minister might compose himself or borrow from elsewhere (e.g. Rome).

HOW TO USE THIS ORDO

FOR EXAMPLE

The Liturgical Colour			Matins and Evensong readings CW			Matins and Evensong readings (1922/1961) for use with BCP
↓			↓	↓	↓	↓ ↓ ↓
MONDAY			Feria (□ S Jane Frances de Chantal, Rel)			
12 P (or W)	MP		Ps: 99, 100 (or 95), 101	Isa 44:24–end		Isa 17
				I Thess 4:13 – 5:11		Mk 4:21–end
	Mass		*of Advent 2; no Gl or Cr; Pref of Advent (1) (or of the Saint)*			
			Isa 35; Ps: 85:7–end; Lk 5:17–26			
	EP			Isa 6		Isa 18
			Ps: 102	Mt 15:21–28		Rev 12

Monday is an ordinary weekday, or 'Feria'.

MP: Two lines in Roman type give Psalms and readings for Matins. EP: ditto.

Mass: Lines of italic give directions for the Eucharist; the second of these lines gives the Roman readings ('The Weekday Lectionary') which are permitted by CW. These form a continuous course of readings, and so are suitable where mass is said (almost) daily. Where mass is not said so often, the mass of last Sunday is more suitable.

Instead, the minister has the discretion to observe the (Colour, Hymns, Collect of the) 'Optional Memorial' of S Jane. □ shows that the Saint is 'unAnglican'; in fact, S Jane is from the Roman Kalender.

TUESDAY			S Lucy, V & M (Ember Day)			
13 R	MP		Ps: 105:1–22	Isa 45:15–end		Isa 21:1–12
				II Thess 1		Mk 5:21–end
	Mass		*of the Saint (**Charles Simeon**)*			
			Isa 40:25–end; Ps: 103:8–13; Mt 11:28–end			
	EP			Isa 8:16 – 9:7		Isa 22:1–14
			Ps: 105:23–end	Mt 16:1–12		Rev 14

Tuesday is a 'Memorial for General Use', and so S Lucy (Colour, Hymns, Collect) displaces, compulsorily, the Feria. The readings given for mass, however, are still the weekday ones, since those saying mass often will probably take advantage of the permission to keep this continuous course of readings as unbroken as possible by using them even on memorials. If preferred, readings for the appropriate class of Saint can be used, and are more suitable where mass is not said daily. The 'Weekday Missal', in its more recent Editions, suggests appropriate readings for most Saints; and so does CW. See Introduction, pages xxvi and following. V & M: abbreviations inside front cover. (**Charles Simeon**) in the Mass line: see Introduction paragraph 3.

ORDER FORM

 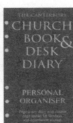  

Advance order for the 2009 editions

Avoid disappointment by ordering the 2009 editions now ! *(All to be published in May 2008)*   quantity

CANTERBURY CHURCH BOOK & DESK DIARY 2009 - *Cased*.................... £16.99 + p&p* ....

CANTERBURY CHURCH BOOK & DESK DIARY 2009 - *Personal Organiser*...£17.99 + p&p* ....

CANTERBURY PREACHERS COMPANION 2009.................................. £16.99 + p&p* ....

ORDER FOR THE EUCHARIST 2009.. £7.99 + p&p* ....

Order a complete set of CANTERBURY CHURCH BOOK AND DESK DIARY *(either cased or personal organiser edition)*, CANTERBURY PREACHERS COMPANION and ORDER FOR THE EUCHARIST at the combined **advance order price of £34.00** + p&p*

Order additional copies of the 2008 editions
Subject to stock availability

Desk Diary £16.99* ....   Organiser £17.99* ....   Preacher's Companion £16.99* ....   Order for the Eucharist £7.99* ....

Ask for details of discounted prices for bulk orders of 6+ copies of any individual title when ordered direct from the Publisher.

Sub-total: £............

* Plus **£2.50** per order to cover post and packing (UK only): £............
All orders over £50 are sent POST FREE to any UK address.
Contact the Publishers office for details of overseas carriage.

TOTAL AMOUNT TO PAY: £............

I wish to pay by...

...**CHEQUE** for £...................... made payable to **SCM-Canterbury Press Ltd**

...**CREDIT CARD**   Visa, Delta, MasterCard and Switch accepted (please delete as appropriate)
Your credit card will not be debited until the books are despatched.

Card number:..   Expiry: ___ / ___

Switch Issue No: ___ ___   Valid from: ___ / ___

Signature of
cardholder:...   Security code: ___ ___ ___
Last three digits on signature panel

Please **PRINT** all details below.

Title:............... Name:...

Delivery address:..

....

....

....

....

....   Post Code:.....................

Telephone:...   Date:............................

Return this order form - with details of payment - to
Canterbury Press Norwich, St Mary's Works, St Mary's Plain, Norwich NR3 3BH, UK

Telephone: 01603 612914   Fax: 01603 624483   Website: www.scm-canterburypress.co.uk

CONTENTS

ALL HALLOWS

ST GABRIELS CONFERENCE CENTRE

St Gabriel's aims to provide a place of welcome for Churches, youth groups, schools and other organisations to come together and experience a relaxed and peaceful Christian environment

- Conference room seating up to 100 people
- Smaller meeting rooms of various sizes
- Full-board accommodation
- Double, twin, single and family bedrooms
- Residential & day groups welcomed
- Traditional home cooked food provided

Tennis courts and an open-air swimming pool available in the summer months.

Contact the Wardens for details and availability

St Gabriel's Centre, Ditchingham, Bungay Suffolk NR35 2DZ   Tel: 01986 892133

saint.gabriels@btinternet.com

a registered charity 230143

INTRODUCTION

1   **THE purpose** of this ORDO is to serve worship needs of Anglicans and Roman
Catholics. For the former, it provides for the recitation of Morning and Evening Prayer
and the celebration of the Holy Communion in accordance with modern forms authorised
or encouraged in the **Provinces of Canterbury and York**. These forms are *selected*,
arranged and *interpreted* in the spirit of what has become generally customary in Western
Christendom since the Second Vatican Council; but notes draw attention also to
Orthodox insights.

It also provides a full Calendar according to the **Modern Roman Rite**, together with
explanatory and catechetical notes. For the convenience of Anglicans, such Roman
material as is not also authorised by General Synod, is given clearly distinguished for use by
those who desire it. The use of this material is covered by Canon B.5.1.

Anglicans who prefer forms of Liturgy based on the *Book of Common Prayer* will find a
Lectionary designed for use with the BCP printed in the far right hand column of each page.

Calendar

2   □ Indicates observances for which there is no Anglican Synodical authority.

✠ Sundays and Holy Days of Obligation ('Principal Feast'; 'Principal Holy Day' CW).

SOLEMNITY: A major 'Red Letter' day or 'Festival' (CW); a Sunday. Those days
normally have a First Evening Prayer.

Festum: A lesser 'Red Letter' day; 'Feast' (Roman); 'Festival' (CW).

Memorial: A 'Black Letter Day' to be generally kept; a 'Lesser Festival' (CW).

Feria: An ordinary weekday.

Feria (. . . . . .): An ordinary weekday (with Optional alternative Memorials).

This ORDO gives a majority of Saints as Optional Memorials (CW says they '*may*' be
used). Rome prefers not to compel 'serious incursion on the weekday cycle' and desires 'to
expand the number of celebrations while reducing the extent of obligation, i.e. to maximise
choice and flexibility'; and CW urges the minister to 'remember the need not to lose the
spirit of the season, especially of Advent and Lent, by too many celebrations that detract
from its character'.

(*Memorials for Optional Use*) are from CW, or ASB, or Rome, or 1662, or 1928; or
the New Roman Calendar for England.

Local, and other commemorations may be added, especially Dedication and Patronal
Festivals (see Appendix 2). Those authorised by the Diocesan are *Optional* (Canon B.6.5).

Scottish, Welsh, and Irish Solemnities, Festa, and Memorials for *General* Use are
included. (Memorials in the Scottish Calendar of 1991 marked '5' or '6' are *Optional*.
Memorials in the Welsh Calendar of 1993 marked 'iv' or 'v' are *Optional*. This Order does
not print them. Nor is the new Church of Ireland list of Diocesan Saints given.)

Rome and CW allow, on a 'green' Feria, the observance, for a good reason, of *any* Saint
listed for that day on an authorised list.

3   **COMMEMORATIONS.** This ORDO follows a CW suggestion by including, in the
line starting '*Mass*', names of uncanonised people who appear in CW as 'lesser
festivals', urging that those who are unhappy to observe them liturgically may nevertheless

incorporate them into the Intercession. Pope John Paul II particularly urged 'local Churches' 'to ensure that the memory of those who have suffered martyrdom should be safeguarded' and calls this 'the most convincing form of Ecumenism'.

4 ✠ DAYS OF EUCHARISTIC OBLIGATION

CANTERBURY & YORK		ORDO	ROMAN []= not in England
Every Sunday	Byz	✠	Every Sunday
			[January 1]
January 6*	Byz	✠	January 6*
February 2*	Byz		
March 25	Byz	(✠)	
			[March 19]
[Ash Wednesday]		(✠)	
[Maundy Thursday]		(✠)	
Ascension	Byz	✠	Ascension*
		✠	Corpus Christi*
	Byz	✠	June 29
	Byz	✠	August 15
November 1*		✠	November 1
			[December 8]
December 25	Byz	✠	December 25

'*Byz*' indicates days which, being among the Twelve Great Festivals of the Byzantine Rites, may be said to have Ecumenical Status. (Byz adds June 24; Aug 6 and 29; Sept 8 and 14; Nov 21)

EAD includes on its list June 29 and August 15, but allows them on the nearest Sunday, as it does the Ascension and Corpus Christi. It omits March 25.

*CW envisages Jan 6, Feb 2, Nov 1 being transferred to a Sunday: see Paragraph 5(C). Parish Priests decide.

*R: envisages Jan 6, Ascension, Corpus Christi being transferred to a Sunday: see Paragraph 5(C). Local hierarchies decide.

*R: envisages Holy Days of Obligation falling on a Saturday or Monday being transferred to a Sunday: see Paragraph 5(B). Local hierarchies decide.

In the Church of England (Canons B6, B14, and C26) Mass is to be celebrated in every Parish Church and (except on Ash Wednesday and Maundy Thursday) every Bishop Priest and Deacon is to celebrate or to be present at Mass.

Good Friday (Canon B.6.4) is "ever to be observed . . . by attendance at Divine Worship." CW added February 2 to the list of Principal Festivals, but, since CW is optional, it is unclear how far this creates obligations under Canon.

The Roman Catholic Church, less clericalist than Anglicanism, expects the participation of *all* God's Holy People.

5   TRANSFER? OMIT?

(A) *External Solemnity.*

When a Solemnity, or a Festum *of Our Lord,* falls in the week after a Sunday in Ordinary Time ('Green'), the Roman Rite allows all the masses and the entire office (including 1 EP) of the Day on the Sunday, *the Holy Day itself also* being celebrated on its proper day.

Transference

(B) Holy Days of Obligation, among English R.C.s, are transferred to the adjacent Sunday when they fall on Saturday or Monday.

(C) A 'Principal Feast' (CW) or 'Solemnity' (R:) supersedes an ordinary ('Green') Sunday 'per annum'. But other 'Festivals' (CW) or 'Feasts' (R:) falling on such a Sunday are, according to R:, omitted that year. According to CW, they must be observed: this may be on the Sunday or the first available day thereafter: see (D) below.

(1) *Epiphany*, in the English Roman Catholic Church and in *some* other countries, is celebrated on the Sunday between January 2 and 8. According to CW, the Epiphany may be transferred to a Sunday between January 2 and 8 'for pastoral reasons'.

(2) *Presentation*, according to CW, may be celebrated *either* on February 2 *or* on the Sunday falling between January 28 and February 3. (According to R:, it could have an External Solemnity on the Sunday *before* but is *still* celebrated on February 2.)

(3) *Ascension*, in the English Roman Catholic Church and in *some* other countries, is celebrated on the Sunday after the appropriate Thursday. There is no General Synod encouragement for this, but EAD permits it.

(4) *Corpus Christi*, in the English Roman Catholic Church and in *some* other countries, is celebrated on the Sunday after the appropriate Thursday. There is no C of E encouragement for this, but Lectionary note 6 would cover it and EAD permits it.

(5) *All Saints*, according to CW, is celebrated on *either* November 1 *or* the Sunday between October 31 and November 6 *or* both. (According to R:, it could have an External Solemnity on the Sunday *before* but is *still* celebrated on November 1. R: also allows local hierarchies to transfer the day.)

(D) *Call it a Votive?* Anglican custom 1928–1980 made a Festum which fell on a 'Green' Sunday supersede that Sunday: CW (C above) allows either observance on the Sunday or transference. Roman rubrics dislike displacing the Sunday because they emphasise the priority of Sunday as the weekly memorial of the Lord's Resurrection. But the older Anglican custom can be harmonised with Roman regulations by regarding the mass of the Festum as a (First Class) Votive 'by command or permission of the Ordinary because of pastoral usefulness' (and *Liturgy of the Hours* permits votive offices). In EAD Ss John Baptist and Peter and Paul; the Assumption; All Saints; the Sacred Heart; Titles; and Dedications; 'may be observed on the nearest Sunday'. But this would not eliminate the observance on the proper day.

6 **EVES.** CW and recent Vatican reforms prefer the Liturgical Day to last from midnight to midnight. However, modern Western usage preserves the ancient custom of considering *Sunday* to begin on the evening of Saturday. So the Collect of each Sunday is used on the Saturday evening before it, and the practice is spreading of celebrating a Sunday mass on the Saturday evening: attendance at this fulfils obligations of Sunday worship. [Do NOT use the CW 'extended preface' for ordinary Sundays at Vigil Masses.]

Solemnities also have a First Evening Prayer. Here, again, obligations of worship can be fulfilled the previous evening. The Roman Missal provides 'Vigil Masses' for Christmas, Pentecost, S John Baptist, SS Peter and Paul, and the Assumption. These masses are said with *Gloria, Creed*, and the colour of the Solemnity, either before or after the First Evening Prayer. The collect of a Vigil Mass is also used at the First Evening Prayer.

Festa do not have a First Evening Prayer. But in years when a Festum displaces a Sunday office, or places where a Festum becomes a Solemnity because it is a Patronal Festival, it acquires a First Evening Prayer.

7 **COLOURS.** The capital letter under the day indicates the colour of the Office. This applies throughout the day, unless another colour appears for Mass and Evening Prayer. The colours suggested in the ORDO are 'traditional', (CW; CW itself suggests, without

being 'mandatory', the use of white up to the Presentation; of red between All Saints and Advent; of red on the Monday, Tuesday, and Wednesday of Holy Week.)

On very solemn days one can use 'festival', or more 'noble' vestments, even if they are not of the colour of the day.

In some churches a 'Lent array' of unbleached linen is used as an alternative to purple during Lent.

Votive Masses may be celebrated in the colour which best suits the character of the chosen Mass, but it is permitted to use instead the colour of the day or season.

Ember and Rogation Masses are said in the seasonal colour. Purple or Black is used at Requiems. In America, Rome allows White.

8 SELF DENIAL etc.

	A	B	C
Roman	PENANCE	ABSTINENCE	FASTING
Canons		Ash Wednesday	Ash Wednesday
1250–1253	Fridays	Fridays EXCEPT	Good Friday
	Lent	Solemnities	
Canterbury	DISCIPLINE AND		
& York (CW)	SELF DENIAL		
	Fridays EXCEPT		
	Solemnities and		
	Festivals outside		
	Lent; and EXCEPT		
	during Eastertide.		
	Weekdays in Lent		

'A' and 'C' are not legally defined in the Universal Canon Law.

Local Episcopates may regulate 'B' and 'C' in detail, substituting charitable works or pious exercises, in whole or in part, for both Abstinence and Fasting.

Abstinence is abstaining from meat. (English Roman Catholics are allowed to substitute some other form of abstinence, or perform some act of piety or charity.) Abstinence binds those above 14 years.

Fasting is defined for English Roman Catholics as 'the amount of food we eat is considerably reduced.' It binds those who are more than eighteen until the beginning of their sixtieth year. It is *recommended* also on Easter Eve up to the Vigil.

9 **'EPIPHANY SEASON'.** The main CW innovation is the suggestion of an Epiphany season modelled on Eastertide: starting on Epiphany and ending on the Presentation. *Arguments in favour* include: it cheers up January and helps to rescue Epiphany and Presentation from oblivion. *Arguments against*: it introduces a new divergence from Roman and Orthodox practice (despite the 1968 pre-ARCIC agreement that we would 'not undertake any significant changes in the seasons') and it mars the (primitive and ecumenical) uniqueness of Easter, the Lord's 50-day-long Great Day of Festival.

If one wishes to follow this CW suggestion, one stays in white vestments and uses Epiphany Office Hymns and an Epiphany Preface until the Presentation; one calls the Sundays 'of' (not 'after') Epiphany; one treats the Presentation as a Solemnity (with 1 EP; Creed at Mass) and as a Day of Obligation. Saturday votives of the Immaculate Heart of Mary (see p. 39) will be particularly appropriate.

Epiphany Hymns: MP 40 (NEH 48) EP 38 (NEH 46).

9A **BIBLICAL TRANSLATIONS** The Vatican now insists on faithfulness to the inspired originals in matters such as grammatical genders and the preservation of as many as possible of the layers of meaning in the original texts, even when these may not be politically correct. 'For example, where the New Testament or the Church's tradition have interpreted certain texts of the Old Testament in a Christological fashion, special care should be observed in the translation of these texts so that a Christological meaning is not precluded ... the word "man" in English should as a rule translate "adam" and "anthropos", since there is no one synonym which effectively conveys the play between the individual, the collectivity and the unity of the human family so important, for example, to expression of Christian doctrine and anthropology.' Among modern translations, such faithfulness can be secured by use of the RSV but NOT the NRSV. Psalter: See Para 29.

Mass

10 **THE LEGALITY OF 'VARIATIONS'.** LHWE and PHG provided forms for 'occasions for which no provision is made' in BCP or ASB. (Such forms of service can be legal if authorised by the Convocations [Canon B:4:1] Archbishop [B:4:2] Ordinary [B:4:3] or Minister having the cure of souls [B:5:2].) *But* LHWE and PHG *also* provided *many* 'variations' in areas where ASB *did* already make *full* and *compulsory* provision; these 'variations' were 'commended by the House of Bishops'; the only legal basis for which can be the words in Canon B:5: 'the minister who is to conduct the service may in his discretion make and use variations which are not of substantial importance'.

Most of the useful material in LHWE and PHG has been superseded by the recently authorised materials. But LHWE and PHG established useful precedents concerning what is a 'variation not of substantial importance' within 'the discretion of the minister who is to conduct the service.' This formula – according to the House of Bishops in 1984 and 1990 – includes **unauthorised Greetings; unauthorised Confessions; unauthorised Collects; unauthorised Readings; unauthorised Prefaces; unauthorised Invitations to Communion.** The fact that some of this material was *subsequently* incorporated in and thus authorised by CW does not change the fact that it was totally unauthorised when the Bishops said it came under the umbrella of Canon B:5:1. So unless the Bishops were wrong in 1984 and 1990, it remains true that Canon B:5:1 still covers the use, at the discretion of the Minister who is to conduct the service, of **unauthorised Greetings; unauthorised Confessions; unauthorised Collects; unauthorised Readings; unauthorised Prefaces; and unauthorised Invitations to Communion. But his discretion is not confined to these areas: see Para 19 below.**

It is to be noted that the Bishops, either collectively or individually, have *no* canonical right to order, *or even allow, any* 'variations' to authorised services. The only right to 'make and use' such 'variations' is that of the 'minister who is to conduct the service' by virtue of Canon B.5.1.. The use of this canon by the Bishops in promoting LHWE and PHG was a creative use of canon law to loosen the straightjacket which otherwise surrounds the law of public worship. And they are still at it: see Para 18 below. But what is sauce for geese . . .

Dix (*Shape* pp. 587–9 and 716–7) wisely sets concepts of 'Liturgical Authority' against their historical background.

11 **CW 'SEASONAL PROVISIONS':** Sentences before the Confession and the Peace; Alleluia before the Gospel; and Proper Prefaces, of different lengths, for some but not all Eucharistic Prayers, appear ('*may* be used') all to be optional. CW does not itself provide, but invites the use of, Entrance and Communion Sentences.

12 **CONFESSION AND KYRIES:** both may be combined into the form of Penitential Rite now popular among Roman Catholics. The sentences prefixed * in the version given below may be varied according to the season. (CW gives three examples, and there are more in PHG and R:.)

The priest invites the people to call to mind their sins, and a pause for silent reflection follows.

Minister:	*You raise the dead to life in the Spirit: Lord, have mercy.	*Priest:*	May almighty God have mercy on us, forgive us our sins,
People:	**Lord, have mercy.**		and bring us to everlasting life.
Minister:	*You bring pardon and peace to the sinner: Christ, have mercy.	*All:*	Amen.
People:	**Christ, have mercy.**		
Minister:	*You bring light to those in darkness: Lord, have mercy.		
People:	**Lord, have mercy.**		

PHG also reminds us of the Asperges (the people are sprinkled with holy water to recall them to their Baptismal commitment; this rite also replaces both the Confession and Kyries and is particularly suitable in Easter Time), giving on p. 249 an abbreviated version of the Roman texts, and on p. 229 versions of the traditional anthems. Or one could 'mine' the materials at CW pp. 48–9. PPL and PHG urge this rite on the Lord's Baptism.

13 **GLORIA IN EXCELSIS** is used on Sundays outside Advent and Lent; Solemnities; Festa; and during Christmas week and Easter week; but not on weekdays and memorials. *Gloria* may be used at special more solemn celebrations.

14 **COLLECTS.** No more than one Collect is ever said at Mass. On Ferias CW orders the collect of the previous Sunday to be used; the Roman usage permits, during the 'green' seasons, any 'green' Sunday Collect to be selected.

On the Sundays between Trinity and All Saints, the Collect to accompany CW readings *will differ from year to year*. While the *readings* come from the 'Sunday of the Year', described by CW as 'Proper number x', the *Collects* are 'after Trinity'.

This new series of CW collects includes a number of the BCP collects from the ancient Roman Sacramentaries, given for use on the same Sunday as in BCP, and very lightly modernised in language (the BCP originals may be used). This welcome development will still leave us using fewer such collects than does the current Roman Rite. Dix (SL p. 367) describes these collects as 'both ancient and beautiful . . . lovely things, grave, melodious and thoughtful, and compact with evangelical doctrine – characteristic products of the liturgical genius of Rome in the fifth and sixth centuries. Cranmer's reputation as a writer of English prose largely rests on his translations . . . and rightly so, for they are among the very best translations ever made . . .'. There is nothing to stop a celebrant using the original, or lightly modernised, versions of those remaining BCP After Trinity collects which CW ignores.

For each weekday in Advent, Christmas, Lent and Easter, Rome provides a separate and seasonally appropriate collect (printed with the readings in the Weekday Missal).

Collects end thus (CW):

Longer Ending (for the Collect itself):

'Through Jesus Christ your Son our Lord, who is alive and reigns with you in the unity of the Holy Spirit, one God, now and for ever'. [But if the Son is addressed: 'for you are alive and reign with the Father in the unity of the Holy Spirit, one God, now and for ever'.]

Shorter Ending (for the prayers Over the Offerings and Post-Communion): 'Through (Jesus) Christ our Lord'. [But if the Son is addressed: 'for you are alive and reign, now and for ever'.]

The College of St Barnabas, Lingfield

The College of St Barnabas is a residential community of retired Anglican clergy. Married couples are very welcome, as are those who have been widowed. Admission is also open to licensed Church Workers and Readers, and there are facilities for visitors and guests.

Residents are encouraged to lead active, independent lives for as long as possible. There is a Nursing Wing providing full nursing care for those who need it, enabling most Residents to remain members of the College for the rest of their lives. Occasionally, it is also possible to offer respite care here.

Sheltered flats in the Cloisters all have separate sitting rooms and bedrooms along with en suite facilities. There are two Chapels; Mass and Evensong are celebrated daily. Meals are served in the Refectory for Cloister Residents.

For further details about life and facilities at the College or to arrange a preliminary visit, please contact the Warden, Fr Howard Such, at:

**The College of St Barnabas,
Blackberry Lane, Lingfield, Surrey, RH7 6NJ**

**Tel. 01342 870260   Fax. 01342 871672
Email: warden@collegeofstbarnabas.com
Website: www.st-barnabas.org**

Charity Commissioners registered number 205220

15 **EUCHARISTIC READINGS: SUNDAYS AND HOLY DAYS** are all in italics.
The *first* line of readings is CW (see paragraph 36 below). This Lectionary was based on the Roman Lectionary in which, S John's Gospel being used particularly in Eastertide, the three Synoptic Gospels take it in turn to dominate the Sundays of the Year (Year A, Matthew; B, Mark; C, Luke). The Roman original has been 'improved' several times by Anglican committees. **Where it is desired to abbreviate a CW reading, R: might be helpful (see below).**

This ORDO assumes that users will prefer the OT readings which will relate thematically to the Sunday Gospel (CW repeats them from R:) rather than the alternative 'continuous' OT readings. 'Typology' is the Bible's own way of using itself intertextually (I Cor 10:1–5; I Pet 3:20, etc.).

The *second* line is the original Roman provision, preceded *R:* (the psalm provision gives the psalm number according to the Anglican system of numbering psalms, but does not specify the detailed uses and combinations of verses).

Advantages in using the Roman version: (a) it will be practical to use books, of R.C. origin, in which the lessons are printed in full; (b) the R: readings generally represent a tighter selection of verses. Whether the differences between CW and R: are slight or greater, the use of R: will constitute a variation 'not of substantial importance' in terms of Canon B.5; and CW itself allows 'the minister' to 'depart from the Lectionary provision for pastoral reasons or preaching or teaching purposes' during 'Ordinary Time', after 'due consultation with the PCC'. (PCCs could pass a resolution 'that this Council has received such due consultation as may be necessary for the Incumbent at his discretion to depart from authorised lectionary provision.')

In the Roman rite, Solemnities have *two* readings before the Gospel; Festa only *one*. Where this ORDO prints two, it is because Rome offers them as alternatives. CW, on the other hand, offers *two* readings even for some 'Lesser Festivals'; i.e. Memorials.

16 **EUCHARISTIC READINGS: WEEKDAY LECTIONARY.** CW continues the authorisation ASB gave to the Roman weekday Eucharistic lectionary; its readings may be used both on Ferias *and* on Memorials. They are printed in full, in italics, although those who wish to use these readings daily at mass will find it simpler to follow the Liturgical Commission's advice and use copies of the small, cheap Roman 'Weekday Missal', containing these readings, than to have to mark up lessons in a Bible each day. See page i for further advice. Psalms follow the CW verse numbers.

Roman Psalms: the complexity of juggling the different versification systems in the Vulgate, King James, BCP and CW Psalters is too much for your compiler. Accordingly, just the psalm number (BCP numeration) is given for the Roman Psalms: which verses are used, how they are combined, and when the Response comes, will have to be discovered from liturgical books.

17 **THE CREED** is to be used on Sundays and Solemnities and *may* be used at special more solemn occasions. The 'Apostles' Creed', the ancient baptismal confession of the Apostolic Roman See (which , together with Quicunque Vult, is also allowed by CW), is particularly recommended by Rome during the baptismal seasons of Lent and Easter and when there are many children present. When it is used, Rome insists that *Carnis Resurrectionem* must be translated *Resurrection of the Flesh* (compare our Article IV). CW institutionalizes an *ad hoc* Vatican custom of omitting *Filioque* when ecumenical considerations urge this.

18 **PREFACES.** ASB and PHG moved, with Rome, in the direction of a generous supply of prefaces; CW only gives a minimum. Rome offers 'extended prefaces' and

others may be found in ASB and books 'commended' by the Bishops (but which have no synodical force). See paragraph 10 above for what is 'legal'.

On Memorials which lack a proper preface, the Common Preface is used (in Advent and Easter, the Seasonal Preface) *or* the appropriate Preface of the Saint.

19 **POST SANCTUS.** Before the 1960s, in both the Roman and Anglican rites, there was but one unchanging 'Consecration Prayer' or 'Canon', so that this part of the service constituted a moment of familiarity, commonality, and invariability deeply sanctified by Tradition. But since CW follows Rome in now offering a dozen or so alternative EuPrs, the authorities in both communions have in effect abrogated this tradition, and transferred discretion to the officiating presbyter.

Does this discretion, combined with the canonical discretion to 'make and use variations' (see Para 10 above), entitle him to use EuPrs not authorised by General Synod or to improve CW EuPrs by introducing ancient, ecumenical and ARCIC verbs such as 'become' and 'offer'? Canons B.5.1, B.5.5 and B.1.3.iii make clear that the celebrant's 'discretion' (see para 10 above) *does* extend to the whole Eucharistic Prayer.

On 26 i 1988, the House of Bishops expressed the view that the use of Eucharistic rites which were once 'canonically authorised' but whose 'authorisation' had 'lapsed' would be a variation 'not of substantial importance' and therefore, in their pastoral judgement, legal. While the Bishops clearly only had in mind some of the temporary rites briefly authorised since 1965, this principle obviously and *a fortiori* also covers 'where well established' the first of the four Roman Eucharistic Prayers, which was frequently used in the Church of England between 597 and 1559. Roman rubrics strongly urge the use of this EuPr on all Sundays; the Octaves of Christmas and Easter; the Apostles and Saints listed in it; the Epiphany and Ascension; and Ritual masses. The Tudor English translation authorised by Rome may be sought from the Compiler. In the judgement of liturgical experts, if this venerable prayer, brought by S Augustine to Canterbury in 597, lacks Twentieth Century Synodical 'legality', it has the 'authority' of nearly a millennium of Anglican use. There are clearly no theological objections to the contents of this Prayer since the House of Bishops (GS Misc 632) has spoken of Anglicans finding 'that they can, with good conscience, say a heartfelt Amen at the end of the [Roman] Eucharistic Prayer.'

The 1988 'statement', so one Bishop points out, also covers ASB EuPrIII, which has a more satisfactory *oblatio* that CW'B', its successor.

It has been suggested that CW EuPr G should not be ignored by Catholics. It breaks new ground in providing a post-consecration intercession into which episcopal names (see para 21) could be inserted. This intercession could be popped into other CW EuPrs.

20 **SAINTS IN THE EUCHARISTIC PRAYER.** The CW Eucharistic Prayers B, E, F, G invite mention by name of Saints, and they are easily inserted into the other Prayers. Rome and Orthodoxy agree that diachronic 'permanence through history' is 'brought into focus' by the mention of the Saints in the Canon. The Ecumenical (Roman and Orthodox) custom since early centuries has been at every mass to name our Lady, and always to do so using her ecumenically agreed official doctrinal title **Mother of God** (*Theotokos*, Ephesus, 431, and Chalcedon, 451; some may be attracted by the ARCIC suggestion of translating this 'Mother of God Incarnate'). The older Byzantine and Latin prayers add another official ecumenical title: **and Ever-Virgin** (*aeiparthenos*, Chalcedon, 451, and Constantinople, 553). Mention of others, in addition to our Lady, (e.g. the Forerunner; Apostles; Patrons; Saints of the Day) varies from rite to rite.

21 **THE BISHOP.** The fundamental sacramental unit of Christ's Church is neither a 'National' Church or Province or 'Communion', nor a parish, but a unity of Bishop,

Presbyterium, and People. So, when a priest offers mass apart from his Bishop, he does so as the Bishop's representative. The Orthodox and Roman Churches agree that it is 'essential' to show this by including his name in the Eucharistic Prayer. This is not merely a prayer *for* the Bishop but an expression of full ecclesial communion *with* him. Where CW formulae are used, at appropriate points after the Consecration the following (see Prayer G) can be interpolated: **Remember, Lord, your Church in every land. Reveal her unity, guard her faith, and preserve her in peace: together with . . .**

A priest says: . . . **our bishop (or whatever) N** adding, if appropriate, **and his assistant bishop N** or, if there are several of them, **and his assistant bishops**.

22 **COMMUNION:** LHWE and PHG print Roman introductions to the Our Father; and the Embolism ('Deliver us, Lord . . .') after the Our Father, as in the Roman rite, is printed in PHG. CW permits the Peace after the Our Father, as in the Roman rite. The (nonR:) CW formulae at the Fraction are only mandatory on Sundays and Principal Holy Days: could this be the moment quietly to dump them? The ASB/CW Zwinglianization of *ECCE Agnus Dei* could be got round in parish leaflets thus: "The priest invites the faithful to receive Jesus, the Lamb of God; they reply . . ."

23 **POSTCOMMUNION.** CW provides, together with the Collects referred to in paragraph 14, post-Communion collects, many of which will be found either eloquent or verbose according to differing tastes. Not one of them is a post-Communion in those same early sacramentaries which provided so many of Cranmer's collects. CW, however, envisages the use of 'another suitable prayer'; which could be found in the Roman selection, or the old one in the 'English Missal'. They replace, *or* are in addition to, '. . . send us out into the world . . .'.

24 **CONCLUSION OF THE MASS.** (i) On Solemnities and Festa outside Lent, and at Requiems, a solemn blessing is encouraged. The deacon or priest says: **Bow your heads and pray for God's blessing**; the blessing follows; and then the dismissal.

(ii) On Sundays and Weekdays in Lent, Prayers Over The People have been optionally restored in the Roman Rite. They are available for 'Green' Sundays. The deacon or priest says: **Bow your heads for God's blessing**; the Prayer is said, followed immediately by **'. . . and the blessing . . .'**; then the dismissal. The new latin Missal provides new texts; until translations are available, the English Missal could be used.

(iii) Otherwise, Mass ends with *The Lord be with you* and its response, the Blessing, and the Dismissal with its response. This applies to Requiems. When a liturgical function immediately follows the Mass, this Conclusion is omitted.

25 **EMBERS & ROGATIONS.** Embers were originally pagan Roman harvest festivals, christianized by being made fasts! Because of the fast, they attracted ordinations. (The Weekday Missal has Votives For Productive Land and the Blessing of Man's Labour.) We indicate the Ember Weeks as given, according to ancient tradition, in BCP and the Roman Tridentine Calendars (the information given in CW being erroneous). But CW allows bishops to transfer them, so that they precede Diocesan Ordinations.

Ember and Rogation Masses may be said on Ferias and Optional Memorials; on Solemnities, Festivals, and General Memorials the expression of Ember and Rogation themes is confined to the Intercession, unless they are Class 1 or Class 2 Votives (see table). The seasonal colour is used at Ember and Rogation Masses.

26 **RITUAL MASSES, REQUIEMS, VOTIVES.** The table opposite indicates when these may and may not be said.

(a) When a Wedding includes a **Nuptial Mass:** On Sundays and Solemnities, the Mass of the Day is said. But one of the Wedding readings may be included, except from Maundy Thursday to Easter Sunday and on Solemnities of Obligation. If the Parochial community is not present at a Wedding on a 'Green' Sunday or a Sunday after Christmas, the entire Nuptial Mass may be said. The ancient 'Nuptial Blessing' is traditionally said over the newly-weds immediately after the Our Father of the Wedding Mass. It is consigned now by CW to oblivion for Political Incorrectness; versions of it will be found in R: and BCP (*O God who by thy mighty power . . .*) and ASB (Additional Prayer 35, on page 299.)

(b) **Our Lady on Saturday** (*in Sabbato*): (i) since at least the Eighth Century liturgical reforms associated with the name of Alcuin of York, our Lady has in the West been particularly commemorated on Saturday (on the Sabbath God the Creator rests from His labour in Mary's womb before His Great New Deed of Creation on His Eighth Day; Mary is the faithful Daughter of Zion, whose Faith begins the New – as Abraham's did the Old – Covenant; in her own Eschatological Rest she prefigures the Sabbath Rest to which God's Pilgrim people is journeying). Post Vatican II legislation confined this usage to when, after Epiphany and Trinity, there is no Solemnity, Festum, or Memorial for General Use. But since IGMR now 'commends' the observance *peculiari modo*, it should be the norm on free Saturdays after Epiphany and Trinity. (As a Class 2 votive – see page xxi – it may be used until December 16, after January 1, and after Low Sunday in Eastertide, and on Memorials for General Use.) (see p. 42 for the **Immaculate Heart**.)

(ii) Variety may be secured by using the **"Collection of Masses of the BVM"**, issued by Rome particularly for use in Marian shrines (where, during pilgrimages, votives from the Collection may also be said on any weekday of Advent, Christmas after January 1, and Lent) and on Saturday. The Compiler (front of volume) can supply a sample mass. *Invariability may be secured from CW pp. 511–2 & 310–1.*

(iii) But, of course, the Feria, or an occuring optional Memorial, may be observed.

(c) **The Sacred Heart on Friday:** see p. 42.

(d) **Votive Masses** may be of the mysteries of the Lord or in honour of the BVM, Angels, any Saint, All Saints; and may be said on any feria when there is not a Memorial for General Use (with the exception of the Immaculate Conception, masses referring to events in the lives of the Lord and His Mother may not be used as votives). *Votive offices*, for a public cause or out of devotion, may be used on *any* day except Solemnities; Sundays of Advent, Lent, or Easter; Ash Wednesday; Palm Sunday to Low Sunday; and 2 November.

Starvation Exploitation Poverty Drought

Who cares?

You do.
And you're not alone.

Twenty-two thousand churches support Christian Aid's work to eradicate poverty. Why? Because we believe in a God of love and justice.

We're here to help you make an impact on poverty in communities all over the world.

To find out more, call 020 7523 2014.
www.christianaid.org.uk

 We believe in life before death

UK registered charity number 1105851 Company number 5171525 Republic of Ireland charity number CHY 6998

MASSES 'FOR VARIOUS OCCASIONS', & VOTIVES / REQUIEMS

	MASSES 'FOR VARIOUS OCCASIONS', & VOTIVES			REQUIEMS		
	CLASS 1 — Permitted or ordered by the Bishop when they have an unusually serious pastoral need or use; and also RITUAL MASSES: e.g. at Baptism, Confirmation or Ordination.	CLASS 2 — When they have a real pastoral need or use; e.g., a First Friday; the Sacred Heart; Rogations. BVM on Saturday	CLASS 3 — Chosen by the Celebrant for the Devotion of the people.	CLASS 1 — at Funerals	CLASS 2 — After hearing the news of a death, on the occasion of the final burial, and on the first Anniversary	CLASS 3 — 'Daily' masses for the Dead.
Solemnities 'of obligation'; Sundays of Advent; Sundays of Lent; Sundays from Easter to Trinity Sunday inclusive; Maundy Thursday to Easter.	NO	NO	NO	NO	NO	NO
Solemnities NOT 'of obligation'; Ash Wednesday; Monday, Tuesday and Wednesday in Holy Week; Easter Week All Souls' Day.	NO	NO	NO	YES	NO	NO
Ordinary ('green') Sundays; Sundays of Christmas; Epiphany Sundays; Festa.	YES	NO	NO	YES	NO	NO
Weekdays December 17–24; the Octave of Christmas; Weekdays of Lent.	YES	NO but see para 26b ii	NO	YES	YES	NO
Memorials for General Use; Weekdays of Advent up to December 16; Weekdays of Christmas after January 1; Weekdays of the Easter Season after Low Sunday.	YES	YES	NO	YES	YES	NO
Ordinary ('green') weekdays of the year; Epiphany weekdays; and Memorials for Optional Use.	YES	YES	YES	YES	YES	YES

Divine Office

This ORDO is arranged on the assumption that clergy will 'say daily the Morning *and* Evening Prayer [at least!] either privately or openly' (1662); 'Bishops, priests and deacons . . . must give due importance to Morning and Evening Prayer . . . and be careful not to omit them except for a grave cause' (Liturgy of the Hours).

27 Versions of the Opus Dei formally prescribed or permitted by Synod in England:

(1) Sarum (1542);

(2) BCP (1662);

(3) 'A Service of the Word' structured in conformity with CW pp. 24–27. These regulations were authorised so that (GS 1342 p. 3) their 'provisions would now give legal "cover" to the use of forms of Daily Office' such as the Roman Breviary ('Liturgy of the Hours') and 'Celebrating Common Prayer'; except that on Sundays and Principal Holy Days when such an Office is the principal service (i.e. in Churches where mass is not said), an Act of Penance, a sermon, and a Creed need to be added to a form which does not already possess them. IT MUST BE CLEARLY NOTED that the forms given in CW pp. 30–45 are purely '*examples* of forms which comply'; they are not mandatory *or even recommended* and take *no* priority over forms which the minister may borrow from elsewhere or devise himself.

Similarly (as one of the Bishops who sat on the Liturgical Commission and helped to write it has explained) *Common Worship: Daily Prayer* is no more than an 'outworking' of 'A Service of the Word' – as is the RC Divine Office.

28 **OFFICE HYMNS**, at Morning and Evening Prayer, are an ancient and integral part of the Divine Office. They now *precede the variable psalms* and state the theme of the Office.

This ORDO provides traditional Office Hymns from the old English Sarum Breviary and the current Latin Office Book, with a very little supplementation, according to the English Hymnal, which covers most needs. *We also give New English Hymnal numbers. But the NEH gives a much poorer selection than EH; we do the best we can with it while recommending EH for those who desire to use the traditional hymns in their daily office.* (The old 'English Catholic Hymn Book' is useful, where it survives).

Hymns for the 'Green' seasons and the Commons are in the table on page xxiii. Hymns for Advent, Christmas, Lent and Easter are indicated in the *Notes before those Seasons*.

Hymns for some other days are in the body of the ORDO; H: 5 (NEH 6) means that 5 is the English Hymnal number; 6 the New English Hymnal number. If no provision is made for Morning Prayer, the evening hymn is to be used; and vice versa.

29 **PSALMS:** arranged as given in GS 1520A. We follow the permission there to use 'Ordinary Time' psalms throughout nearly all the year, as Rome does. We assume also the traditional use of substantial psalmody. But any arrangement of the psalms is equally lawful. CW includes a psalter; but it was not passed by General Synod and has no more authority than any other translation. Nevertheless the Compiler has tried consistently to give verse numbers according to CW. 'The Revised Psalter' of 1964 (BCP sensitively adjusted by biblical scholars in collaboration with T.S. Eliot and C.S. Lewis) is considered by many the best English version.

Office Hymns

PER ANNUM (The 'Green' Seasons after Epiphany and Pentecost)

	Morning Prayer		Evening Prayer	
	EH	NEH	EH*	NEH
Sunday	50	53 or 149	51/164	150 or 54
Monday	52 or 632		58/81	61,
Tuesday	165	149	59/264	241,
Wednesday	54	or	60/262	248,
Thursday	55, 53 or 254	151	61/269	or
Friday	56		62/265	152
Saturday	57		49/280	
BVM on Saturday	213, 214, or 215	180, 181 or 183		

COMMONS for the entire year.

N.B. On days which are memorials, R: allows *either* the weekday hymns (according to season), *or* these hymns from the Commons.

	EH	NEH	EH	NEH
BVM	214&215	181&183	213	180
Apostles, Evangelists	174 (R: Proper)	‡	176	214
in Eastertide	124 pt 2	‡	123 pt 2	100 vv4–end
Several Martyrs	175† or 183	213†	182	218
One Martyr	180 or 185	217	181	218
A Virgin Martyr	180 or 185	‡	191	222
A Virgin	‡	‡	192	222
A Holy Man	‡	‡	189	223
A Holy Woman	‡	‡	193	222
[Group Commem]	‡	‡	[253: 1&7–13]	[223]

* The first hymn is from the Seventh Century Weekly Cycle celebrating the Days of Creation; the second is a suggested alternative.
† *Correct to* The Martyrs' glorious deeds . . .
‡ Use the Evening Hymn.

(None of the Roman hymns for 'Pastors' is to be found in Anglican hymnals. EH 188(NEH 220), the traditional hymn for 'Confessors', is now confined to S Martin, for whom it was composed.)

VOTIVE OFFICES: as on the day. See paragraph 26 (d).

Those who feel like spending $30 (Canadian) on a volume containing all the traditional Office Hymns – mainly translated by J. M. Neale – should contact:
The Parish of St John the Evangelist
990 Falmouth Road
Victoria, BC
Canada V8X 3A3

The Church does not use the psalms in an individualistic way, or academically as pieces of historical Hebrew poetry; but corporately and Christologically according to the *sensus messianicus* (cf. Mt 22: 41–46; Lk 24: 44; Acts 2: 25–28 & 34–35; Hebrews passim). The Fathers received and explained the Psalter as a prophecy of Christ and the Church, and in the psalms, heard Christ crying to the Father, or the Father speaking with the Son, or the voice of the Church ('Christ prays for us as our Priest; in us as our Head; He is prayed to as our God'). Thus, in praying the psalms, the Body of Christ enters into the relationship between Son and Father.

So it is irrelevant whether the 'mood' of a psalm suits that of a particular worshipper at a particular moment. Nevertheless, the modern Roman Office, no less than Anglican equivalents, avoids some 'bloodthirsty' places because of their 'psychological difficulty'.

30 **OFFICE READINGS.** From Advent 3 to the Baptism, and from Palm Sunday to Trinity, CW expects 'authorised' readings to be used. Otherwise . . .

In the middle column the readings of the text are based on CW. ('Second Service' provides the 2 EP, and 'Third Service' the MP, on Sundays; on weekdays we use the lectionary contained in GS 1520A/B. *In the third column* the readings are according to the 1961 lectionary, designed to accompany the BCP. Although technically the authorisation for this has lapsed, it is but a light revision and improvement of the 1922 lectionary . . . which *is* still legal! Thus your Compiler regards the use of the 1961 lectionary as a 'variation not of substantial importance' according to the Canons.

Technically, CW covers interchanging readings between MP, EP, and Mass, but the distribution of readings as given in this ORDO is to be recommended.

When a reading begins with a personal pronoun the reader may substitute the appropriate noun.

Verses printed within (parentheses) are permitted additions to the appointed passages. Verse numbers followed by 'a' or 'b' indicate the first or second part of the verse. Verse numberings generally follow the *(New) Revised Standard Version*. When other versions are used, such adaptations may be made as are necessary.

31 **CANTICLES & FINAL ANTHEMS.** The ancient Canticles of the Western Church (R: and BCP) are: MP *Benedictus* EP *Magnificat* and *Nunc Dimittis*. MP includes the *Te Deum* on all Sundays outside Lent, and on Solemnities and Festa. By long custom encouraged by an Archbishop of Canterbury, this Office concludes with an anthem to our Lady (Celebrating Common Prayer pp. 265–7).

32 **RITUAL.** Rome still anticipates the Sign of the Cross at *O God make speed* . . . , and the beginnings of the Gospel Canticles; the Cross on the mouth at *O Lord open* . . . ; and, **together with Byzantium expects the congregation to be standing for the proclamation of a Gospel reading!** PHG encourages a service of Light before EP, the ancient *Lucernarium*. It is not always realised that, since MP and EP occupy the time of the Temple morning and evening offerings of incense, its traditional use at the *Benedictus* and *Magnificat* is more than just a piece of highchurchery. EAD urges consideration also of 'a proper focus on the Blessed Sacrament, exposed for adoration.' Elliot (Int P38) tells you how to do it.

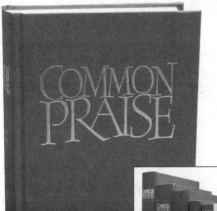

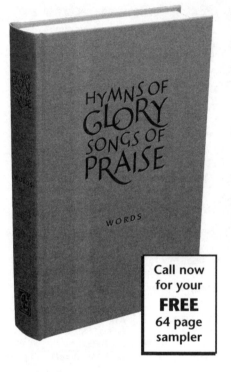

Resources

33 **'TRADITIONAL LANGUAGE' LITURGY.** While the Prayer Book Communion may be used as it is printed, for many years it was universally modified (e.g. omission of long exhortations). Nearly all the customary modifications of the 1662 eucharistic rite, including the 'Interim Rite', have now been given legal 'cover' by recent legislation.

With this rite one may add to the BCP propers the bulk of the additional *collects and propers from the 1928 Prayer Book* (and Old Testament readings from the old Series I), which were authorised by General Synod in 2000.

As far as *Series One and Two* are concerned, on 26 i 1988 the House of Bishops 'agreed in regarding the continued use, where well established, of any form of service which has, at any time since 1965, been canonically authorised (notwithstanding the fact that such authorisation was not renewed after it lapsed) as not being of 'substantial importance' within the meaning of Canon B5.4' . . . a creatively cheeky use of Canon Law.

34 **'LENT • HOLY WEEK • EASTER:** Services and Prayers', (LHWE) 'commended by the House of Bishops' provides forms of traditional liturgy for the period from Ash Wednesday to Pentecost. This may be used under the Diocesan's authority (Canon B4) or by decision of the Parish Priest (Canon B5). Since (LHWE) 'the Services . . . are set out so that they can be used as they stand. Alternatively, they may be used as source material . . . Every part of these services is optional . . .', it is clearly not illegal to borrow from other Churches and Rites.

Many priests have found the existence of LHWE an influential pastoral tool in recommending traditional Lenten and Holy Week rites to congregations unfamiliar with them. The texts provided for Holy Week are in fact the Roman texts with mostly insignificant alterations. Some of these changes slightly improve the Roman (ICEL) wording; unfortunately, LHWE lacks the detailed rubrical directions required (e.g.) for the traditional rites surrounding the Paschal Candle; and, for example, has seen fit to eliminate such memorable pieces of liturgical poetry as *O felix culpa*.

On Good Friday, the earlier tradition, preserved by the Roman rite, is for the intercessions to come between the Passion and the Veneration of the Cross; LHWE makes 'The Proclamation of the Cross' precede the Intercessions.

35 **'THE PROMISE OF HIS GLORY'** (PHG) contains a great deal of liturgical material beyond the scope of this ORDO. It provides Mass (R:) and Office for the Holy Family, and the (R:) Eucharistic readings for the Solemnities of Our Lady (Dec 8 and Jan 1); but in its movement towards the three-year Lectionary it has now been superseded by CW. This ORDO draws attention to such PHG material, from All Saints to the Presentation, as remains relevant.

36 **CALENDAR LECTIONARY AND COLLECTS 2000** finally sanctioned the three-year Roman Sunday and Festival Eucharistic Lectionary. This had already been 'improved', and the 'improved' version called the Revised Common Lectionary. Before General Synod promulgated it, it 'improved' it some more (although not as much as some pressure groups desired). There is NO *single* version of this Lectionary with readings printed out in full which is authorised by General Synod. *Any* translation of the Bible may be used. Mowbray/Cassell have published a version with NRSV texts; Hodder and Stoughton favour the NIV; etc; but none of these possesses any exclusive 'official' status.

CW accommodates Evangelical dislike of the Deuterocanonical books by providing alternatives to readings from them (a recent custom; 1549 and 1662 denied such alternatives). This ORDO assumes that users have no problems with those Deuterocanonical books which the C of E and the Roman Catholic Church both receive.

37 **SUNDAY MISSAL; WEEKDAY MISSAL.** The cheapest and simplest way of using the Roman Sunday readings (which are much the same as those now authorised in CW) is by purchasing a small Collins 'Sunday Missal'. The Collins 'Weekday Missal' prints in full the readings of the CW Daily Eucharistic Lectionary, propers for all the Saints in the Roman Universal Calendar, and a small Supplement of the main National Saints.

38 **CEREMONIES OF THE MODERN ROMAN RITE** by Msgr P.J. Elliot. This gives full, intelligent, and sensitive advice about the performance of Mass and Office in the Western tradition; it is modern, yet sensitive to the desire to do God's Work in a decent and orderly way not totally divorced from earlier traditions. It is the modern replacement for both 'Fortescue' and our own 'Ritual Notes'. It includes information about what to do with the Bishop! It costs £21.95 (+£2.20 p/p in the UK). It may be bought from Faith House Bookshop. (The same author's follow-up of 1998 is called "Liturgical Question Box", and another volume deals with the Seasons.)

39 **AKATHIST HYMN:** that great explosion of Byzantine wit and of Sixth Century devotion to our Lady is suitable, as the late Fr Colin Stephenson of Walsingham used to urge, for use in the Mary Month of May. PPL warmly encourages it. (During the Jubilee Year of 2000 it was used in Rome on October 1 and December 8). Two English translations (by Bishop Kallistos Ware and Roger Green) are suitable. A limited number of copies is available from the Ecumenical Society of the BVM at £1.35 each including p&p (cheques to ESBVM).

40 **COLLECTION OF MASSES:** see paragraph 26b ii.

The following observance of the Principal Joys of Mary by daily votives has received strong episcopal encouragement in the Diocese of Exeter. The bracketed numbers are the Compiler's suggestions as to which votives in the 'Collection' (above) fit.

Sunday: Nativity of BVM (20)
Monday: Annunciation (2)
Tuesday: Nativity of the Lord (4, 5, 19)
Wednesday: Adoration of the Magi (6)
Thursday: Purification of BVM (7)
Friday: Compassion of BVM (11, 12)
Saturday: Assumption of BVM (29)

---

41 *A MANUAL OF ANGLO-CATHOLIC DEVOTION* by the Bishop of Ebbsfleet contains a wealth of traditional resources.

42 *THE DIRECTORY ON POPULAR PIETY AND THE LITURGY*, a Vatican production, offers 'principles' and takes us through the liturgical year. Fun.

43 **THE ENGLISH MISSAL**, reprinted by the Tufton Press, may be found useful, as long as one remembers that it prints rubrics in black. The rite of which it is a translation has now been confirmed by the Holy Father as at the lawful disposal of every presbyter, without any futher permission being needed.

Appendix 1: Particular days

JANUARY 1: The Vatican observes World Peace Day. Leo the Great pointed out that the association of Peace with Christmastime is based as much on dogma as on sentiment. The Old Covenant community, defined by Circumcision, is replaced by Christ, the Father's One New Creation, into whom we are incorporated by Baptism. All peoples are called to this Unity and Peace. See the readings at the Office for Mary, Mother of God.

JANUARY 18 (PHG) OR ☐ FEBRUARY 22 (R:)

The { **Confession (PHG)** / **☐ Chair (R:)** } **of S Peter, Apostle**

W	MP	Ezek 34:11–16
	Ps: 30, 34	Jn 21:15–22
	Mass — *Gl; R: Pref of Apostles; CW, of a Saint*	
	Ps 23, I Pet 5:1–4; Mt 16:13–19	
	EP — H: 226 (NEH 171) vv 3&6	Ezek 3:4–11
	Ps: 71, 145	Acts 11:1–18 (= R:)

The *Week of Prayer for Christian Unity* began in 1908 (among Anglicans who sought unity around the See of Peter) as the *Chair of Unity Octave*. It linked the Feasts of S Peter's Chair (January 18) and S Paul's Conversion (January 25). In 1969 Rome suppressed the former feast because it duplicated the Fourth Century Feast of the Chair (i.e. 'Episcopal Consecration') of S Peter in February (which R: retains). PHG put S Peter back at the start of our annual Prayer for Unity and, despite the lack of interest of CW, he survives there in some Diocesan Calendars. Even those who prefer the more ancient date and title in February might like to begin the Week of Prayer with a votive mass and office of S Peter.

MP commemorates the Pastoral Charge to Peter; in the Gospel at mass Peter's Confession of Christ leads to the granting of the keys; and EP shows Peter unlocking the Church's doors to the Gentiles.

At mass, the texts in the Missal for February 22 may conveniently be used on either day. PHG suggests the ASB Collect on p. 780 (a more prolix version of the Roman).

SUNDAY IN THE CHAIR OF UNITY OCTAVE

PHG follows the old English R.C. practice in allowing a mass for Unity on this Sunday (in green vestments). The Missal has texts towards the end; PHG on pp. 246 ff with Collects on pp. 366 f.

R: = CW = PHG Sunday Mass: *Gl; Cr; Pref of Unity, PHG p. 257 (= R:)*
Ps 100, 122; Zeph 3:16–end; Eph 4:1–6 or Col 3:9–17 or
I Jn 4:9–15; Jn 11:45–52 or Jn 17:11b–19 (20–23)

MOTHERING SUNDAY (LENT 4)

On 'Mothering' or 'Refreshment' Sunday, rose colour is sometimes used; together with the organ and flowers.
Mothering Sunday can be combined with Lent if its theme is **Our Lady of Sorrows**. For texts, see Missal September 15. CW *Readings: Exod 2:1–10; 2 Cor 1:3–7 or Col 3:12–17; Ps 34:11–20; 127:1–4; Jn 19:25–27 or Lk 2:33–35; Preface PHG p. 278 (second pref).*

HARVEST

CW offers

Year A	*Deuteronomy 8:7–18* or *Deuteronomy 28:1–14;*
	Psalm 65;
	2 Corinthians 9:6–15;
	Luke 12:16–30 or *Luke 17:11–19.*
Year B	*Joel 2:21–27;*
	Psalm 126;
	1 Timothy 2:1–7 or *1 Timothy 6:6–10;*
	Matthew 6:25–33.
Year C	*Deuteronomy 26:1–11;*
	Psalm 100;
	Philippians 4:4–9 or *Revelation 14:14–18;*
	John 6:25–35.

REMEMBRANCE SUNDAY

PHG recommended the original R: Sunday lections (inappropriately 'improved' by CW) as suitable themes for Remembrance. CW also provides a votive for Peace. In many places the traditional practice of a Solemn Requiem on this day is continued, with appropriate propers related to the Resurrection Hope and the duty of Prayer for the Dead. CW considers the Collects for the Third Sunday before Advent most suitable for Remembrance Sunday.

THE BISHOP AND THE SOVEREIGN PONTIFF

On the Anniversary of the Pope's Inauguration and the 'Episcopal Ordination' (Consecration) or Translation of the Diocesan or the Provincial Bishop, a class 2 Votive (p. xxi) may be said. Texts in the Missal, or CW p. 237. (In the Collect, change 'your servant now to be *enthroned*' to 'your chosen servant *N*'.)

THE MONARCH

Office and Mass: Josh 1:1–10; Prov 8:1–16; Rom 13:1–10; Rev 21:22–22:4; Ps 20; 101; 121; Mt 22:16–22; Lk 22:24–30.

Hope on
the Horizon

Imagine a ship staffed by surgeons, doctors, nurses, water engineers and other specialists. Now imagine their services offered free of charge to the world's poorest people. That is Mercy Ships.

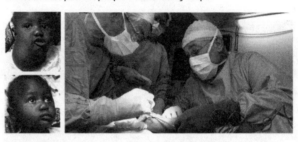

Visit www.mercyships.org.uk to support us

Phone us now

01438 727 800

Registered Charity No. 1053055

E-mail us now

fundraising@mercyships.org.uk

Appendix 2: Local days

THE DEDICATION OF THE LOCAL CHURCH

is a Solemnity observed on the date of the church's Consecration; if this Solemnity falls on a Sunday in Advent, Lent or Easter the seasonal notes will indicate how to transfer it. (The Dedication of the Cathedral is a Festum.)

When the Day of Consecration is unknown, CW allows the first Sunday in October. R: and CW suggest the Sunday before All Saints, in order to focus on the unity between the Church on Earth and the Church in Heaven. See Introduction paragraph 5 (External Solemnities, etc.). Clergy who serve several (country) churches may observe their Dedications as they get around them Sunday by Sunday 'on suitable dates chosen locally' (CW).

Hymns: 1 & 2 EP: 169 (NEH 204); MP 170 (NEH 205)
Mass: Gl; Cr; R: Pref of Dedication (ASB 26)

R:		Mass	*II Chron 5:6–11 & 13–6:2 (in Eastertide, Acts 7:44–50) I Cor 3:9–13 & 16–17; Jn 4:19–24*		
CW	W	1st EP of foll;	II Chron 7:11–16		Gen 28:10–end
		Ps: 24	Jn 4:19–29		Rev 21:9–16
	W	MP	Hag 2:6–9		I Chron 29:6–11
		Ps: 48	Heb 10:19–25		Eph 2:8–end
		Mass	*Year A: I Kings 8:22–30 or Rev 21:9–14; Ps 122; Heb 12:18–24; Mt 21:12–16.*		
			Year B: Gen 28:11–18 or Rev 21:9–14; Ps 122; 2 Pet 2:1–10; Jn 10:22–29.		
			Year C: I Chron 29:6–19; Ps 122; Eph 2:19–22; Jn 2:13–22.		
		2 EP	Year A	Jer 7:1–11	I Kgs 8:22–30
			Ps: 132	I Cor 3:9–17	Heb 10:19–25
			Years B & C	Jer 7:1–11	
			Ps: 132	Lk 19:1–10	

THE DEDICATION OF THE CATHEDRAL

is a Festum throughout the Diocese: no 1 EP or Creed at mass, but otherwise as above.

THE PATRON OF A CHURCH, CITY OR TOWN
is a Solemnity; Gloria and Creed are said at Mass, a first EP is said. The readings used in the Office should be the CW Proper Readings given by the middle column of the ORDO, supplemented by readings for the first EP from the list below, or else readings from the Commons. Or the generous provision in the Weekday Missal may be found helpful.

Appropriate readings should be selected if neither the ORDO nor this Appendix nor the Weekday Missal make adequate provision. August 6 is traditionally the Title of Churches dedicated to Christ; August 15 of those dedicated to S Mary.

If this Solemnity falls on a Sunday in Advent, Lent or Easter, the seasonal notes will indicate how to transfer it. See Introduction, paragraph 5, External Solemnity.

THE PRINCIPAL PATRON OF A DIOCESE is a Solemnity *or* Festum. Anglican Diocesan Calendars tend not to use this term, but it is often clear that particular Saints are so regarded (e.g. Chichester: Ss Richard and Wilfrid; Truro: Ss Piran and Petroc). When more than one Saint is clearly regarded as of more than 'Memorial' status, they should all probably be regarded as Co-Principal Patrons. When such Calendars tend to assume that these Saints can displace a 'Green' Sunday, they may be regarded as Solemnities (1 EP; Gl and Cr at Mass). Rome and EAD prefer such Patrons only to be Festa; no 1 EP; Gl only.

THE TITLE OF THE LOCAL CHURCH is a Solemnity.

THE TITLE OF THE CATHEDRAL is not observed outside the Cathedral unless (which tends particularly to be true in 'Celtic' areas) he/she – may be regarded as also the Diocesan Patron.

WHEN A SOLEMNITY REQUIRES A FIRST EVENING PRAYER (CW):

HYMNS are the same as for the Second EP.

	Psalm	OT Reading	NT Reading
S Paul	149	Isa 49:1–13	Acts 22:3–16
Presentation	118	I Sam 1:19b–28	Heb 4:11–16
S Mark	19	Isa 52:7–10	Mk 1:1–15
Ss P and James	25	Isa 40:27–31	Jn 12:20–26
S Matthias	147	Isa 22:15–22	Phil 3:13b–4:1
Visitation	45	Songs 2:8–14	Lk 1:26–38
S Barnabas	1 & 15	Isa 42:5–12	Acts 14:8–28
S Thomas	27	Isa 35	Heb 10:35–11:1
S Mary Magdalen	139	Isa 25:1–9	II Cor 1:3–7
S James	144	Deut 30:11–20	Mk 5:21–43
Transfiguration	99 & 110	Exodus 24:12–18	Jn 12:27–36a
S Bartholomew	97	Isa 61:1–9	II Cor 6:1–10
Holy Cross Day	66	Isa 52:13–53:12	Eph 2:11–22
S Matthew	34	Isa 33:13–17	Mt 6:19–34
S Michael etc	91	II Kgs 6:8–17	Mt 18:1–6 & 10
S Luke	33	Hos 6:1–3	II Tim 3:10–17
Ss S and Jude	124, 125, & 126	Deut 32:1–4	Jn 14:15–26
S Andrew	48	Isa 49:1–9a	I Cor 4:9–16

Appendix 3

CW COMMONS

Arranged for use at mass; but available to be used at the Office when, for example, a Patron is to be celebrated.
*coincides with or overlaps Roman reading. †Reading supplied from R:

	1st READING		PSALMS	2nd READING	GOSPEL
	OT: Outside Eastertide	NT: Within Eastertide			
MARTYRS	II Chron 24:17–21*	Rev 12:10–12a*	31:1–5*	Rom 8:35–39*	Mt 10:16–22*
	Wisd 4:10–15		126*	II Cor 4:7–15*	Mt 10:28–39*
	Isa 43:1–7		3; 11	II Tim 2:3–7(8–13)*	Jn 12:24–26*
	Jer 11:18–20		44:19–24	I Pet 4:12–19*	Jn 15:18–21*
				Heb 11:32–40	Mt 16:24–26
BISHOPS AND PASTORS	I Sam 16:1 & 6–13*	Acts 20:28–35*	15*; 96*	I Cor 4:1–5*	Jn 10:11–16*
	Isa 6:1–8*		110*	II Cor 4:1–10*	Jn 21:15–17*
	Jer 1:4–10*		1; 16:5–11	II Cor 5:14–20*	Mt 11:25–30
	Ezek 3:16–21*			I Pet 5:1–4*	Mt 24:42–46
	Mal 2:5–7				

	1st READING				
	OT: Outside Eastertide	NT: Within Eastertide	PSALMS	2nd READING	GOSPEL
DOCTORS	I Kgs 3:(6–10)11–14* Wisd 7:7–10 & 15–16* Ecclus 39:1–10* Prov 4:1–9	Acts 13:26–33†	19:7–10* 37:30–35* 119:89–96* 119:97–104 34:11–17	I Cor 1:18–25* I Cor 2:1–10* I Cor 2:9–16* Eph 3:8–12* II Tim 4:1–8* Titus 2:1–18	Mt 5:13–19* Mt 23:8–12* Mk 4:1–9* Mt 13:52–58 Jn 16:12–15
VIRGINS	Song S 8:6–7* Hos 2:14–15 & 19–20*	Rev 19:1 & 5–9*	45†; 149†	II Cor 10:17–11.2*	Mt 19:3–12*
HOLY MEN AND WOMEN	Gen 12:1–14* Mic 6:6–8* Ecclus 2:7–13(14–17)* Prov 8:1–11	Rev 21:(1–4)5–7*	33:1–5 32; 119:1–8; 139:1–4(5–12); 145:8–14	Eph 3:14–19* Eph 6:11–18* Jas 2:14–17* I Jn 4:7–16* Heb 13:7–8 & 15–16	Mt 25:1–13* Mt 25:14–30* Jn 15:1–8* Jn 17:20–26* Mt 19:16–21
RELIGIOUS As for Virgins; and—	I Kgs 19:9–18* Prov 10:27–32 Isa 61:10–62.5	Acts 4:32–35*	34:1–8* 112:1–9* 131* 119:57–64 123	Phil 3:7–14* I Jn 2:15–17	Mt 11:25–30* Mt 19:3–12 Lk 9:57–62* Lk 12:32–37* Mt 19:23–30
MISSIONARIES	Isa 52:7–10 Isa 61:1–3a Ezek 34:11–16 Jonah 3:1–5	Acts 2:14 & 22–36 Acts 13:46–49 Acts 16:6–10 Acts 26:19–23	67; 87; 97; 100; 117	Rom 15:17–21 II Cor 5:11–6:2	Mt 9:35–38 Mt 28:16–20 Mk 16:15–20 Lk 5:1–11 Lk 10:1–9
Those who worked for the UNDER-PRIVILEGED	Isa 58:6–11*	Acts 4:32–35†	82; 146: 5–10	I Jn 3:14–18* Heb 13:1–3	Mt 5:1–12* Mt 25:31–46*
MARRIED	Tobit 8:4–7* Prov 31:10–31*	Rev 19:1 & 5–9†	128* 127	I Pet 3:1–9*	Mk 3:31–35* Lk 10:38–42*
RULERS	I Sam 16:1–13a I Kgs 3:3–14	Rev 3:14 & 20–22†	72:1–7 99	I Tim 2:1–6	Lk 14:27–33* Mk 10:42–45
SCHOLARS	Prov 8:22–31 Ecclus 44:1–15	Rev 21:5–7†	36:5–10 49:1–4	Phil 4:7–8*	Mt 13:44–46 & 52* Jn 7:14–18

Office of the Dead (a selection)

MP	Ps: 40, 42		Isa 25:6–9 Phil 3:10–21	Isa 38:10–20 I Cor 15:51–end
EP	H: 350 vv 1 & 4–7 (NEH 327) Ps: 121, 130		Lam 3:22–26 & 31–33 Jn 14:1–6	Isa 43:1–7 Rev 1:9–18

Appendix 4

'LESSER FESTIVALS' AND 'COMMEMORATIONS'

in The Christian Year: Calendar, Lectionary and Collects=Common Worship.

This list contains two distinct categories:

(a) the *Roman type* names, followed (mostly without description) by: are those (only) of the CW 'lesser festivals' for which CW provides optional proper readings. Some, but not all, of these suggested readings coincide with Roman optional suggestions for the same Saint; those which do are marked †.

(b) the *Italic* names, with brief descriptions, are those recommended, as 'commemorations': i.e. for naming in the prayers of intercession and thanksgiving. The Liturgical Commission admitted that it had not been 'scrupulous in reflecting on questions of orthodoxy or even baptismal status' with regard to some of these. Your compiler, see front of volume, may be able to provide information about some of them. 'RefM' means 'Reformation Martyr'.

(BRACKETS) distinguish those who have not been canonised or enjoyed a traditional cultus in the Latin or Byzantine rites. Your compiler accepts that different ecclesiological presuppositions will lead different users to regard some of these as having been definitively raised to the altars of the Church; or as suited to a real but restricted cultus ('Beati'); or as orthodox Christians judged to have had cardinal and theological virtues to a heroic degree and deserving therefore a private cultus ('Venerabiles'); or as still needing to have the Holy Sacrifice offered for them. (Those listed for 'commemoration' on the CW list who have been canonised, or enjoyed a long-standing traditional cultus, are mostly omitted from this list since they are incorporated into the main body of the ORDO as having (CW) 'an established celebration in the wider church'.)

JAN:
- 2 Basil and Gregory: II Tim 4:1–8; Mt 5:13–19
- 2 *Seraphim, Monk*
- 2 *(Vedanayagam Samuel Azariah, Bishop)*
- 10 *(William Laud, Bishop, Martyr)*
- 11 *(Mary Slessor, Missionary)*
- 12 Aelred: Ecclus 15:1–6
- 13 Hilary: I Jn 2:18–25†; Jn 8:25–32
- 13 *(George Fox)*
- 17 Antony: Phil 3:7–14; Mt 19:16–26†
- 17 *(Charles Gore, Bishop)*
- 19 Wulfstan: Mt 24:42–46
- 20 *Richard Rolle, Religious*
- 21 Agnes: Rev 7:13–17
- 24 Francis de Sales: Prov 3:13–18; Jn 3:17–21
- 28 Thomas Aquinas: Wisd 7:7–10 & 15–16; I Cor 2:9–16; Jn 16:12–15
- 30 Charles: Ecclus 2:12–17; I Tim 6:12–16

FEB:
- 3 Anskar: Isa 52:7–10; Rom 10:11–15
- 14 Cyril and Methodius: Isa 52:7–10; Rom 10:11–15
- 15 *(Thomas Bray, Priest)*
- 17 *(Janani Luwum, Bishop, Martyr)* Ecclus 4:20–28; Jn 12:24–32
- 23 Polycarp: Rev 2:8–11†
- 27 *(George Herbert, Priest:* Mal 2:5–7; Mt 11:25–30; Rev 19:5–9

MAR:
- 1 David: II Sam 23:1–4; Ps 89:19–22 & 24
- 7 Perpetua, etc.: Rev 12:10–12a; Wisd 3:1–7
- 8 *(Geoffrey Studdert Kennedy, Priest)*
- 8 *(Edward King, Bishop:* Heb 13:1–8)
- 17 Patrick: Ps 19:1–4 & 13–16; Lk 10:1–12 & 17–20
- 21 *(Thomas Cranmer, Bishop, RefM.)*
- 24 *(Walter Hilton, Religious)*
- 24 *(Oscar Romero, Bishop, Martyr)*
- 26 *(Harriet Monsell, Religious)*
- 31 *(John Donne, Priest)*

APR: 1 (*Frederick Denison Maurice, Priest*)
9 (*Dietrech Bonhoeffer, Martyr*)
10 (*William Law, Priest:* I Cor 2:9–16;
Mt 17:1–9)
10 (*William of Ockham*)
11 (*George Augustus Selwyn, Bishop*)
16 (*Isabella Gilmore, Deaconess*)
19 Alphege: Heb 5:1–4
21 Anselm: Wisd 9:13–18; Rom 5:8–11
27 (*Christina Rossetti*)
29 Catherine: Prov 8:1 & 6–11; Jn 17:12–26
30 (*Pandita Mary Ramabai*)

MAY: 2 Athanasius: Ecclus 4:20–28; Mt 10:24–27
8 (*Julian:* I Cor 13:8–13; Mt 5:13–16)
16 (*Caroline Chisholm*)
19 Dunstan: Mt 24:42–46; Exod 31:1–5
20 (*Alcuin, Deacon, Abbot:* Col 3:12–16;
Jn 4:19–24)
24 (*John and Charles Wesley, Priests:* Eph
5:12–20)
25 Bede: Ecclus 39:1–10
26 Augustine: I Thess 2:2b–8; Mt 13:31–33
26 (*John Calvin, Priest*)
28 (*Lanfranc, Bishop*)
30 (*Josephine Butler:* Isa 58:6–11;
I Jn 3:18–23; Mt 9:10–13
30 (*Apolo Kivebulaya, Priest*)

JUNE: 1 Justin: Jn 15:18–21; I Macc 2:15–22;
I Cor 1:18–25
5 Boniface: Acts 20:24–28
6 (*Ini Kopuria, Religious*)
8 (*Thomas Ken, Bishop:* II Cor 4:1–10;
Mt 24:42–46)
9 Columba: Titus 2:11–15
14 (*Richard Baxter, Priest*)
15 (*Evelyn Underhill*)
16 Richard: Jn 21:15–19
16 (*Joseph Butler, Bishop*)
17 (*Samuel, Priest, and Henrietta Barnett*)
18 (*Bernard Mizeki, Martyr*)
19 (*Sundar Singh of India*)
22 Alban: II Tim 2:3–13; Jn 12:24–26
23 Etheldreda: Mt 25:1–13
28 Irenæus: II Pet 1:16–21

JULY: 1 (*John and Henry Venn, Priests*)
11 Benedict: I Cor 3:10–11; Lk 18:18–22
14 (*John Keble, Priest:* Lam 3:19–26;
Mt 5:1–8)
15 Swithun: Jas 5:7–11 & 13–18
18 (*Elizabeth Ferard, Deaconess*)
19 Gregory, and Macrina: I Cor 2:9–13;
Wisd 9:13–17
20 (*Bartolomé de las Casas, Bishop*)
27 (*Brooke Foss Westcott, Bishop*)
30 (*William Wilberforce:* Job 31:16–23;
Gal 3:26–29 & 4:6–7; Lk 4:16–21)

AUG: 5 Oswald: I Pet 4:12–19; Jn 16:29–33
7 (*John Mason Neale, Priest*)
8 Dominic: Ecclus 39:1–10
9 (*Mary Sumner:* Heb 13:1–5)
10 Laurence: II Cor 9:6–10†
11 Clare: Song S 8:6–7
11 (*John Henry Newman, Priest*)
13 (*Jeremy Taylor, Bishop:* Titus 2:7–8 &
11–14)
13 (*Florence Nightingale*)
13 (*Octavia Hill*)
20 Bernard: Rev 19:5–9
20 (*William and Catherine Booth*)
27 Monica: Ecclus 26:1–3 & 13–16
28 Augustine: Ecclus 39:1–10; Rom 13:11–13
30 (*John Bunyan:* Heb 12:1–2; Lk 21:2 1 &
34–36)
31 Aidan: I Cor 9:16–19

SEPT: 2 (*The Martyrs of Papua New Guinea*)
3 Gregory: I Thess 2:3–8
4 Cuthbert: Ezek 34:11–16; Mt 18:12–14
6 (*Allen Gardiner, Missionary*)
9 (*Charles Fuge Lowder, Priest*)
13 John Chrysostom: Mk 5:13–19; Jer 1:4–10
15 Cyprian: I Pet 4:12–19; Mt 18:18–22
16 Ninian: Acts 13:46–49; Mk 16:15–20
16 (*Edward Bouverie Pusey, Priest*)
17 Hildegard: I Cor 2:9–13; Lk 10:21–24
20 (*John Coleridge Patteson, Bishop and Comps
Martyrs:* II Chron 24:17–21;
Acts 7:55–60
25 (*Lancelot Andrewes, Bishop:* Isa 6:1–8)
25 *Sergei of Radonezh, Religious*
26 (*Wilson Carlile, Priest*)
27 Vincent de Paul: I Cor 1:25–31†;
Mt 25:34–40

OCT: 1 (*Anthony Ashley Cooper*)
4 Francis: Gal 6:14–18†; Lk 12:22–34
6 (*William Tyndale, RefM:* Prov 8:4–11;
II Tim 3:12–17
9 (*Robert Grosseteste, Bishop*)
10 Paulinus: Mt 28:16–20
10 (*Thomas Traherne*)
11 (*James the Deacon*)
12 Wilfrid: Lk 5:1–11; I Cor 1:18–25
12 (*Elizabeth Fry*)
12 (*Edith Cavell*)
13 Edward the Confessor: II Sam 23:1–5;
I Jn 4:13–16
15 Teresa of Avila: Rom 8:22–27†
16 (*Nicholas Ridley, Bishop, and Hugh Latimer,
Bishop, RefMs*)
17 Ignatius: Phil 3:7–12; Jn 6:52–58
19 (*Henry Martyn:* Mk 16:15–20; Isa 55:6–11)
26 (*Alfred the Great:* II Sam 23:1–5; Jn
18:33–37)
26 Chad/Cedd: I Tim 6:11b–16
29 (*James Hannington, Bishop and Martyr:* Mt
10:28–39)
31 (*Martin Luther, Priest, Religious*)

OIL IN INITIATION

1. The main thrust of the ancient Western, and particularly Roman, tradition is to use two distinct sets of terms:
   (a) line[i]re or ung(u)ere (or simply tangere) – to *smear* oil on; and
   (b) (con)signare – to 'seal' with the *sign* of (usually) the Cross.
2. The use of oil may feature at three points:
   (i) Before the act of Baptism, when the Oil of the Catechumens, often nowadays called the Oil of Baptism, is used. Historically, 1(a) terms were used, and the candidates were smeared on their *chests* and *backs* (in the modern Roman Rite, only on their chests) *not* on (the one place required in *Common Worship*!) their heads.
   Concepts of exorcism or of the Christian Athlete can be associated with this.
   (ii) Immediately after the act of baptism. Historically, a presbyter smeared (1(a)) *the top of the head* (*not* the forehead) of the new Christian with Chrism. This is still Roman practice.
   (iii) In Confirmation, when the Bishop sealed (1(b)) the *forehead* of the candidates, usually (but see 3, below) having dipped his thumb in Chrism. This is still Roman practice.
3. One way of reading the evidence is to see 2(ii) as a preliminary to 2(iii); the presbyter (as S. Ambrose's description appears to suggest) poured generously and smeared oil from the top of the head downwards, and the Bishop then thumbed the sign of the Cross on the already oily forehead. When the current Western practice of splitting 'Baptism' and 'Confirmation' results in 2(ii) and 2(iii) having several years between them, one could, catechetically, explain 2(ii) in 'Baptism' as a 'pointer' to 2(iii) in 'Confirmation'.
4. SUMMARY. If it is desired to use CW texts as they stand:
   (i) CW Section "Signing with the Cross":
   – Make the sign of the Cross on the **chest**. If using oil, use the "Oil of Baptism".
   (ii) CW Section "Baptism," after the words ". . . inheritance of the Saints in glory. Amen.":
   – Do **not** make the sign of the Cross. If using oil, simply smear Chrism on the **top** of the head, **saying nothing**.
   (iii) The sign of the Cross on the forehead is proper to Confirmation alone.

Advent 2008 until Christ the King 2009 inclusive:
CW and the ROMAN SUNDAY LECTIONARY . . . . *CYCLE B*
    This year's readings are dominated by S Mark's Gospel.

DAILY EUCHARISTIC AND OFFICE LECTIONARIES . . . . *CYCLE 1*

ADVENT AND DECEMBER

UNTIL DECEMBER 16

1 Nothing may displace the Sunday Mass and Office. Any Solemnity (e.g. Dedication or Patron) is transferred to the Monday. Festa and Memorials are suppressed. (CW orders a Festum to be so transferred to Monday, and allows Dedication and Patronal festivals except on Advent 1.)

2 Altars are not decorated with *flowers* except on Solemnities, Festa, and Advent 3; and apart from these days the *organ* and other instruments are only played at liturgical services to sustain singing.

3 **Office Hymns. Until 16 December: EH: MP 2 EP 1. *NEH: MP 2 EP 1.***

4 On the Sundays of Advent, *Te Deum* is said at MP even though the *Gloria* is not used at Mass.

5 A seasonal form of the **Penitential Rite** (Introduction 12) is given in PHG p. 128, 2a (=R:).

6 Of the two prefaces provided in the Roman missal, Advent (I) is to be used from Advent Sunday to 16 December. This **preface** is the first of the 'extended' CW prefaces. On memorials, *either* the *seasonal* preface is used, *or* that of the Saint.

7 November 29 is, in Anglican Calendars, a Day of Intercession for the Missionary Work of the Church.

DECEMBER 17 – 31

8 On December 17 the Great Antiphons begin. They are found at EH 734 and NEH 503, and they are all now a day later than the medieval/BCP dates given in EH and NEH. They are said before and after the Magnificat at EP. (PHG suggests other uses for these Antiphons.)

9 In the Roman rite, the second Advent **preface** is now used. This preface is the second of the 'extended' CW prefaces.

10 **Office Hymns: EH: MP 14 EP 5. *NEH: MP 19 EP5.***

11 On the remaining weekdays of December, the propers in the Daily Eucharistic Lectionary are according to the *date in the month*.

12 On the remaining weekdays of December, Memorials are indicated [within square brackets] which means the following: Mass and Office of the Feria. The Memorial may be *either* totally ignored; *or* its Collect may be said *after* the Collect of the day at MP and EP, and *instead* of the Collect of the day at Mass.

13 Advent 4 is the Sunday of the Fathers of the Old Testament, and of Our Lady seen as the climax of God's ancient Covenant and Scriptures. The ancient Western celebration of January 1 as the Solemnity of Mary, Mother of God (Theotokos), is not a duplication of this, since it concentrates more on Our Lady as guarantee of the dogmatic truths of the Incarnation: Christ, Man and God; one Person, two Natures. (CW provides the R: mass readings of this Solemnity.) 'The . . . Council of Ephesus used *Theotokos* . . . to affirm the oneness of Christ's person by identifying Mary as the Mother of God the Word incarnate.' (ARCIC 2005)

IMMACULATE CONCEPTION OF THE BVM

1 'The Immaculate Conception was a feast (and a doctrine) first developed in the West in the Anglo-Saxon England of the early eleventh century on an older and rather different Byzantine basis.' (Gregory Dix). (It had to fend off assaults by Norman Romanizers who pointed out that it was not observed by the Papal Court.)

2 'As a result of our study, the Commission offers the following agreements, which we believe significantly advance our consensus regarding Mary. We affirm together . . . that in view of her vocation to be the Mother of the Holy One, Christ's redeeming work reached "back" in Mary to the depths of her being and to her earliest beginnings.' (ARCIC 2005)

3 While CW only offers the Commons, we follow PHG, which provides the (R:) mass readings and the full provision for MP and EP (Collect 89) as being 'appropriate to the season of Advent'. 'In the night of the Advent expectation, Mary began to shine like a true *Stella Matutina*. For just as the Morning Star, together with the Dawn, precedes the rising of the Sun, so Mary from the time of her Immaculate Conception preceded the coming of the Saviour, the rising of the Sun of Righteousness.' (JP2). PPL urges a Novena.

4 The *Office Hymns* now used are not in EH or NEH but may be obtained from the Compiler. The Common Hymns are 213, 214, 215 (NEH 180, 181, 183). EH 229 vv 1–3 & 7 is appropriate.

5 S John Diego Cuahtlatoatzin (Dec 9) was the visionary who saw our Lady of Guadalupe (Dec 12), Patron of the Americas. They have both been added optionally to the Universal Calendar as an expression of the Church's universality. For obtaining the Collects, see *PRAENOTANDA*.

S NICOLAS, BISHOP, PATRON: Mass: Isa 61:1–3; I Tim 6:6–11; Mk 10:13–16
    1 EP: Ezek 34:11–16, Mt 25:14–30   MP: Isa 6:1–8, I Cor 4:1–6
    2 EP: Isa 52:7–10; I Tim 4:1–5   Psalms, 1, 15, 23 (CW and PHG.)

✠ *SUNDAY* | **ADVENT 1**

30   P   MP   Ps: 44   Isa 2:1–5   Isa 1:1–20
   Lk 12:35–48   Mt 24:1–28

R: Ps I   Mass   *no Gl; Cr; Pref of Advent (1)*
   (Anniversary of the Episcopal Ordination, in 2000, of Andrew, third Bishop of Ebbsfleet)
   CW: Isa 64:1–9; Ps 80:1–7 & 18–20; I Cor 1:3–9; Mk 13:24–37
   R: Isa 63:16–17 & 64:1 & 3–8; Ps 80; I Cor 1:3–9; Mk 13:33–7 (Waiting for the Lord)

   2 EP   Isa 1:1–20   Isa 2:10–end
   Ps: 25   Mt 21:1–13   I Thess 5

D E C E M B E R

MONDAY   Feria (S Andrew, Sol, in Scotland)

1   P   MP   Ps: 1, 2, 3   Isa 42:18–end   Isa 3:1–15
   Rev 19   Mk 1:1–20

   Mass   *of Sunday or the day in Advent; no Gl or Cr; Pref of Advent (1)* (**Charles de Foucauld**)
   Isa 2:1–5; Ps 122; Mt 8:5–11

   EP   Isa 25:1–9   Isa 4:2–end
   Ps: 4, 7   Mt 12:1–21   Rev 6

TUESDAY   Feria

2   P   MP   Ps: 5, 6, 8   Isa 43:1–13   Isa 5:1–17
   Rev 20   Mk 1:21–end

   Mass   *as Monday*
   Isa 11:1–10; Ps 72:1–4 & 18–19; Lk 10:21–24

   EP   Isa 26:1–13   Isa 5:18–end
   Ps: 9, 10   Mt 12:22–37   Rev 7

WEDNESDAY   S Francis Xavier, Pr

3   W   MP   Ps: 119: 1–32   Isa 43:14–end   Isa 6
   Rev 21:1–8   Mk 2:1–22

   Mass   *of the Saint*
   Isa 25:6–10a; Ps 23; Mt 15:29–37

   EP   Isa 28:1–13   Isa 8:16 – 9:7
   Ps: 11, 12, 13   Mt 12:38–end   Rom 8

THURSDAY   Feria (☐ S John of Damascus, Pr, Dr)

4   P   MP   Ps: 14, 15, 16   Isa 44:1–8   Isa 9:8 – 10:4
   (or W)   Rev 21:9–21   Mk 2:23 – 3:12

   Mass   *as Monday (or of the Saint)* (**Nicolas Ferrar, Dcn, Rel**)
   Isa 26:1–6; Ps 118:18–27a; Mt 7:21 & 24–27

   EP   Isa 28:14–end   Isa 10:5–23
   Ps: 18   Mt 13:1–23   Rev 9

FRIDAY   Feria (☐ S Birinus, B*)

5   P   MP   Ps: 17, 19   Isa 44:9–23   Isa 10:24 – 11:9
   Rev 21:22 – 22:5   Mk 3:13–end

   Mass   *as Monday (First Friday: Sacred Heart, see p. 42)*
   Isa 29:17–end; Ps 27:1–4 & 16–17; Mt 9:27–31

   EP   Isa 29:1–14   Isa 11:10–12 end
   Ps: 22   Mt 13:24–43   Rev 10

SATURDAY   Feria (S Nicolas, B, see p. xxxvi)

6   P   MP   Ps: 20, 21, 23   Isa 44:24 – 45:13   Isa 13:1 – 14:2
   (or W)   Rev 22:6–end   Mk 4:1–20

   Mass   *as Monday (or of the Saint) (First Saturday: Immaculate Heart, see p. 42)*
   Isa 30:19–21 & 23–26; Ps 146:4–9; Mt 9:35 – 10:1 & 6–8

   P   1 EP of foll   Isa 29:15–end   Isa 14:3 – 27
   Ps: 24, 25   Mt 13:44–end   Rev 11

---

* His traditional date. CW prefers September 4.

✠ *SUNDAY*   **ADVENT 2**

7   P   MP   Ps: 80   Zeph 3:14–20 or Baruch 5:1–9   Isa 5:1–16
                                                 Lk 1:5–20   Mt 24:29–end

R: Ps II   Mass   *no Gl; Cr; Pref of Advent (1)*
                      CW: Isa 40:1–11; Ps 85:1–2 & 8–13; II Pet 3:8–15a; Mk 1:1–8
                      R: Isa 40:1–5 & 9–11; Ps 85; II Pet 3:8–14; Mk 1:1–8 (The Good News)
           2 EP of Sunday   I Kgs 22:1–28   Isa 5:18–end
                                   Ps: 40   Rom 15:4–13   II Tim 3:14 – 4:8

MONDAY   **IMMACULATE CONCEPTION OF THE BVM (PHG)** (transferred)
                 (see page xxxvi)

8   W   MP   Ps: 46, 87   Isa 61:10 – 62:5   ◁
                                               I Cor 1:26–30   ◁

           Mass   *Cl; Cr; Proper Pref (or CW Annunciation)*
                    Gen 3:9–15 & 20; Ps 98; Eph 1:3–6 & 11–12; Lk 1:26–38
           EP   Zeph 3:14–17   ◁
                    Ps: 94   Rev 11:19 & 12:1–6 & 10   ◁

TUESDAY   *Feria (☐ S John Diego Cuahtlatoatzin)*

9   P   MP   Ps: 32, 36   Isa 46   Isa 19:1–17
        (or W)   I Thess 2:1–12   Mk 5:1–20

           Mass   *of Sunday or the day in Advent; no GL or Cr; Pref of Advent (1) (or of the Saint)*
                    Isa 40:1–11; Ps 96:1 & 10–end; Mt 18:12–14
           EP   Isa 30:19–end   Isa 19:18–end
                    Ps: 33   Mt 14:13–end   Rev 13

WEDNESDAY   *Feria*

10   P   MP   Ps: 34   Isa 47   Isa 21:1–12
                                               I Thess 2:13–end   Mk 5:21–end

           Mass   *as Tuesday (**The Holy House: Loretto, Walsingham and Glastonbury**)**
                    Isa 40:25–end; Ps 103:8–13; Mt 11:28–end
           EP   Isa 31   Isa 22:1–14
                    Ps: 119:33–56   Mt 15:1–20   Rev 14

THURSDAY   *Feria (☐ S Damasus I, Pp)*

11   P   MP   Ps: 37   Isa 48:1–11   Isa 24
        (or W)   I Thess 3   Mk 6:1–13

           Mass   *as Tuesday (or of the Saint)*
                    Isa 41:13–20; Ps 145:1 & 8–13; Mt 11:11–15
           EP   Isa 32   Isa 28:1–13
                    Ps: 39, 40   Mt 15:21–28   Rev 15

FRIDAY   *Feria (☐ Our Lady of Guadalupe)*

12   P   MP   Ps: 31   Isa 48:12–end   Isa 28:14–end
        (or W)   I Thess 4:1–12   Mk 6:14–29

           Mass   *of the Saint (or of our Lady)*
                    Isa 48:17–19; Ps 1; Mt 11:16–19
           EP   Isa 33:1–22   Isa 29:1–14
                    Ps: 35   Mt 15:29–end   Rev 16

SATURDAY   *S Lucy, V, M*

13   R   MP   Ps: 41, 42, 43   Isa 49:1–13   Isa 29:15–end
                                               I Thess 4:13–end   Mk 6:30–end

           Mass   *of the Saint (**Samuel Johnson**)*
                    Ecclus 48:1–4 & 9–11; Ps 80:1–4 & 18–19; Mt 17:10–13
           P   1 EP of Advent 3   Isa 35   Isa 30:1–18
        (or Rose)   Ps: 45, 46   Mt 16:1–12   Rev 17

---

* The shrine at Loretto was particularly highly profiled in late fifteenth century, and an abbot who had seen it reproduced it at Glastonbury. The English Missal has the old mass for this day.

✠ *SUNDAY*
14 P (or Rose)
R: Ps III

ADVENT 3 *(O Rex)*

MP	Ps: 50:1–6 & 62	Isa 12	Isa 25:1–9
		Lk 1:57–66	Mt 25:1–30
Mass	*no Gl; Cr; Pref of Advent (1) or (2)*		
	CW: Isa 61:1–4 & 8–11; Ps Mag; I Thess 5:16–24; Jn 1:6–8 & 19–28		
	R: Isa 61:1–2 & 10–11; Ps Mag; I Thess 5:16–24; Jn 1:6–8 & 19–28 (S John Baptist)		
2 EP		Mal 3:1–4 & 4	Isa 26:1–13
	Ps: 68:1–20	Phil 4:4–7	I Tim 1:12 – 2:8

MONDAY
15 P

Feria

MP	Ps: 44	Isa 49:14–25	Isa 30:19–end
		I Thess 5:1–11	Mk 7:1–23
Mass	*of Sunday or the day in Advent; no Gl or Cr; Pref of Advent (1)*		
	Num 24:2–7 & 15–17; Ps 25:3–9; Mt 21:23–27		
EP		Isa 38:1–8, 21–22	Isa 31
	Ps: 47, 49	Mt 16:13–end	Rev 18

TUESDAY
16 P

Feria

MP	Ps: 48, 52	Isa 50	Isa 38:1–20
		I Thess 5:12–end	Mk 7:24 – 8:10
Mass			
	Zeph 3:1–2 & 9–13; Ps 34:1–6 & 21–22; Mt 21:28–32		
EP		Isa 38:9–20	Isa 40:1–11
	Ps: 50	Mt 17:1–13	Rev 19

WEDNESDAY
17 P

Feria* (O Sapientia) (NEW LITURGICAL DIRECTIONS pages xxxv–xxxvi)

MP	Ps: 119:57–80	Isa 51:1–8	Isa 40:12–end
		II Thess 1	Mk 8:11 – 9:1
Mass	*no Gl or Cr; of the date in Advent; Pref of Advent (2)* (**Eglantine Jebb**)		
	Gen 49:2 & 8–10; Ps 72:1–5 & 18–19; Mt 1:1–17		
EP		Isa 39	Isa 41
	Ps: 59, 60, 67	Mt 17:14–21	Rev 20

THURSDAY
18 P

Feria (O Adonal)

MP	Ps: 56, 57, 63	Isa 51:9–16	Isa 42:1–17
		II Thess 2	Mk 9:2–32
Mass	*as Wednesday (obit of Michael, second Bishop of Ebbsfleet, in 1999)*		
	Jer 23:5–8; Ps 72:1–2 & 12–13 & 18–end; Mt 1:18–24		
EP		Zeph 1:1 – 2:3	Isa 42:18 – 43:13
	Ps: 61, 62, 64	Mt 17:22–end	Rev 21:1–14

FRIDAY
19 P

Feria (O Radix)*

MP	Ps: 144, 146	Isa 51:17–end	Isa 43:14 – 44:5
		II Thess 3	Mk 9:33–end
Mass	*as Wednesday*		
	Judg 13:2–7 & 24–end; Ps 71:3–8; Lk 1:5–25		
EP		Zeph 3:1–13	Isa 44:6–23
	Ps: 10, 57	Mt 18:1–20	Rev 22:15 – 22:5

SATURDAY
20 P

Feria (O Clavis)*

MP	Ps: 46, 95	Isa 52:1–12	Isa 44:24 – 45:13
		Jude	Mk 10:1–31
Mass	*as Wednesday (**Our Lady of the Annunciation:2**)*		
	Isa 7:10–14; Ps 24:1–6; Lk 1:26–38		
P 1 EP of foll		Zeph 3:14–end	Isa 45:14–end
	Ps: 4, 9	Mt 18:21–end	Rev 22:6–end

---

* Ember Days. See Introduction, paragraph 25.

✠ *SUNDAY*   **ADVENT 4** *(O Oriens)*

21   P   MP   Ps: 144   Isa 7:10–16   Isa 32:1–8
                         Rom 1:1–7   Mt 25:31–end

R: Ps IV   Mass   *no Gl; Cr; Pref of Advent (2) (Anniversary of the Episcopal Ordination in 1996 of David, Bishop in Wales)*
CW: II Sam 7:1–11 & 16; Ps 89:1–4 & 19–26; Rom 16:25–27; Lk 1:26–38
R: II Sam 7:1–5 & 8–11 & 14a & 16; Ps 89; Rom 16:25–27; Lk 1:26–38 (our Lady)

         2 EP   Zech 2:10–13   Isa 40:1–11
                Ps: 113, 131   Lk 1:39–55   II Pet 3:1–14

MONDAY   **Feria** *(O Rex)*

22   P   MP   Ps: 124, 125, 126, 127   Isa 52:13–53 end   Isa 46
                         II Pet 1:1–15   Mk 10:32–end

         Mass   *of the DATE in December; Pref of Advent (2)*
I Sam 1:24–end; Ps 113 ; Lk 1:46–56

         EP   Mal 1:1 & 6–end   Isa 47
              Ps: 24, 48   Mt 19:1–12   Jude 1–16

TUESDAY   **Feria** *(O Emmanuel)* **[Com ☐ S John de Kety, Pr]**

23   P   MP   Ps: 128, 129, 130, 131   Isa 54   Isa 48
                         II Pet 1:16 – 2:3   Mk 11:1–26

         Mass   *as Monday*
Mal 3:1–4 & 4:5–end, Ps 25:3–9; Lk 1:57–66

         EP   Mal 2:1–16   Isa 50:4–10
              Ps: 89:1–37   Mt 19:13–15   Jude 17–end

WEDNESDAY

24   P   MP   Ps: 45, 113   Isa 55   Isa 51:1–16
                         II Pet 2:4–end   Mk 11:27 – 12:12

         Mass   *as Monday*
II Sam 7:1–5 & 8–11 & 16; Ps 89:2 & 19–27; Lk 1:67–79

         1 EP   See Christmas
         Virgil Mass: See Christmas

KING CHARLES THE MARTYR
JANUARY 30

The 1662 Prayer Book put him into the Calendar as a Red Letter Day. This provision has never been legally varied, although the printers took it upon themselves to remove it when the State ceased to provide special services for this day.

As far as Charles Stuart's status is concerned, your Compiler offers these considerations.

(1) As late as the seventeenth century, local churches in the West continued to beatify upon their own authority.

(2) In the seventeenth century, beatification consisted simply of publishing and authorizing liturgical propers.

(3) The texts authorized from 1662 described Charles, not as Saint, but as 'Blessed'.

The old Office Readings were:
MP Ps 9, 10, 11; II Sam 1; Mt 27
EP Ps 79, 94, 85; Jer 12; Heb 11:32 & 12:1–7.

The Society of King Charles the Martyr provides Propers.

✠ NATIVITY OF THE LORD
24-25
CHRISTMAS EVE and CHRISTMAS DAY   GOLD OR WHITE

All the masses of Christmas—*including* the Vigil Mass (see note 1 below) — are celebrated in white vestments, with Gloria, Creed (Kneel for the *Incarnatus*), and Preface of the Incarnation (see note 4 below).

EVE	Evening ('Vigil') Mass: *Isa 62:1–5; Ps 89:3–4 & 15–16 & 26 & 28; Acts 13:16–17 & 22–25*		
	Mt (1–17) 18–end		
	1 EP	Zech 2 (R: Isa 11:1–10)	Zech 2:10–end
	Ps: 85	Rev 1:1–8	Titus 2:11–14
NIGHT	Midnight Mass:		
	CW = R: Isa 9:2–7; Ps 96; Titus 2:11–14; Lk 2:1–14		
DAY	MP Ps: 110, 117	Isa 62:1–5	Isa 9:2–7
		Mt 1:18–25	Lk 2:1–20
	Mass at Dawn:		
	CW: Isa 62:6–12; Ps 97; Titus 3:4–7; Lk 2 (1–7) 8–20		
	R: Isa 62:11–12; Ps 97; Titus 3:4–7; Lk 2:15–20		
	Mass of the Day:		
	CW: Isa 52:7–10; Ps 98; Heb 1:1–4 (5–12); Jn 1:1–14		
	R: Isa 52:7–10; Ps 98; Heb 1:1–6; Jn 1:1–18 or 1–5 & 9–14		
	2 EP	Isa 65:17–25	Isa 35
	Ps: 8	Phil 2:5–11	I Jn 4:7–end

NOTES FOR CHRISTMASTIDE AND EPIPHANY

1 **The Eve.** The Vigil mass of Christmas is the first of the four masses of Christmas, and is celebrated festally as such. Its Collect in the Roman Rite is the ancient one which CW mistakenly assigns to the Advent mass in *purple* vestments said in the *earlier* part of the 24th. This Collect is also used at 1 EP.

2 **Penitential Rite.** Seasonal forms (Introduction, Paragraph 12) are given in PHG: *Christmas* p. 196, 1; *Epiphany* p. 233, a and b (all=R:).

3 **Collects.** *Eve*: see Note 1. *Midnight*: CW gives the Roman Collect in a better translation than R:. *Dawn*: the R: Collect, which is not in CW, is also used at MP. *Day*: CW continues to offer Cranmer's elegant composition.

The ancient Christmas Collect *Almighty God who wonderfully created* ... was introduced by 1928 for Christmas II, transferred by ASB and CW to Christmas I, (where it will unfortunately be in competition with the Holy Family) and is now the Roman Collect for Christmas Day itself.

On *ferial days* from Christmas until the Sunday after Ephiphany, R: has a different Collect for each day. Anglican custom expects the Christmas Day and Epiphany Collects to be used until the following Sundays, and otherwise the Collect of the previous Sunday to be used. Your compiler recommends that it is best *either* to use the daily Roman Collects: *or* to stay with *Almighty God who wonderfully created* ... until Epiphany, and thereafter to use the Epiphany Collect. **Memorials:** see page xxxv note 12.

4 **Prefaces.** The CW 'extended' Preface is a lengthened version of the Roman Preface. R: offers two more Christmas Prefaces. PHG gives us a version of the Roman Epiphany Preface on p. 238 (b); and the Roman Preface for the Baptism on p. 231. On the Feasts of Christmas Week, the Christmas Prefaces are used. On memorials after January 1, the Preface of the Season or of the Saint is used.

5 **Evening Prayer.** The great festival of the Incarnation should dominate its octave. Accordingly, from S Stephen to the Holy Innocents, Rome, endorsed by PHG but not CW, has *MP only* of the Festum; EP of Christmastide (H:17 NEH 19). *Your Order follows this usage*, while giving readings for the Saints *in the right-hand column* for those who follow the other practice, or who need to treat these Saints as Patronal Solemnities. (The readings in both columns are CW.)

6 **Office hymns until Epiphany: EH: MP 18 EP 17 *NEH: MP 20 EP 19.***

FRIDAY   **S Stephen, First Martyr**

26   R   MP   H: 31 (NEH 218)   Jer 26:12–15   ◁
                  Ps: 13, 31:1–8, 150   Acts 6 (=R:)   ◁
         Mass   *Gl; Pref of Incarnation*
                CW: from: II Chron 24:20–22; Acts 7:51–60; Ps 119:161–168; Gal 2:16b–20;
                Mt 10:17–22
                R: Acts 6:8–10 & 7:54–9; Ps 31; Mt 10:17–22

                                                                      [EP of the Saint
         W   EP of Christmas H: 17 (NEH 19)   Isa 41:1–5   Ps 57, 86; Gen 4:1–10
                  Ps: 19   Jn 12:20–26   Mt 23:34–end]

SATURDAY   **S John, Apostle and Evangelist**

27   W   MP   Hymn from Common   Exod 33:12–end   ◁
                  Ps: 21, 147:13–20   I Jn 2:1–11 (=R:)   ◁
         Mass   *Gl; Pref of Christmas*
                CW: Exod 33:7–11a; Ps 117; I Jn 1; Jn 21:19b–25
                R: I Jn 1:1–4; Ps 97; Jn 20:2–8

                                                                      [EP of the Saint:
EITHER W   1 EP of Christmas H: 17 (NEH 19) Isa 41:8–16   Ps 97: Isa 6:1–8
                  Ps: 45   Jn 12:27–33   1 Jn 5:1–12]
   OR   W   1 EP of Holy Family   Prov 4:1–6
                  Ps: 122   Mt 2:12–15 & 19–end

✠ *SUNDAY*   **CHRISTMAS 1 (CW)**

28   MP   Ps: 105:1–11   Isa 63:7–9   Isa 41:8–20
                                            Eph 3:5–12   Col 1:1–20
R: Ps I   Mass   *Gl; Cr; Pref of Christmas*
                   CW: Isa 61:10 – 62:3; Ps 148; Gal 4:4–7; Lk 2:15–21
             EP   Isa 35   Isa 12
                  Ps: 132   Col 1:9–20   Phil 2:1–11

   OR   **HOLY FAMILY SUNDAY (ROMAN & PHG)**
             MP   Ps: 132   Isa 35   ◁
                                             Col 1:1–20   ◁
             Mass   *Gl; Cr; Pref of Christmas*
                    Ecclus 3:2–6 & 12–14; Ps 128; Col 3:12–21; Lk 2:22 (23–38) 39–40
                    OR Gen 15:1–6 & 21:1–3;
                    Ps 105; Heb 11:8 & 11–12 & 17–19; Lk 2:22 (23–38) 39–40
             EP   H: 46 (NEH 45)   Isa 41:21–end   ◁
                  Ps: 84   Phil 2:1–11   ◁

MONDAY   **In the Octave of Christmas (Holy Innocents: PRAENOTANDA)***

29   W   MP   H: 18 (NEH 20)   Isa 57:15–end   Isa 55
                  Ps: 19, 20   Jn 1:1–18   Jn 1:14–18
         Mass   *Gl; Pref of Christmas*
                I Jn 2:3–11; Ps 96:1–4; Lk 2:22–35
         EP   H: 17 (NEH 19)   Jonah 1   Isa 60:1–12
                  Ps: 131, 132   Col 1:1–14   Mt 11:2–6

TUESDAY   **In the Octave of Christmas**

30   W   MP   H: 18 (NEH 20)   Isa 59:1–15a   Isa 60:13–end
                  Ps: 111, 112, 113   Jn 1:19–28   Jn 3:16–21
         Mass   *Gl; Pref of Christmas*
                I Jn 2:12–17; Ps 96:7–10; Lk 2:36–40
         EP   Jonah 2   Isa 61
                  Ps: 65, 84   Col 1:15–23   Mt 16:13–20

* Where S Thomas Becket (Red) is patron, this day is a Solemnity; its first EP supersedes the Sunday 2EP on the 28th. Propers from whatever Missal you use CW: see p. xxxiv; supplemented by CW Commons p. xxx. Elsewhere, there is an optional Commemoration of the Martyr as on p. xxxv, para. 12.

WEDNESDAY			**In the Octave of Christmas** [*Com* □ *(S Silvester) Pp*]	
31	W	MP	Ps: 102	Isa 59:15b–end	Isa 62
				Jn 1:29–34	Jn 6:41–58
		Mass	*as Monday (**John Wycliff, Pr**)*	
			I Jn 2:18–21; Ps 96:1 & 11–end; Jn 1:1–18	
EITHER			1 EP of The Holy Name of Jesus*	Jer 23:1–6	Numb 6:22–26
			Ps: 148, 90	Col 2:8–15	Lk 21:25–36
OR			1 EP of Mary Mother of God (R:)*	Gen 17:1–12a & 15–16	◁
			Ps: 90, 148	Col 2:8–15	◁

* Hymn from tomorrow's EP.

J A N U A R Y   2 0 0 9

THURSDAY			**THE MOST HOLY NAME OF JESUS (CW)**	
1	W	MP	H: 238 (NEH 291)	Gen 17:1–13	Deut 10:12 – 11:1
			Ps: 103, 150	Rom 2:17–29	Rom 2:17–end
		Mass	*Gl; Cr; Pref of Incarnation*	
			Num 6:22–27; Ps 8; Gal 4:4–7; Lk 2:15–21	
		2 EP	H: 237 (NEH 153)	Deut 30: (1–10) 11-20	Deut 30
			Ps: 115	Acts 3:1–16	Col 2:8–15
OR			**MARY MOTHER OF GOD (ROMAN)**	
	W	MP	H: 214 (NEH 181)	Mic 5:2–5a	◁
			Ps: 103	Heb 2:9–17 (=R:)	◁
		Mass	*Gl; Cr; Pref I of BVM*	
			Num 6:22–27; Ps 67; Gal 4:4–7; Lk 2:16–21 (given by PHG & CW)	
		2 EP	H: 613:1 & 3–6		
			(NEH 33)	Baruch 4:36 – 5:4	◁
			Ps: 115	Eph 2:11–22	◁
			WORLD PEACE DAY. SEE Appendix 1.	
FRIDAY			*Ss Basil the Great and Gregory Nazianzen, Bs and Drs*	
2	W	MP	Ps: 18:1–30	Isa 60:1–12	Isa 63:1–6
				Jn 1:35–42	Mt 1:18–end
		Mass	*of the Saints; no Gl; Pref of Christmas (**S Seraphim of Sarov, Rel**)*	
			*(**Vedanayagam Samuel Azariah, B**)*	
			1 Jn 2:22–28; Ps 98:1–4; Jn 1:19–28	
			(Printed in Weekday Missal as 'Readings for 2–12 January: 2 January')	
			(First Friday: Sacred Heart, see p. 42)	
		EP	Ruth 1	Isa 63:7–end	
			Ps: 45, 46	Col 2:8–end	I Thess 1
SATURDAY			*Feria (□ Most Holy Name of Jesus*)*	
3	W	MP	Ps: 127, 128, 131	Isa 60:13–end	Isa 64
				Jn 1:43–end	Mt 2
		Mass	*CW: of Sunday. Weekday Missal: 'Masses for Weekdays of the Christmas Season'**	
			no Gl or Cr; Pref of Christmas (First Saturday: Immaculate Heart, see p. 42)	
			I Jn 2:29 – 3:6; Ps 98:2–7; Jn 1:29–34	
			Holy Name: Phil 2:1–11; Ps 8; Lk 2:21–24	

1 EP of the Epiphany, if it is being observed tomorrow, Sunday. Otherwise, EP as follows:

		EP		Ruth 2	Isa 65:1–16
			Ps: 46; 48	Col 3:1–11	I Thess 2:1–16

* CW texts for January 1 could be used.

The English Roman Catholic Church and the General Synod of the Church of England prefer the Epiphany to be celebrated on the Sunday. The propers are printed here.

✠   **EPIPHANY OF THE LORD**

	1 EP*	H: 38 (NEH 46)	Isa 49:1–13	Isa 42:1–9
		Ps: 96, 97	Jn 4:7–26	Rom 15:8–21
W	MP	H: 40 (NEH 48)	Jer 31:7–14	Isa 49:1–13
		Ps: 113, 132	Jn 1:29–34	Lk 3:15–22

        Mass   *Gl; Cr; Pref of Epiphany (p. 5, note 4)*
               CW: Isa 60:1–6; Ps 72: (1–9) 10–15; Eph 3:1–12; Mt 2:1–12
               R: Isa 60:1–6; Ps 72; Eph 3:2–3a & 5–6; Mt 2:1–12

| | 2 EP | H: 38 (NEH 46) | Isa 60:1–9 (10–22) (= R:) or Baruch 4:36 – 5:9 | Isa 60:9–end |
| | | Ps: 98, 100 | Jn 2:1–11 | Jn 2:1–11 |

Those who prefer to observe the Epiphany on January 6 will observe Christmas 2 as follows:

                          CHRISTMAS 2

| MP | | Zech 8:1–8 | Isa 41:21–end |
| | Ps: 87 | Lk 2:41–52 | I Jn 1:1 – 2:6 |

        Mass   *CW: Ecclus 24:1–12; Wisd 10:15–21; Eph 1:3–14; Jn 1:1–18*
               R: Ecclus 24:1–2 & 8–12; Ps 147; Eph 1:3–6 & 15–18; Jn 1:1–18

| EP | | Isa 46:3–13 | Isa 12 |
| | Ps: 135 | Rom 12:1–8 | Phil 2:1–11 |

and, where Epiphany has been kept on the 6th, the propers for the weekdays after it are as follows:

Jan 7	Wednesday:	Day (A) on p. 9
Jan 8	Thursday:	Day (B) on p. 9
Jan 9	Friday:	Day (C) on p. 9
Jan 10	Saturday:	Day (D) on p. 9

But Saturday EP is the first EP of the Baptism.

* Rome now provides a *Vigil mass of Epiphany*; its Collect should be used also at 1 EP. (We beseech thee/beg you, Lord; may the splendour of thy/your majesty pour its light into our hearts, so that we may be able to pass through the darkness of this world and come to the country of everlasting glory.)

ALL TIMES BELONG TO HIM: THE PASCHAL CANDLE

In many parts of the West, a desire to show, on the Paschal Candle, not only the year 'from the Incarnation' but also other chronological information, led to the fixing onto the Candle each year of a piece of paper – the *charta*. This custom survived at Amiens until 1969.

The following, for Easter 2009, translates, simplifies, and updates French examples of *Charta* texts; some of which were very long.

Year since the Lord's Incarnation	2009
Year since the Lord's Passion	1976
Year since our Lady's Nativity	2023
Year since her Glorious Assumption	1959
Year of the Pontificate of Pope Benedict XVI	4
Year of the Ebbsfleet Apostolic District	15
Year of the Episcopate of Bishop Andrew	9

The Sovereign's year; Since the Creation (6009, according to Rouen); Since the foundation of the Church of England (1412); Since the Foundation of the Diocese or Parish . . . scope for eccentricity is endless. The Compiler, if asked, will supply texts in Latin. (Concept by Fr Roger Russell.)

MONDAY   *Feria*
(A) 5 ^W   MP   H: 40 (NEH 48)   Isa 63:7–end   Hos 2:14–3 end
                         Ps: 71   I Jn 3   Mt 5:17–end
              Mass   *CW: of Epiphany; R: from 'Masses for weekdays of the Christmas season'.*
                       no Gl or Cr; Pref of Christmas or Epiphany.
                       I Jn 3:22 – 4:6; Ps 2:7–end; Mk 4:12–17 & 23–end (Printed in Weekday Missal as 'Readings
                       for 2–12 January: 7 January or Monday after Epiphany'.)
              EP   H: 38 (NEH 46)   Baruch 1:15 – 2:10   Hos 4:1–11
                       Ps: 72, 75   Mt 20:1–16   I Thess 4:1–12

TUESDAY   *Feria*
(B) 6 ^W   MP   H: 40 (NEH 48)   Isa 64   Hos 5:8 – 6:6
                         Ps: 73   I Jn 4:7–end   Mt 6:1–18
              Mass   *as above*
                       I Jn 4:7–10; Ps 72:1–8; Mk 6:34–44
              EP   H: 38 (NEH 46)   Baruch 2:11–end   Hos 8
                       Ps: 74   Mt 20:17–28   I Thess 4:13 – 5:11

WEDNESDAY   *Feria (☐ S Raymund of Penyafort, Pr on the 7th)*
(C) 7 ^W   MP   H: 40 (NEH 48)   Isa 65:1–16   Hos 9
                         Ps: 77   I Jn 5:1–12   Mt 6:19–end
              Mass   *as above*
                       I Jn 4:11–18; Ps 72:1 & 10–13; Mk 6:45–52
              EP   H: 38 (NEH 46)   Baruch 3:1–8   Hos 10
                       Ps: 119:81–104   Mt 20:29–end   I Thess 5:12–end

THURSDAY   *Feria*
(D) 8 ^W   MP   H: 40 (NEH 48)   Isa 65:17–end   Hos 11
                         Ps: 78:1–39   I Jn 5:13–end   Mt 7
              Mass   *as above*
                       I Jn 4:19 – 5:4; Ps 72:1 & 17–end; Lk 4:14–22
              EP   H: 38 (NEH 46)   Baruch 3:9 – 4:4   Hos 12
                       Ps: 78:40–end   Mt 23:1–12   II Thess 1

FRIDAY   *Feria*
(E) 9 ^W   MP   H: 40 (NEH 48)   Isa 66:1–11   Hos 13:1–14
                         Ps: 55   II Jn   Mt 8:1–17
              Mass   *as above*
                       I Jn 5:5–13; Ps 147:13–end; Lk 5:12–16
              EP   H: 38 (NEH 46)   Baruch 4:21–30   Hos 14
                       Ps: 69   Mt 23:13–28   II Thess 2

SATURDAY   *Feria*
(F) 10 ^W   MP   H: 40 (NEH 48)   Isa 66:12–23   Joel 1
                         Ps: 76, 79   III Jn   Mt 8:18–end
              Mass   *as above **(William Laud, B, M)***
                       I Jn 5:14–end; Ps 149:1–5; Jn 3:22–30
                       Saturday Evening before the Baptism of the Lord:
              W   1 EP of foll H: 47   Isa 61   ◁ [Joel 2:1–14]
                         Ps: 36   Titus 2:11–14 & 3:4–7   ◁ [II Thess 3]

✠ *SUNDAY* W   MP   **THE BAPTISM OF THE LORD**

11

		Ps: 89:19–29	I Sam 16:1–3 & 13	[Isa 49:13–23]
			Jn 1:29–34	[Mt 17:1–13]

R: Ps I   Mass   *Gl; Cr; Pref (5) (p. 35 note 3)*
CW: Gen 1:1–5; Ps 29; Acts 19:1–7; Mk 1:4–11
R: Isa 42:1–4 & 6–7; Ps 29; Acts 10:34–38; Mk 1:7–11 (or Isa 55:1–11; Ps Isa 12:2–6; I Jn 5:1–9; Mk 1:7–11)

	2 EP	H: 38 (NEH 58)	Isa 42:1–9	[Isa 61]
		Ps: 46, 47	Eph 2:1–10	[Mt 2]

'ORDINARY TIME' – 'PER ANNUM' – 'THE GREEN SEASON' – BEGINS

1st WEEK of YEAR

MONDAY G   MP   *Feria (S Aelred of Rievaulx, Ab)*

12 (or W)

	MP	Ps: 80, 82	Amos 1	Joel 2:15–end
			I Cor 1:1–17	Mt 9:1–17

Mass   *CW: of Epiphany 1; R: of the first week of the year; no Gl or Cr; Common Pref (or of the Saint)*
(Benedict Biscop, Ab)
Heb 1:1–6; Ps 97:1–2 & 6–10; Mk 1:14–20

	EP		Gen 1:1–19	Joel 3
		Ps: 85, 86	Mt 21:1–17	Gal 1

TUESDAY G   MP   *Feria (S Hilary, B, Dr; Scotland: S Kentigern, B, Feast)*

13 (or W)

	MP	Ps: 87, 89:1–18	Amos 2	Amos 1
			I Cor 1:18–end	Mt 9:18–34

Mass   *as Monday (or of the Saint)* **(George Fox)**
Heb 2:5–12; Ps 8; Mk 1:21–28

	EP		Gen 1:20 – 2:3	Amos 2
		Ps: 89:19–end	Mt 21:18–32	Gal 2

WEDNESDAY G   *Feria*

14

	MP	Ps: 119:105–128	Amos 3	Amos 3
			I Cor 2	Mt 9:35 – 10:23

Mass   *as Monday*
Heb 2:14–end; Ps 105:1–9; Mk 1:29–39

	EP		Gen 2:4–end	Amos 4
		Ps: 91, 93	Mt 21:33–end	Gal 3

THURSDAY G   *Feria*

15

	MP	Ps: 90, 92	Amos 4	Amos 5
			I Cor 3	Mt 10:24–end

Mass   *as Monday*
Heb 3:7–14; Ps 95:1 & 8–end; Mk 1:40–end

	EP		Gen 3	Amos 6
		Ps: 94	Mt 22:1–14	Gal 4:1 – 5:1

FRIDAY G   *Feria*

16

	MP	Ps: 88, 95	Amos 5:1–17	Amos 7
			I Cor 4	Mt 11

Mass   *as Monday*
Heb 4:1–5 & 11; Ps 78:3–8; Mk 2:1–12

	EP		Gen 4:1–16, 25–26	Amos 8
		Ps: 102	Mt 22:15–33	Gal 5:2–end

SATURDAY W   *S Antony, Abbot*

17

	MP	Ps: 96, 97, 100	Amos 5:18–end	Amos 9
			I Cor 5	Mt 12:1–21

Mass   *of the Saint* **(Charles Gore, B)**
Heb 4:12–16; Ps 19:7–end; Mk 2:13–17

G	1 EP of foll		Gen 6:1–10	Obadiah
		Ps: 104	Mt 22:34–end	Gal 6

✠ SUNDAY   **2nd SUNDAY and WEEK of YEAR; EPIPHANY 2**

18   G   MP   Ps: 145:1–12   Isa 62:1–5   Isa 43:14 – 44:5
                                      I Cor 6:11–20   Eph 1
R: Ps II   Mass   *Gl; Cr; Sunday Preface. CHRISTIAN UNITY: see Introduction Appendix I*
                        CW: I Sam 3:1–10 (11–20); Ps 139:1–5 & 12–18; Rev 5:1–10; Jn 1:43–51
                        R: I Sam 3:3–10 & 19; Ps 40; I Cor 6:13–15 & 17–20; Jn 1:35–42 (Answering God's Call)
         2 EP   Isa 60:9–22   Isa 44:6–23
                  Ps: 96   Heb 6:17 – 7:10   Mk 1:35–end

MONDAY   *Feria (S Wulfstan, B)*

19   G   MP   Ps: 98, 99, 101   Amos 6   Jonah 1 & 2
      (or W)   I Cor 6:1–11   Mt 152:22–end
         Mass   *of Sunday; no Gl or Cr; Common Pref (or of the Saint)*
                Heb 5:1–10; Ps 110:1–4; Mk 2:18–22
         EP   Gen 6:11 – 7:10   Jonah 3 & 4
                  Ps: 103, 105   Mt 24:1–14   I Cor 1:1–25

TUESDAY   *Feria (S Fabian, Pp, M; ☐ S Sebastian, M)*

20   G   MP   Ps: 106   Amos 7   Micah 1
      (or R)   I Cor 6:12–end   Mt 13:1–23
         Mass   *as Monday (or of the Saint)* (**Richard Rolle**)
                Heb 6:10–end; Ps 111; Mk 2:23–end
         EP   Gen 7:11–end   Micah 2
                  Ps: 107   Mt 24:15–28   I Cor 1:26–2 end

WEDNESDAY   *S Agnes, V, M*

21   R   MP   Ps: 110, 111, 112   Amos 8   Micah
                                      I Cor 7:1–24   Mt 13:24–43
         Mass   *of the Saint*
                Heb 7:1–3 & 15–17; Ps 110:1–4; Mk 3:1–6
         EP   Gen 8:1–14   Micah 4:1 – 5:1
                  Ps: 119:129–152   Mt 24:29–end   I Cor 3

THURSDAY   *Feria (S Vincent, Dcn, M)*

22   G   MP   Ps: 113, 115   Amos 9   Micah 5:2–end
      (or R)   I Cor 7:25–end   Mt 13:44–end
         Mass   *as Monday (or of the Saint)*
                Heb 7:25 – 8:6; Ps 40:7–10 & 17–end; Mk 3:7–12
         EP   Gen 8:15 – 9:7   Micah 6
                  Ps: 114, 116, 117   Mt 25:1–13   I Cor 4:1–17

FRIDAY   *Feria*

23   G   MP   Ps: 139   Hos 1:1 – 2:1   Micah 7
                                      I Cor 8   Mt 14
         Mass   *as Monday (**Espousals of the BVM**)*
                Heb 8:6–end; Ps 85:7–end; Mk 3:13–19
         EP   Gen 9:8–19   Nahum 1
                  Ps: 130, 131, 137   Mt 25:14–30   I Cor 4:18–5 end

SATURDAY   *S Francis de Sales, B, Dr*

24   W   MP   Ps: 120, 121, 122   Hos 2:2–17   Nahum 2
                                      I Cor 9:1–14   Mt 15:1–28
         Mass   *of the Saint*
                Heb 9:2–3 & 11–14; Ps 47:1–8; Mk 3:20–21
         G   1 EP of foll   Gen 11:1–9   Nahum 3
                  Ps: 118   Mt 25:31–end   I Cor 6

✠ *SUNDAY*   **3rd SUNDAY and WEEK of YEAR; EPIPHANY 3***

25   G   MP   Ps: 113   Jonah 3:1–5 & 10   Isa 45:9–end
                                       Jn 3:16–21   Eph 2

R: Ps III   Mass   *Gl; Cr; Sunday Pref*
                      CW: Gen 14:17–20; Ps 128; Rev 19:6–10; Jn 2:1–11
                      R: Jonah 3:1–5 & 10; Ps 25; I Cor 7:29–31; Mk 1:14–20 (Preaching Repentance)

               2 EP   Jer 3:21 – 4:2   Isa 46:3–end
                      Ps: 33   Titus 2:1–8 & 11–14   Mk 7:24–end

MONDAY   **Ss Timothy & Titus, Bs**

26   W   MP   Ps: 123, 124, 125, 126   Hos 2:18–3 end   Hab 1
                                       I Cor 9:15–end   I Cor 7

             Mass   *of the Saints*
                    Heb 9:15 & 24–end; Ps 98:1–7; Mk 3:22–30

             EP   Gen 11:27 – 12:9   Hab 2
                    Ps: 127, 128, 129   Mt 26:1–16   I Cor 8

TUESDAY   **Feria (☐ S Angela Merici, V)**

27   G   MP   Ps: 132, 133   Hos 4:1–16   Hab 3:2–end
     (or W)   I Cor 10:1–13   I Cor 9

             Mass   *of Sunday; no Gl or Cr; Common Pref (or of the Saint)*
                    Heb 10:1–10; Ps 40:1–5 & 7–10; Mk 3:31–end

             EP   Gen 13:2–end   Zeph 1
                    Ps: 134, 135   Mt 26:17–35   I Cor 10:1 – 11:1

WEDNESDAY   **S Thomas Aquinas, Pr, Dr**

28   W   MP   Ps: 119:153–end   Hos 5:1–7   Zeph 2
                                       I Cor 10:14 – 11:1   I Cor 11:2–end

             Mass   *of the Saint*
                    Heb 10:11–18; Ps 110:1–4; Mk 4:1–20

             EP   Gen 14   Zeph 13
                    Ps: 136   Mt 26:36–46   I Cor 12:1–27

THURSDAY   **Feria**

29   G   MP   Ps: 143, 146   Hos 5:8 – 6:6   Zech 11
                                       I Cor 11:2–16   I Cor 12:27–13 end

             Mass   *as Tuesday*
                    Heb 10:19–25; Ps 24:1–6; Mk 4:21–25

             EP   Gen 15   Zech 13
                    Ps: 138, 140, 141   Mt 26:47–56   I Cor 14:1–19

FRIDAY   **Feria (Bl Charles Stuart, M? see p. 4)**

30   G   MP   Ps: 142, 144   Hos 6:7 – 7:2   Mal 1
     (or R)   I Cor 11:17–end   I Cor 14:20–end

             Mass   *as Tuesday (or of the Blessed)*
                    Heb 10:32–end; Ps 37:3–6 & 40–41; Mk 4:26–34

             EP   Gen 16   Mal 2:1–16
                    Ps: 145   Mt 26:57–end   I Cor 15:1–34

SATURDAY   **S John Bosco, Pr**

31   W   MP   Ps: 147   Hos 8   Mal 2:17 – 3:12
                                       I Cor 12:1–11   I Cor 15:35–end

             Mass   *of the Saint*
                    Heb 11:1–2 & 8–19; Benedictus 1–6; Mk 4:35–end

             1 EP   Gen 17:1–22   Mal 3:13–4 end
                    Ps: 148, 149, 150   Mt 27:1–10   I Cor 16

* S Paul: see PRAENOTANDA.

FEBRUARY

The *Presentation*, according to CW, may be celebrated *either* on Sunday February 1 *or* on Monday February 2. In either case it is, for CW, a Solemnity with a 1 EP and the Creed at Mass. (According to R: it is observed on Friday, with *no* 1 EP: and, additionally, an 'External Solemnity' – all Masses and Offices including a 1 EP – may be observed on Sunday.) We print the entire provision separately for insertion according to local decision.

Presentation of the Lord

[IEP	Ps: 118	I Sam 1:19b–28		Exod 13:1–16
		Heb 4:11–16		Gal 4:1–7]
W	MP	Ps: 48; 146	Exod 13:1–16 (=R:)	I Sam 1:21–end
			Rom 12:1–5	Heb 10:1–10
	Mass	*Ceremonies*; Gl; Pref of Presentation (Missal or CW)*		
		CW: Mal 3:1–5; Ps 24:(1–6) 7–10; Heb 2:14–18; Lk 2: 22–40		
		R: Mal 3:1–4; Ps 24; Heb 2:14–18; Lk 2:22–32 (33–40)		
	(2)EP	HL 208 (NEH 156*)	Hag 2:1–9	Hag 2:1–9
		Ps: 122, 132	Jn 2:18–22	Rom 12:1–5

* In H: NEH 156, NEH seems curiously intent on eliminating *Theotokos*. The Presentation ceremonies traditionally take place before the main mass (R: & PHG pp. 283 ff); PHG envisages they might follow it (pp. 280ff). R: and PHG both envisage the omission of the Penitential Rite.

HOLY OILS

We talk about 'the holy oils'. The oil of the sick, and the oil of baptism with which we touch the candidate for baptism before he is baptized – traditionally, upon the chest – are sacramentals demanding our respect, but it is the Chrism which goes back to within a stone's throw of the New Testament; is full of significance; and calls for greater reverence. It is also a potential source of catechesis as we draw our people into a deeper understanding of the Paschal Mystery.

'We are called Christians because we are anointed with the oil of God'*; 'by it Christians are made and priests and kings and prophets'†, a phrase associated with the oil of chrism in the ancient and modern liturgies of East and West. Since the second century it has been called the oil of eucharist because it is consecrated by a prayer of thanksgiving, just as the eucharistic elements are. As the Lord breathed the Holy Spirit upon his disciples‡, your bishop breathes the Spirit upon the Chrism which you will take back to your people. S Cyril of Jerusalem informed his neophytes that they should 'not mistake the Chrism for ordinary ointment. Just as the bread of the Eucharist after the invocation of the Holy Spirit is not ordinary bread but the Body of Christ, so also the holy Chrism after the invocation is no more merely ointment, but the gracious endowment of Christ and the Holy Spirit, being made operative by the presence of his Divinity'§.

The current liturgical books encourage you to teach the faithful about the oils as you (or lay members of your congregation) bring them into your church, either before the Maundy Thursday Mass of the Last Supper, or at some other suitable time. When you baptize, by ancient custom, immediately after the act of water-baptism, you daub the top of the head of the new christian with Chrism: an action which can be seen as a pointer and preliminary to Confirmation. Your people will be interested to know that this is also the oil used in the ordination of priests and bishops, in the consecration of altars and churches, and in the coronation of christian monarchs.

The oils are kept reverently in an aumbry, but not in an aumbry or tabernacle in which the Blessed Sacrament is reserved. Nor should they be kept in a tabernacle which has the appearance of being used for the reservation of the Blessed Sacrament. Where the font is still used for baptisms, it may be appropriate to reserve the oils nearby. If no suitable aumbry is available, perhaps the church safe or a decent place in the priest's house will have to serve. The aumbry for the oils sometimes has *OLEA SANCTA – THE HOLY OILS* – on the door, or a purple veil hanging in front of it. A recent idea is to have an aumbry with a glass door and an internal light, so that the people, being able to see the oils, may easily be instructed. At the end of the year, what remains of the three oils is decently burnt, preferably in the oil lamp which burns before the Blessed Sacrament.

* Theophilus of Antioch (*c.* 180).   † Aphraates *Dem.*23.3 (*c.* 340).   ‡ John 20:22.   § *Cat.* xxi.3 (348).

✠ *SUNDAY*   **4th SUNDAY and WEEK of YEAR; EPIPHANY 4**
                          (PRESENTATION see p. 13)

1   W   MP   Ps: 71:1–6 & 15–17   Jer 1:4–10   Isa 48:12–end
                                           Mk 1:40–45   Eph 3
R: Ps IV   Mass *Gl; Cr; Sunday Pref*
                   CW: Deut 18:15–20; Ps 111; Rev 12:1–5a; Mk 1:21–28
                   R: Deut 18:15–20; Ps 95; I Cor 7:32–35; Mk 1:21–28
             EP   I Sam 3:1–20   Isa 54:1–14
                   Ps: 34   I Cor 14:12–20   Lk 13:1–17

MONDAY   **Feria (PRESENTATION see p. 13)**

2   G   MP   Ps: 1, 2, 3   Joel 1:1–14   Jer 1
                                           Jn 15:1–11   II Cor 1:1 – 2:11
             Mass *of the 5th [sic] before Lent or 4th of the Year; no Gl or Cr; Common Pref (or of the Saint) (Anniversary*
                   of the Episcopal Ordination in 1994 of Martyn, third Bishop of Beverley)*
                   Heb 11:32–end; Ps 31:19–end; Mk 5:1–20
             EP   Lev 19:1–18 & 30–end   Jer 2:1–13
                   Ps: 4, 7   I Tim 1:1–17   II Cor 2:12–3 end

TUESDAY   **Feria (S Blaise, B, M; S Ansgar, B)**

3 G (or R MP   Ps: 5, 6, 8   Joel 1:15–end   Jer 4:1–18
       or W)   Jn 15:12–17   II Cor 4
             Mass *as Monday (or of the Saint)*
                   Heb 12:1–4; Ps 22:26–end; Mk 5:21–end
             EP   Lev 23:1–22   Jer 5:1–19
                   Ps: 9, 10   I Tim 1:18–2 end   II Cor 5

WEDNESDAY   **Feria (S Gilbert of Sempringham, Pr Founder)**

4   G   MP   Ps: 119:1–32   Joel 2:1–17   Jer 5:20–end
      (or W)   Jn 15:18–end   II Cor 5:20 – 7:1
             Mass *as Monday (or of the Saint)*
                   Heb 12:4–7 & 11–15; Ps 103:1–2 & 13–18; Mk 6:1–6
             EP   Lev 23:23–end   Jer 6:1–21
                   Ps: 11, 12, 13   I Tim 3   II Cor 7:2–end

THURSDAY   **S Agatha, V, M**

5   R   MP   Ps: 14, 15, 16   Joel 2:18–27   Jer 7:1–28
                                           Jn 16:1–15   II Cor 8
             Mass *of the Saint*
                   Heb 12:18–19 & 21–24; Ps 48:1–3 & 8–10; Mk 6:7–13
             EP   Lev 24:1–9   Jer 8
                   Ps: 18   I Tim 4   II Cor 9

FRIDAY   **Ss Paul Miki & Comp, Ms**

6   R   MP   Ps: 17, 19   Joel 2:28–end   Jer 9:1–24
                                           Jn 16:16–22   II Cor 10
             Mass *of the Saints (First Friday: Sacred Heart, see p. 42)*
                   Heb 13:1–8; Ps 27:1–6 & 9–12; Mk 6:14–29
             EP   Lev 25:1–24   Jer 10
                   Ps: 22   I Tim 5:1–16   II Cor 11

SATURDAY   **Our Lady on Saturday†**

7   W   MP   Ps: 20, 21, 23   Joel 3:1–3 & 9–end   Jer 14
      (or G)   Jn 16:23–end   II Cor 12:1–13
             Mass *Introduction Paragraph 26(b) (First Saturday: Immaculate Heart, see p. 42)*
                   Heb 13:15–17 & 20–21; Ps 23; Mk 6:30–34
        G   1 EP of foll   Num 6:1–5 & 21–end   Jer 15
                   Ps: 24, 25   I Tim 5:17–end   II Cor 12:14–13 end

---

* CW Collect and Past Communion this week from 'The Fifth (sic) Sunday before Lent.'
† A full explanation, historical and theological, of this custom is found on page xx.

✠ *SUNDAY*   **5th SUNDAY and WEEK of YEAR; CW 3rd before LENT; BCP SEPTUAGESIMA**

8   G   MP   Ps: 2, 3   Jer 26:1–16   Gen 1:1 – 2:3
                                                      Acts 3:1–10   Jn 1:1–18

R: Ps I   Mass   Gl; *Sunday Pref (CW Proper 1)*
                          CW: Isa 40:21–31; Ps 147:1–12 & 21c; I Cor 9:16–23; Mk 1:29–39
                          R: Job 7:1–4 & 6–7; Ps 147:1–12; I Cor 9:16–19 & 22–23; Mk 1:29–39 (Christ, Healer)
                  2 EP   Num 13:1–2 & 27–33   Gen 2:4–end
                          Ps: 5   Phil 2:12–28   Rev 4

MONDAY   *Feria*

9   G   MP   Ps: 27, 30   Eccles 1   Gen 3
                                                      Jn 17:1–5   Mt 15:29 – 16:12
                  Mass   *of Sunday; no Gl or Cr; Common Pref*
                          Gen 1:1–19; Ps 104:1–2 & 6–13 & 26; Mk 6:53–end
                  EP   Gen 24:1–28   Gen 4:1–16
                          Ps: 26, 28, 29   I Tim 6:1–10   Rom 1

TUESDAY   *S Scholastica, V*

10   W   MP   Ps: 32, 36   Eccles 2   Gen 6:5–end
                                                      Jn 17:6–19   Mt 16:13–end
                  Mass   *of the Saint*
                          Gen 1:20 – 2:4a; Ps 8; Mk 7:1–13
                  EP   Gen 24:29–28 end   Gen 7
                          Ps: 33   I Tim 6:11–end   Rom 2

WEDNESDAY   *Feria (☐ Our Lady of Lourdes: World Day for the Sick, and compulsory in EAD)*

11   G   MP   Ps: 34   Eccles 3:1–15   Gen 8:1–14
         (or W)   Jn 17:20–end   Mt 17:1–23
                  Mass   *as Monday (or of our Lady: Isa 66:10–14; Jn 2:1–11)*
                          Gen 2:4b–9 & 15–17; Ps 104:12 & 29–32; Mk 7:14–23
                  EP   Gen 25:7–11 & 19–end   Gen 8:15 – 9:17
                          Ps: 119:33–56   II Tim 1:1–14   Rom 3

THURSDAY   *Feria*

12   G   MP   Ps: 37   Eccles 3:16–4 end   Gen 11:1–9
                                                      Jn 18:1–11   Mt 17:24 – 18:14
                  Mass   *as Monday*
                          Gen 2:18–25; Ps 128; Mk 7:24–30
                  EP   Gen 26:34 – 27:40   Gen 11:27 – 12:10
                          Ps: 39, 40   II Tim 1:15 – 2:13   Rom 4

FRIDAY   *Feria*

13   G   MP   Ps: 31   Eccles 5   Gen 13
                                                      Jn 18:12–27   Mt 18:15–end
                  Mass   *as Monday*
                          Gen 3:1–8; Ps 32:1–8; Mk 7:31–end
                  EP   Gen 27:41–28 end   Gen 14
                          Ps: 35   II Tim 2:14–end   Rom 5

SATURDAY   **Ss Cyril, Monk, and Methodius, B, Patrons of Europe**

14   W   MP   [Ps: 41, 42, 43]   [Eccles 6]   [Gen 15]
                                                      [Jn 18:28–end]   [Mt 19:1–15]
                  Mass   *Office: Appendix 3 (Religious)*
                          of the Saints; Gl, no Cr; R: Pref of Saints. CW = R: Acts 13:46–49; Ps 117; Lk 10:1–9
                          (S Valentine, B, M)
                          [Gen 3:9–end; Ps 90:1–12; Mk 8:1–10]
           G   1 EP of foll   Gen 29:1–30   Gen 16
                          Ps: 45, 46   II Tim 3   Rom 6

✠ *SUNDAY*

15   G

R: Ps II

6th SUNDAY and WEEK of YEAR; CW 2nd before LENT SEXAGESIMA

	MP	Ps: 29, 67	Deut 8:1–10	Gen 3
			Mt 6:25–34	I Cor 10:1–13
	Mass	*Gl; Cr; Sunday (CW Proper 2)*		
		CW: Prov 8:1 & 22–31; Ps 104:26–37; Col 1:15–20; Jn 1:1–14		
		R: Lev 13:1–2 & 45–46; Ps 32; I Cor 10:31 – 11:1; Mk 1:40–45 (The Friend of Outcasts)		
	2 EP		Gen 2:4b–25	Gen 4:1–16
		Ps: 65	Lk 8:22–35	I Jn 3:1–15

MONDAY

16   G

Feria

	MP	Ps: 44	Eccles 7:1–14	Gen 17:1–22
			Jn 19:1–16	Mt 19:16 – 20:16
	Mass	*of Sunday; no Gl or Cr; Common Pref*		
		Gen 4:1–15 & 25; Ps 50:1 & 8 & 16–end; Mk 8:11–13		
	EP		Gen 29:31 – 30:24	Gen 18
		Ps: 47, 49	II Tim 4:1–8	Rom 7

TUESDAY

17   G
(or W)

Feria (☐ Seven Founders of the Servite Order)

	MP	Ps: 48, 52	Eccles 7:15–end	Gen 19:1–3 & 12–29
			Jn 19:17–30	Mt 20:17–end
	Mass	*as Monday (or of the Saints) (**Janani Luwum, B, M**)*		
		Gen 6:5–8 & 7:1–5 & 10; Ps 29; Mk 8:14–21		
	EP		Gen 31:1–24	Gen 21
		Ps: 50	II Tim 4:9–end	Rom 8:1–17

WEDNESDAY

18   G

Feria

	MP	Ps: 119:57–80	Eccles 8	Gen 22:1–19
			Jn 19:31–end	Mt 21:1–22
	Mass	*as Monday*		
		Gen 8:6–13 & 20–22; Ps 116:10–end; Mk 8:22–26		
	EP		Gen 31:25 – 32:2	Gen 23
		Ps: 59, 60, 67	Titus 1	Rom 8:18–end

THURSDAY

19   G

Feria

	MP	Ps: 56, 57, 63	Eccles 9	Gen 24:1–28
			Jn 20:1–10	Mk 21:23–end
	Mass	*as Monday*		
		Gen 9:1–13; Ps 102:16–23; Mk 8:27–33		
	EP		Gen 32:3–30	Gen 24:29–end
		Ps: 61, 62, 64	Titus 2	Rom 9

FRIDAY

20   G

Feria

	MP	Ps: 51, 54	Eccles 11:1–8	Gen 25:7–11 & 19–end
			Jn 20:11–18	Mt 22:1–33
	Mass	*as Monday*		
		Gen 11:1–9; Ps 33:10–15; Mk 8:34 – 9:1		
	EP		Gen 33:1–17	Gen 27:1–40
		Ps: 38	Titus 3	Rom 10

SATURDAY

21   W
(or G)

Our Lady on Saturday (or the Feria or ☐ S Peter Damian, B, Dr)

	MP	Ps: 68	Eccles 11:9–12 end	Gen 27:41–28 end
			Jn 20:19–end	Mt 22:34 – 23:12
	Mass	*Introduction Paragraph 26(b)*		
		Heb 11:1–7; Ps 145:1–10; Mk 9:2–13		
G	1 EP of foll		Gen 35	Gen 29:1–20
		Ps: 65, 66	Philemon	Rom 11

NOTES FOR LENT

1 The faithful are encouraged to see Lent as their preparation for the *Paschal* Mystery of the Death and Resurrection of the Lord, the Easter Triduum, rather than as a mere imitation of the Forty Days in the Wilderness. Preachers might notice that CW texts now follow Rome in expecting congregations to understand the word 'Paschal'. Those who are to be baptized and/or confirmed at Easter are prepared for the Sacraments, and the rest of the faithful express their penitence sacramentally and in communal Services of Penitence. Ash Wednesday is a day of fasting and abstinence (p. xiv).

2 *On Sundays in Lent,* any Solemnity (e.g. Dedication or Patron) is transferred to the Monday; Festa and Memorials are suppressed. (CW also allows a Festum to be transferred to Monday, and permits a Dedication or Patronal Festival on Sundays 2, 3, and 4).

3 *On Weekdays in Lent,* Solemnities and Festa are observed; Memorials are indicated [within square brackets] which means the following: Mass and Office are of the Feria. The memorial may be *either* totally ignored *or* its collect may be said *after* the Collect of the day at MP and EP, and *instead* of the Collect of the day at Mass. (The new R: Calendar for England has moved S Chad from 2 March to 26 October; and S Cuthbert from 20 March to 4 September: to get them out of Lent. CW permits this optionally. Local Saints will prefer to have a non-Lenten date found for them: e.g. as of a Translation.)

4 **Office Hymns: EH: Sundays: MP 65 EP 66; Ferias: MP 67 or 68 EP 69. *NEH: MP 59 EP 60.***

5 Altars are not decorated with *flowers* except on Solemnities, Festa, and Lent 4, Refreshment Sunday; and apart from these days the organ and other instruments are only played at liturgical services to sustain poor singing. All use of *Alleluia* is avoided.

6 *Prefaces:* R: provides, in the Weekday Missal, four Lenten Prefaces, the first of which beautifully brings out the character of Lent as preparation for the *Pascha*, followed now in this by the (less generously provided) CW prefaces. R: also encourages marking Lent 1 with the Litany at the Entrance of the Mass.

7 **Sunday Themes and Readings**
  (a) On *Lent 1,* CW and Rome remember the Temptation in the Wilderness.
  (b) On *Lent 2,* Rome recalls the Transfiguration (Lent calls us to a participation in the Lord's own Paschal Transfiguration). CW transferred this perception to the Sunday *before* Lent.
  (c) On *Lent 3, 4, and 5* CW and Rome reflect an ancient Christian association of Lent with Eschatological, Paschal, and Redemptive themes. Rome (see also CW) allows (even in Years B and C) the Year A Gospels (together with their associated readings and proper prefaces) which are given below. These are the readings anciently used in the preparation of candidates for Baptism and Confirmation. They may also be used on weekdays. (Compare also the Byzantine rite.)

  ### Roman Sundays in Year A
  3 Living Water [The Samaritan Woman]
    Exod 17:3–7; Rom 5:1–2 & 5–8; Jn 4:5–42 (or 5–15 & 19–26 & 39–42)
  4 Enlightenment [the Man Blind from Birth]
    I Sam 6:1 & 6–7 & 10–13; Eph 5:8–14; Jn 9:1–41 (or 1 & 6–9 & 13–17 & 34–38)
  5 New Life [Lazarus]
    Ezek 37:12–14; Rom 8:8–11; Jn 11:1–45 (or 3–7 & 17–27 & 33b–45)

8 Customary ways of observing Lent include: *Thursdays* Eucharistic Adoration *Fridays* Way of the Cross and penitential celebrations *Saturdays* Rosary. PPL urges also: venerating relics of the Cross; reading the Passion; the *Via Matris.*

✠ *SUNDAY*   **7th SUNDAY and WEEK of YEAR; CW NEXT before LENT QUINQUAGESIMA**

22	G	MP	Ps: 27, 150	Exod 24:12–18	Gen 12:1–9
				II Cor 3:12–18	I Cor 12:4–end
R: Ps III		Mass	*Gl; Cr; Sunday Pref*		
			CW: II Kgs 2:1–12; Ps 50:1–6; II Cor 4:3–6; Mk 9:2–9		
			R: Isa 43:18–19 & 21–22 & 24–25; Ps 41; II Cor 1:18–22; Mk 2:1–12 (Only He Forgives)		
		2 EP		I Kgs 1–16	Gen 6:5–end
			Ps: 2, 99	II Pet 1:16–21	Lk 17:20–end

MONDAY   **S Polycarp, B, M**

23	R	MP	Ps: 71	Jer 1	Gen 31:1–9 & 14–21
				Jn 3:1–21	Mt 23:13–end
		Mass	*of the Saint*		
			Ecclus 1:1–10; Ps 93; Mk 9:14–29		
		EP		Gen 37:1–11	Gen 31:22 – 32:2
			Ps: 72, 75	Gal 1	Rom 12

TUESDAY   **Feria**

24	G	MP	Ps: 73	Jer 2:1–13	Gen 32:3–30
				Jn 3:22–end	Mt 24:1–28
		Mass	*of Sunday; no Gl or Cr; Common Pref*		
			Ecclus 2:1–11; Ps 37:3–6 & 27 & 28; Mk 9:30–37		
		EP		Gen 37:12–end	Gen 33
			Ps: 74	Gal 2:1–10	Rom 13

(✠) *WEDNESDAY*   **ASH WEDNESDAY**

25	P	MP	Ps: 38	Dan 9:3–6 & 17–19	Isa 58
				I Tim 6:6–19	Mk 2:13–22
		Mass	*of the day; the penitential rite is omitted; Blessing & imposition of Ashes takes place after the Homily;*		
			R: Pref 4 of Lent; CW, Pref 1 of Lent		
			CW: Joel 2:1–2 & 12–17; Ps 51:1–18; II Cor 5:20b – 6:10; Mt 6:1–6 & 16–21		
			R: Joel 2:12–18; Ps 51; II Cor 5:20 – 6:2; Mt 6:1–6 & 16–18		
		EP		Isa 1:10–18 [R: Isa 58:1–12]	Dan 9:3–19
			Ps: 102	Lk 15:11–32	Heb 3:12 – 4:13

THURSDAY   **Feria**

26	P	MP	Ps: 78:1–39	Jer 2:14–32	Gen 35:1–20
				Jn 4:1–26	Mt 24:29–end
		Mass	*of the day; Pref of Lent*		
			Deut 30:15–20; Ps 1: Luke 9:22–25		
		EP		Gen 39	Gen 37
			Ps: 78:40–end	Gal 2:11–end	Rom 14

FRIDAY   **Feria**

27	P	MP	Ps: 55	Jer 3:6–22	Gen 39
				Jn 4:27–42	Mt 25:1–30
		Mass	*as Thursday (**George Herbert, Pr**)*		
			Isa 58:1–9a; Ps 51:1–5 & 17 &18; Mt 9:14 & 15		
		EP		Gen 40	Gen 40
			Ps: 69	Gal 3:1–14	Rom 15

SATURDAY   **Feria**

28	P	MP	Ps: 76, 79	Jer 4:1–18	Gen 41:1–40
				Jn 4:43–end	Mt 25:31–end
		Mass	*as Thursday (**Foundation of SSC; Votive of the Holy Cross?**)*		
			Isa 58:9b–14; Ps 86:1–7; Lk 5:27–32		
		1 EP of foll		Gen 41:1–24	Gen 41:41–end
			Ps: 81, 84	Gal 3:15–22	Rom 16

✠ *SUNDAY*   **LENT 1***

1   P   MP   Ps: 77   Exod 34:1–10   Gen 13
                                         Rom 10:8b–13   Lk 15:1–10

R: Ps I   Mass   *Cr; Proper Pref; CW, of Lent*
                        CW: Gen 9:8–17; Ps 25:1–9; I Pet 3:18–22; Mk 1:9–15
                        R: Gen 9:8–15; Ps 25; I Pet 3:18–22; Mk 1:12–15 (Water and Covenant)

                 2 EP   Gen 2:15–17 & 3:1–7   Gen 8:15 – 9:17
                        Ps: 119:17–32   Rom 5:12–19   Mk 14:1–26

MONDAY   **Feria***

2   P   MP   Ps: 80, 82   Jer 4:19–end   Gen 42
                                         Jn 5:1–18   Mt 26:1–30

                 Mass   *of the day; Pref of Lent*
                        Lev 19:1 & 2 & 11–18; Ps 19:7–end; Mt 25:31–46

                 EP   Gen 41:25–45   Gen 43
                        Ps: 85, 86   Gal 3:23 – 4:7   Phil 1

TUESDAY   **Feria†**

3   P   MP   Ps: 87, 89:1–18   Jer 5:1–19   Gen 44
                                         Jn 5:19–29   Mt 26:31–56

                 Mass   *as Monday*
                        Isa 55:10 & 11; Ps 34:4–6 & 21 & 22; Mt 6:7–15

                 EP   Gen 41:46 – 42:5   Gen 45:1–15
                        Ps: 89:19–end   Gal 4:8–20   Phil 2

WEDNESDAY   **Feria‡ [☐ S Casimir]**

4   P   MP   Ps: 119:105–128   Jer 5:20–end   Gen 45:16 – 46:7
                                         Jn 5:30–end   Mt 26:57–end

                 Mass   *as Monday*
                        Jonah 3:1–10; Ps 51:1–5 & 17 & 18; Lk 11:29–32

                 EP   Gen 42:6–17   Gen 46:26 – 47:12
                        Ps: 91, 93   Gal 4:21 – 5:1   Phil 3

THURSDAY   **Feria [CORNWALL: Solemnity of S Piran]**

5   P   MP   Ps: 90, 92   Jer 6:9–21   Gen 47:13–end
                                         Jn 6:1–15   Mt 27:1–26

                 Mass   *as Monday*
                        Esth 14:1–5 & 12–14; Ps 138; Mt 7:7–12

                 EP   Gen 42:18–28   Gen 48
                        Ps: 94   Gal 5:2–15   Phil 4

FRIDAY   **Feria‡**

6   P   MP   Ps: 88, 95   Jer 6:22–end   Gen 49:1–32
                                         Jn 6:16–27   Mt 27:27–56

                 Mass   *as Monday*
                        Ezek 18:21–28; Ps 130; Mt 5:20–26

                 EP   Gen 42:29–end   Gen 49:33–50 end
                        Ps: 102   Gal 5:16–end   Col 1:1–20

SATURDAY   **Feria‡ [Ss Perpetua and Felicity, Ms]**

7   P   MP   Ps: 96, 97, 100   Jer 7:1–20   Exod 1:1–14 & 22 – 2:10
                                         Jn 6:27–40   Mt 27:57–28 end

                 Mass   *as Monday*
                        (Anniversary of the Episcopal Ordination in 2002 of Keith, second Bishop of Richborough.)
                        Deut 26:16–19; Ps 119:1–8; Mt 5:43–48

                 1 EP of foll   Gen 43:1–15   Exod 2:11–22
                        Ps: 104   Gal 6   Col 1:21 – 2:7

---

* Where S David is Patron, his Solemnity is transferred to Monday.
† Rome keeps S Chad on October 26, to keep him out of Lent.
‡ Ember Masses Introduction paragraph 25.

✠ *SUNDAY*
8   P   **LENT 2**

		MP	Ps: 105:1–6 & 37–45	Isa 51:1–11	Gen 18:1–16
R: Ps II				Gal 3:1–9 & 23–29	Lk 15:11–end
		Mass	*Cr; Pref of Lent*		
			CW: Gen 17:1–7 & 15–16; Ps 22:23–31; Rom 4:13–25; Mk 8:31–38		
			R: Gen 22:1–2 & 9–13 & 15–18; Ps 116; Rom 8:31–34; Mk 9:2–10		
			(The Father Gives His Son)		
		2 EP		Gen 12:1–9	Gen 11:1–9
			Ps: 135	Heb 11:1–3 & 8–16	Mk 14:27–52

MONDAY
9   P   Feria [☐ S Frances of Rome, Rel]

		MP	Ps: 98, 99, 101	Jer 7:21–end	Exod 2:23–3 end
				Jn 6:41–51	Jn 1:1–28
		Mass	*of the day; Pref of Lent*		
			Dan 9:4–10; Ps 79:8 & 9 & 12 & 14; Lk 6:36–38		
		EP		Gen 43:16–end	Exod 4:1–23
			Ps: 103, 105	Heb 1	Col 2:8 – 3:11

TUESDAY
10   P   Feria [SCOTLAND: Feast of S John Ogilvie, Pr, M]

		MP	Ps: 106	Jer 8:1–15	Exod 4:27 – 6:1
				Jn 6:52–59	Jn 1:29–end
		Mass	*of the day; Pref of Lent*		
			Isa 1:10 & 16–20; Ps 50:8 & 16–end; Mt 23:1–12		
		EP		Gen 44:1–17	Exod 6:2–13 & 7:1–7
			Ps: 107	Heb 2:1–9	Col 3:12 – 4:1

WEDNESDAY
11   P   Feria

		MP	Ps: 110, 111, 112	Jer 8:18 – 9:11	Exod 7:8–end
				Jn 6:60–end	Jn 2
		Mass	*as Tuesday*		
			Jer 18:18–20; Ps 31:4–5 & 14–18; Mt 20:17–28		
		EP		Gen 44:18–end	Exod 8:1–9
			Ps: 119:129–152	Heb 2:10–end	Col 4:2–end

THURSDAY
12   P   Feria

		MP	Ps: 113, 115	Jer 9:12–24	Exod 8:20 – 9:12
				Jn 7:1–13	Jn 3:1–21
		Mass	*as Tuesday*		
			Jer 17:5–10; Ps 1; Lk 16:19–31		
		EP		Gen 45:1–15	Exod 9:13–end
			Ps: 114, 116, 117	Heb 3:1–6	Philemon

FRIDAY
13   P   Feria

		MP	Ps: 139	Jer 10:1–16	Exod 10:1–20
				Jn 7:14–24	Jn 3:22–end
		Mass	*as Tuesday*		
			Gen 37:3 & 4 & 12 & 13 & 17–28; Ps 105:16–22; Mt 21:33–43 & 45 & 46		
		EP		Gen 45:16–end	Exod 10:21–11 end
			Ps: 130, 131, 137	Heb 3:7–end	Eph 1

SATURDAY
14   P   Feria

		MP	Ps: 120, 121, 122	Jer 10:17–24	Exod 12:1–20
				Jn 7:25–36	Jn 4:1–26
		Mass	*as Tuesday (**Our Lady of Kostroma**)*		
			Mic 7:14–15 & 18–20; Ps 103:1–4 & 9–12; Lk 15:1–3 & 11–end		
		1 EP of foll		Gen 46:1–7 & 28–end	Exod 12:21–36
			Ps: 118	Heb 4:1–13	Eph 2

✠ *SUNDAY*
15 P MP — **LENT 3**

	P	MP	Ps: 18:1–25	Jer 38	Gen 18:17–end
				Phil 1:1–26	Lk 18:1–14

R: Ps III Mass *Cr; Pref of Lent*
CW: *Exod 20:1–17; Ps 19; I Cor 1:18–25; Jn 2:13–22*
R: *Exod 20:1–3 (4–6) 7–8 (9–11) 12–17; Ps 19; I Cor 1:22–25; Jn 2:13–25*
(Christ, Wisdom Incarnate)

2 EP   Exod 5:1 – 6:1   Gen 24:1–28
Ps: 11, 12   Phil 3:4b–14   Mk 14:53–end

MONDAY
16 P   **Feria**
MP   Ps: 123, 124, 125, 126   Jer 11:1–17   Exod 12:37–end
   Jn 7:37–52   Jn 4:27–end

Mass   *of the day, Pref of Lent (**Walter Hilton, Rel; Oscar Romero, B, M**)*
II Kgs 5:1–15; Ps 42:1–2 & 43:1–4; Lk 4:24–30

EP   Gen 47:1–27   Exod 13:1–16
Ps: 127, 128, 129   Heb 4:14 – 5:10   Eph 3

TUESDAY
17 W   **S Patrick, B (Ireland: Solemnity)**
MP   Ps: 132, 133   Jer 11:18 – 12:6   Exod 13:17 – 14:14
   Jn 7:53 – 8:11   Jn 5:1–23

Mass   *Office from Appendix B.*
of the Saint; Gl; Cr only in Ireland; Pref of Saints. Missal: National Appendix
[Song of the Three* 2:11–20; Ps 25:3–10; Mt 18:21–25]

EP   Gen 47:28–48 end   Exod 14:15–end
Ps: 134, 135   Heb 5:11 – 6:12   Eph 4:1–16

WEDNESDAY
18 P   **Feria (S Cyril of Jerusalem, B, Dr)**
MP   Ps: 119:153–end   Jer 13:1–11   Exod 15:1–26
   Jn 8:12–30   Jn 5:24–end

Mass   *as Monday*
Deut 4:1 & 5–9; Ps 147:13–end; Mt 5:17–19

S JOSEPH, HUSBAND OF THE BVM
W   1 EP of foll   Hos 11:1–9   ◁
   Ps: 132   Lk 2:41–52   ◁

THURSDAY
19 W   MP   H: 46   Isa 11:1–10   ◁
   Ps: 25, 147:1–12   Mt 13:54–58   ◁

Mass   *Gl; Cr; R: Proper Pref; CW: of a Saint*
CW: *II Sam 7:4–16; Ps 89:27–36; Rom 4:13–18; Mt 1:18–25*
R: *II Sam 7:4–5a & 12–14a & 16; Ps 89; Rom 4:13 & 16–18 & 22;*
Mt 1:16 & 18–21 & 24a or Lk 2:41–51a

EP   H: NEH 160   Gen 50:22–26   ◁
   Ps: 1, 112   Mt 2:13–23   ◁

FRIDAY
20 P   **Feria†**
MP   Ps: 142, 144   Jer 15:10–end   Exod 19
   Jn 8:48–end   Jn 6:22–40

Mass   *as Monday*
Hos 14:2–10; Ps 81:6–10 & 13 & 16; Mk 12:28–34

EP   Exod 1:1–14   Exod 20:1–21
Ps: 145   Heb 7:11–end   Eph 5:22 – 6:9

SATURDAY
21 P   **Feria**
MP   Ps: 147   Jer 16:10 – 17:4   Exod 22:20 – 23:17
   Jn 9:1–17   Jn 6:41–end

Mass   *as Monday (**Thomas Cranmer, B, Ref M**)*
Hos 5:15 – 6:6; Ps 51:1 & 2 & 17–end; Lk 18:9–14

P‡   1 EP of foll   Exod 1:22 – 2:10   Exod 23:20–end
   Ps: 148, 149, 150   Heb 8   Eph 6:10–end

---

* Apocryphal/Deuterocanonical Books, 'Prayer of Azariah and Song of the Three Young Men/Jews/Children? King James-based and Vulgate-based Bibles have different verse-systems; we follow the former.

† Rome keep S Cuthbert on September 4, to keep him out of Lent.

‡ Rose colour is sometimes used this evening and tomorrow; similarly, organ and flowers. Mothering Sunday, Introduction Appendix 1.

✠ *SUNDAY*
22 P (or Rose)

R: Ps IV

	MP	**LENT 4**	
		Ps: 27	
		I Sam 16:1–13	Exod 1:8–14 & 22 – 2:10
		Jn 9:1–25	Lk 18:35 – 19:10
	Mass	*Cr; Pref of Lent. MOTHERING SUNDAY pxxi*	
		CW: Num 21:4–9; Ps 107:1–3 & 17–22; Eph 2:1–10; Jn 3:14–21	
		R: II Chron 36:14–16 & 19–23; Ps 137; Eph 2:4–10; Jn 3:14–21 (The Redeemer)	
	2 EP	Exod 6:2–13	Gen 24:29–end
		Ps: 13, 14	
		Rom 5:1–11	Mk 15:1–21

MONDAY
23 P

	MP	*Feria* [□ *S Turibius of Mongrovejo, B*] THE ANNOTINE EASTER	
		Ps: 1, 2, 3	
		Jer 17:5–18	Exod 24
		Jn 9:18–end	Jn 7:1–24
	Mass	*of the day; Pref of Lent*	
		Isa 65:17–21; Ps 30:1–5 & 8 & 11 & 12; Jn 4:43–54	
	EP	Exod 2:11–22	Exod 25:1–22
		Ps: 4, 7	
		Heb 9:1–14	I Tim 1:1–17

TUESDAY
24 P

	MP	*Feria*	
		Ps: 5, 6, 8	
		Jer 18:1–12	Exod 28:1–4 & 29:1–9
		Jn 10:1–10	Jn 7:25–end
	Mass	*as Monday (**Our Lady 'of the Way'**)*	
		*(**Walter Hilton, Rel; Oscar Romero, B, M**)*	
		Ezek 47:1–9 & 12; Ps 46:1–8; Jn 5:1–3 & 5–16	

(✠)
W

	1 EP	**ANNUNCIATION OF THE LORD**	
		Wisd 9:1–12 or Gen 3:8–15	◁
		Ps: 85	
		Gal 4:1–5	◁

WEDNESDAY
25 W

	MP	H: 214 (NEH 181)	
		I Sam 2:1–10 (R: I Chron 17:1–15)	Isa 52:7–12
		Ps: 111, 113	
		Rom 5:12–21	Heb 2:5–end
	Mass	*Gl; Cr (Kneel for Incarnatus); R: and CW Proper Prefaces*	
		R = CW: Isa 7:10–14; Ps 40:5–11; Heb 10:4–10; Lk 1:26–38	
	2 EP	Isa 52:1–12	I Sam 2:1–10
		Ps: 131, 146	
		Heb 2:5–18	Mt 1:18–23

THURSDAY
26 P

	MP	*Feria*	
		Ps: 14, 15, 16	
		Jer 19:1–13	Exod 34
		Jn 10:22–end	Jn 8:31–end
	Mass	*as Monday (**Harriet Monsell**)*	
		Exod 32:7–14; Ps 106:19–23; Jn 5:31–47	
	EP	Exod 4:27 – 6:1	Exod 35:20 – 36:7
		Ps: 18	
		Heb 10:19–25	I Tim 4

FRIDAY
27 P

	MP	*Feria*	
		Ps: 17, 19	
		Jer 19:14 – 20:6	Exod 40:17–end
		Jn 11:1–16	Jn 9
	Mass	*as Monday*	
		Wis 2:1 & 12–22; Ps 34:15–end; Jn 7:1 & 2 & 10 & 25–30	
	EP	Exod 6:2–13	Lev 6:8–end
		Ps: 22	
		Heb 10:26–end	I Tim 5

SATURDAY
28 P

P*

	MP	*Feria*	
		Ps: 20, 21, 23	
		Jer 20:7–end	Lev 19:1–18 & 30–end
		Jn 11:17–27	Jn 10:1–21
	Mass	*as Monday*	
		Jer 11:18–20; Ps 7:1–2 & 8–10; Jn 7:40–52	
	1 EP of foll	Exod 7:8–end	Lev 25:1–24
		Ps: 24, 25	
		Heb 11:1–16	I Tim 6

* Before this EP, crosses, statues and pictures may be veiled in purple.

✠ SUNDAY
29   P
R: Ps IV

LENT 5*

MP	Ps: 107:1–22	Exod 24:3–8		Exod 2:23 – 3:20
		Heb 12:18–29		Mt 20:17–28
Mass	*Cr; Pref of Lent (CW: Pref of Fifth Sunday onwards)*			
	CW: Jer 31:31–34; Ps 51:1–13; Heb 5:5–10; Jn 12:20–33			
	R: Jer 31:31–34; Ps 51; Heb 5:7–9; Jn 12:20–33 (Christ's Prayer was heard)			
2 EP		Exod 7:8–24		Exod 4:27 – 6:1
	Ps: 34	Rom 5:12–21		Mk 15:22–39

MONDAY
30   P

Feria

MP	Ps: 27, 30	Jer 21:1–10		Num 6
		Jn 11:28–44		Jn 10:22–end
Mass	*of the day; Pref 1 of Passion (CW: Pref of Fifth Sunday onwards)*			
	Susanna 1–9 & 15–17 & 19–30 & 33–62 or 41–62; Ps 23; Jn 8:1–11			
EP		Exod 8:1–19		Num 9:15–end & 10:29–end
	Ps: 26, 28, 29	Heb 11:17–31		Titus 1:1–28

TUESDAY
31   P

Feria

MP	Ps: 32, 36	Jer 22:1–5, 13–19		Num 11:10–23
		Jn 11:45–end		Jn 11:1–44
Mass	*as Monday (**John Donne, Pr**)*			
	Num 21:4–9; Ps 102:1–3 & 16–23; Jn 8:21–30			
EP		Exod 8:20–end		Num 12
	Ps: 33	Heb 11:32 – 12:2		Titus 2:9–3 end

A P R I L
WEDNESDAY
1   P

Feria

MP	Ps: 34	Jer 22:20 – 23:8		Num 13:1–3 & 17–end
		Jn 12:1–11		Jn 11:45–end
Mass	*as Monday (**Frederick D Maurice, Pr**)*			
	Dan 3:14–20 & 24 & 25 & 28; Benedicite (short form); Jn 8:31–42			
EP		Exod 9:1–12		Num 14:1–25
	Ps: 119:33–36	Heb 12:3–13		II Tim 1

THURSDAY
2   P

Feria [☐ S Francis de Paolo, hermit]
(Obit, in 2005, of the Ven. John Paul the Great)

MP	Ps: 37	Jer 23:9–32		Num 16:1–35
		Jn 12:12–19		Jn 12:1–19
Mass	*as Monday*			
	Gen 17:3–9; Ps 105:4–9; Jn 8:51–59			
EP		Exod 9:13–end		Num 16:36–17 end
	Ps: 39, 40	Heb 12:14–end		II Tim 2

FRIDAY
3   P

Feria

MP	Ps: 31	Jer 24		Num 20
		Jn 12:20–36a		Jn 12:20–end
Mass	*as Monday (**There is a new Roman Collect today for our Lady of Sorrows**)*			
	Jer 20:10–13; Ps 18:1–6; Jn 10:31–42			
EP		Exod 10		Num 22:1–35
	Ps: 35	Heb 13:1–16		II Tim 3

SATURDAY
4   P

Feria [☐ S Isidore, B, Dr]

MP	Ps: 41, 42, 43	Jer 25:1–14		Num 22:36 – 23:26
		Jn 12:36b–end		Jn 13
Mass	*as Monday*			
	Ezek 37:21–28; Jer 31:10–13; Jn 11:45–57			
P 1 EP of foll		Exod 11		Num 23:27–24 end
	Ps: 45, 46	Heb 13:17–end		II Tim 4

---

* Confusion may arise from the fact that this Sunday is no longer called 'Passion Sunday' in the Roman Rite, which has transferred this title to next Sunday (Palm Sunday). But the Roman Office allows the use of the 'Passion' Hymns on the Weekdays of this Week: MP 95 or 96 (NEH 78 or 517); EP 94 (NEH 79). CW continues talk of 'Passiontide'.

HOLY WEEK AND THE END OF LENT

Lent lasts until the Evening of Maundy Thursday. The Mass of the Last Supper until the EP of Easter Sunday inclusively constitutes the Easter Triduum, which is of even greater antiquity than the Season of Lent.

1   From Palm Sunday onwards, Solemnities are transferred to after Low Sunday; Festivals and Memorials are suppressed.

2   **The Chrism Mass** provides the Oils for use at Baptism and Confirmation at Easter and thereafter. It should take place towards the end of Lent at a time when priests and peoples can easily gather. (Oils in Initiation: see p. xxxiv and 13.)

In some places, the Oils are subsequently 'received' into Parish Churches, and their purpose explained. Before the Mass of the Lord's Supper is a popular time for this, but undeniably complicates the occasion. Earlier in Holy Week, or at MP on Good Friday or Holy Saturday, may be convenient occasions.

3   **Confessions and Penitential Celebrations** for the whole Christian community (LHWE pp. 38 ff) should take place at the end of Lent, *before* the Easter Triduum, but not immediately before the Mass of the Lord's Supper.

4   **PALM SUNDAY** The colour of the day is red. Palms are held during the Palm gospel and procession, but not during the Passion gospel. The processional cross is carried unveiled. After the procession, when the celebrant arrives at the altar, he reverences (and censes) it. Then he goes to his chair and Mass begins with the collect of the day. Rome allows, for pastoral reasons, one or both of the readings before the Passion to be omitted.

The Passion gospel may be read by three deacons or by laymen. If possible, the priest should read the part of Christ. The Passion may be read by the deacon of the Mass, or if necessary by the celebrant. Neither lights nor incense are used. At the beginning the greeting and signing of the book are omitted. At the end the book is not kissed. LHWE permits the omission of the Creed.

5   **MAUNDY THURSDAY** Before the Evening, holy water stoups are emptied, the Blessed Sacrament taken to a private place of reservation, and lamps extinguished. Those who have concelebrated or communicated with the Bishop in the morning may celebrate concelebrate or communicate again in the evening.

6   The practice of attenuating the Office during the Triduum, mentioned by LHWE (p. 90), was discontinued by Rome in 1971.

THE PASCHAL CANDLE: page 8.

✠ *SUNDAY*   **PALM SUNDAY OF THE LORD'S PASSION**

5   R   MP   H: 95 or 96 (NEH 78)   Zech 9:9–12   Exod 11
                          Ps: 61, 62   I Cor 2:1–12   Mt 26
R: Ps II   Mass   *Cr; Pref Proper (CW: 'from the Fifth Sunday of Lent')*
                          Gospel for Palms Ceremony: Mt 11:1–11 (R: 1–10)
                          CW: Isa 50:4–9a; Ps 31:9–16; Phil 2:5–11; Mk 14:1 – 15:47 or 15:1–39 (40–47)
                          R: Isa 50:4–7; Ps: 22; Phil 2:6–11; Mk 14:1 – 15:47 or 15:1–39
                  EP   H: 94 (NEH 79)   Isa 5:1–7   Isa 52:13–53
                          Ps: 69:1–20   Mk 12:1–12   Lk 19:29–end

MONDAY   **MONDAY IN HOLY WEEK**

6   P   MP   H: 95 or 96 (NEH 78)   Lam 1:1–12a   ◁
                          Ps: 41   Lk 22:1–23   Jn 14:1–14
                  Mass   *of the day; R: Pref of Passion II; CW, Pref of Fifth Sunday onwards*
                          CW: Isa 42:1–9; Ps 36:5–11; Heb 9:11–15; Jn 12:1–11
                          *ASB = R: = LHWE: Isa 42:1–7; Ps 27:1–3 & 16–17; Jn 12:1–11
                  EP   H: 94 (NEH 79)   Lam 2:8–19   Lam 2:8–19
                          Ps: 25   Col 1:18–23   Jn 14:15–end

TUESDAY   **TUESDAY IN HOLY WEEK**

7   P   MP   H: 95 or 96 (NEH 78)   Lam 3:1–18   Lam 3:1–30
                          Ps: 27   Lk 22:24–53 (or 39–53)   Jn 15:1–16
                  Mass   *as Monday*
                          CW: Isa 49:1–7; Ps 71:1–14; I Cor 1:18–31; Jn 12:30–36
                          *ASB = R: = LHWE: Isa 49:1–6; Ps 71:1–6 & 15–16; Jn 13:21–33 & 36–38
                  EP   H: 94 (NEH 79)   Lam 3:40–51   Lam 3:40–51
                          Ps: 55:13–24   Gal 6:11–18   Jn 15:17–end

WEDNESDAY   **WEDNESDAY IN HOLY WEEK**

8   P   MP   H: 95 or 96 (NEH 78)   Jer 11:18–20 or Wisd 1:16 – 2:1 & 2:12–22   Isa 42:1–9
                          Ps: 102   Lk 22:54–71   Jn 16:1–15
                  Mass   *as Monday*
                          CW: Isa 50:4–9a; Ps 70: Heb 12:1–3; Jn 13:21–32
                          *ASB = R: = LHWE: Isa 50:4–9a; Ps 69:8–910 & 32–35; Mt 26:14–25
                  EP   H: 94 (NEH 79)   Isa 63:1–9   Num 21:4–9
                          Ps: 88   Rev 14:18 – 15:4   Jn 16:16–end

THURSDAY   **THURSDAY IN HOLY WEEK (Morning)**

9   P   MP   H: 95 or 96 (NEH 78)   Lev 16:2–24   Exod 24:1–11
                          Ps: 42, 43   Lk 23:1–25   Jn 17
           P   EP   H: 331 (NEH 308)   Exod 11   Lev 16:2–24
                          vv 2–4
                          Ps: 39   Eph 2:11–18   ◁ or Jn 13:1–35

* Readings at Mass: ASB = R: = LHWE: are the originally Roman propers authorised by ASB p. 1074 and repeated in LHWE, printed in the Weekday Missal. Psalms are adjusted to the CW verse numbers.

THE EASTER TRIDUUM

1   **THE EASTER FAST**, more ancient than Lent, should be observed both on Friday and Saturday, until the Vigil.

2   **R:** the following anthem is said before Benedictus and Magnificat from EP on Maundy Thursday to Holy Saturday: **Christ humbled himself for us, and, in obedience, accepted death**. Good Friday add **even death on a cross**.
Holy Saturday add **Therefore God raised him to the heights and gave him the name which is above all other names**.

3   **MAUNDY THURSDAY** For the evening Mass of the Lord's Supper, white vestments are worn, the altar is decorated as on feasts, and the cross is veiled in white. Bells may

be rung at *Gloria in excelsis* and then are silent until the Easter Vigil. The Washing of Feet may follow the Sermon. The Creed is omitted. The Institution Narrative begins *Who in this night when* . . . It is appropriate that authorised lay people take Communion to the sick or elderly at Communion time. Immediately after the post-communion prayer the procession to the altar of repose follows, where the watch takes place. John 13–17 may be read. After midnight, flowers and candles are removed; one lamp or two candles are to be left burning. After the procession altars are privately stripped and crosses removed (or covered with a purple veil).

If there will be no Good Friday Liturgy in the same church, the Blessed Sacrament is replaced in the Tabernacle and Mass ends in the ordinary way.

4 **GOOD FRIDAY** The colour for the day is red. Public MP is encouraged. For the Solemn Liturgy, which should begin about 3 pm but may for pastoral reasons take place between noon and 9 pm, the sacred ministers wear Mass vestments throughout. The altar should be completely bare at the start of the service. Afterwards, it is stripped again, the Cross and four candles being left upon it.

The Passion According To John, Chapters 18 & 19, is, according to ancient tradition (preserved in CW and the Roman Rite) read in its entirety at the Solemn Liturgy. CW, and BCP allow it to be divided: MP Jn 18; Liturgy Jn 19:1–37; EP Jn 19:38–end.

The priest may remove his chasuble and shoes to venerate the Cross; and *Stabat Mater* (EH 115, NEH 97) or another piece about our compassionate Mother is added to the texts which may accompany the Veneration.

5 **HOLY SATURDAY BEFORE THE VIGIL** The *Anglican* tradition has been for a Liturgy of the Word – 'Antecommunion' or 'Altar Prayers' – in purple stole (and cope); MP; and EP; the 'Principal Service' readings should be used at the main Office attended by the faithful. *Rome* recommends the Office of Readings, and Morning Prayer, with the participation of the people – or at least 'some celebration of the Word of God, or some suitable act of devotion'. Representations of Christ crucified or entombed or visiting Hell, or of our Lady of Sorrows, may be placed in Church for the veneration of the faithful.

EP must be said, and veiled statues and pictures unveiled, before the Vigil.

6 **THE EASTER VIGIL** is the 'Solemnity of Solemnities', and the people (even those who will be away from their home parishes on holiday) are urged to see it as the greatest observance of the Christian Year and the foretaste of the Everlasting Easter; and as the Celebration of the Resurrection Night rather than as a service that happens at the end of Holy Saturday. The dignity and festive character of the Vigil may be enhanced if smaller groups and parishes celebrate it together. Both Rome and LHWE are adamant that there *must still only be one Paschal Candle*; LHWE adds that 'if it is desired to take Easter Candles back to other churches, they may be lit from the first candle at the end of the service and carried in procession out of the building'.

The Vigil should begin after nightfall and end before daybreak; the bonfire should, if possible, be big enough for its flames truly to scatter the darkness of this Night; and the Paschal Candle should be large. The marking of the Candle is compulsory.

The service of Light and Fire should precede the Vigil readings from the OT: for the Christian tradition, the OT is not a period of darkness but a divine dispensation illuminated and elucidated by Christ our Light: 'only in the light of Resurrection can we comprehend the unfolding revelation of the prophecies that point to the Paschal Mystery'. The 'Light of Christ' is proclaimed at: church door; mid-church; sanctuary.

The sacred ministers wear white Mass vestments throughout. At *Gloria in excelsis* bells are rung (and statues and pictures unveiled). At the Gospel incense is carried, but not candles. Before he shows the *Lamb of God* the priest may briefly address any new communicants. After the Mass, the Blessed Sacrament is replaced in the aumbry or tabernacle. Priests who celebrate or concelebrate the Vigil Mass may celebrate or concelebrate the Mass of Easter Day. Those who receive Holy Communion at the Vigil Mass may communicate again at Mass on Easter Day. But they *have* already fulfiled their Easter duty.

THE EASTER TRIDUUM

(✠) THURSDAY
9   W   Mass   **MAUNDY THURSDAY EVENING**
Gl; R: Pref of Eucharist; CW, Proper Pref
CW: Exod 12:1–4 (5–10) 11–14; Ps 116:1 & 10–17;
I Cor 11:23–26; Jn 13:1–17 & 31b–35
R: Exod 12:1–8 & 11–14; Ps 116; I Cor 11:23–26; Jn 13:1–15

FRIDAY   **GOOD FRIDAY, IN THE LORD'S PASSION**
10   R   MP   H: 95 or 96 (NEH 78)   Gen 22:1–18   Gen 22:1–18
                    Ps: 69   Heb 10:1–10   see note, or ◁
The Solemn Liturgy

Readings (CW = R:): Isa 52:13 – 53:12; Ps 22 (R: 31:1 & 5 & 11–12 & 14–16 & 24);
Heb 4:14–16 & 5:7–9; Jn 18 & 19 (see note)

          EP   H: 94 (NEW 79)   Lam 5:15–22   Isa 50:4–18
                    Ps: 130, 143   Col 1:18–23   see note; or I Pet 2:11–end

SATURDAY   **HOLY SATURDAY**
11   P   CW 'Principal Service': Job 14:1–14 or Lam 3:1–9 & 19–24; Ps 31:1–4 & 15–16;
                                       I Pet 4:1–8; Mt 27:57–66 or Jn 19:38–42
                 CW 'Morning Service': Ps 142; Hos 6:1–6; Jn 2:18–22
                 CW 'Evening Service': Ps 116; Job 19:21–27; I Jn 5:5–12
                 1961: MP: Zech 9:9–12 & I Pet 2:19–end; EP: Job 19:21–27 & Jn 2:13–22
                 R: MP: Hos 5:15d – 6:2; Office of Readings Heb 4:1–13; EP I Pet 1:18–21
                 Byzantium: Liturgy: I Cor 5:6–9 & Gal 3:13–14; Mt 27:62–66

EASTER TIME
11–12   W   **EASTER NIGHT: THE EASTER VIGIL**

There should be at least three readings before the Epistle and Gospel. The account of the Crossing of the Red Sea (Exodus) must always be read. (CW and LHWE make suggestions additional to those listed).

	Roman Rite	**CW (or LHWE)**
1.	*Gen 1:1 – 2:2	*Gen 1:1 – 2:4a
	(or 1:1 & 26–31a)	(or 1:1–5 & 26–end: LHWE)
		*Gen 7:1–5 & 11–18 & 8:6–18 & 9:8–13
2.	*Gen 22:1–18	*Gen 22:1–18
	(or 22:1–2 & 9a & 10–13 & 15–18)	(or 22:1–2 & 9–13 & 15–18: LHWE)
3.	*Exod 14:15 – 15:1	*Exod 14:10–31 & 15:20–21
		(or Exod 14:15 – 15:1a: LHWE)
4.	Isa 54:5–14	(Isa 54:5–14: LHWE)
5.	*Isa 55:1–11	*Isa 55:1–11
6.	*Baruch 3:9–15 & 32 – 4:4	*Baruch 3:9–15 & 32 – 4:4
7.	Ezek 36:16–17a & 18–28	Ezek 36:24–28
		*Ezek 37:1–14
	Rom 6:3–11	Rom 6:3–11
	Mk 16:1–8	Mk 16:1–8

For Reading 7, R: allows, where baptisms are happening, Isa 12:2–6.

[In Churches where the Vigil is not observed, the Principal Eucharist on Easter Sunday morning is the Great Easter Liturgy; it may start with the blessing of the Paschal Candle (LHWE).

It fittingly includes Baptisms and Confirmations or else the Renewal of Baptismal Vows, e.g., CW 'Initiation' pp. 127–8) after the Gospel; if so, the Creed is omitted.]

---

* Readings from the ancient Roman Vigil.

✠ *SUNDAY*   **EASTER DAY IN THE LORD'S RESURRECTION**

12	W	MP	Ps: 114; 117	Gen 1:1–5 & 26–31	Exod 12:1–14
				II Cor 5:14 – 6:2	Rev 1:4–18

R: Ps I   Mass   *Gl; (R: Seq compulsory: EH 130 NEH 519) Cr; R: Pref I of Easter; CW, Pref of Easter.*

                           CW: Acts 10:34–43; Ps 118*:1–2 & 14–24; I Cor 15:1–11; Jn 20:1–18 (or Mk 16:1–8)
                           R: Acts 10:34a & 37–43; Ps 118*:1–2 & sequence; 15–17 & 22–23; Col 3:1–4 (or
                           I Cor 5:6b–8); Jn 20:1–9 (or Mk 16:1–8 or, at an Evening Mass, Lk 24:13–35)
                           [OT readings: see Note 9 below. For those who particularly desire an OT reading, CW provides
                           Isa 65:17–25]

		EP		Ezek 37:1–14	Exod 14
			Ps: 105 or 66:1–11	Lk 24:13–35	Jn 20: (1–10) 11–23

* Ps 118, last of the Passover Hallel psalms, quoted by the Lord and in the Easter Kerygma. Verses 24 & 1 are anciently associated with the readings at Rome and Byzantium.

NOTES FOR EASTER WEEK ONLY

1 During the octave of Easter, that is, from Easter Day *until the evening of Low Sunday*, two alleluias are added to the dismissals at the end of Mass, and at the end of Morning and Evening Prayer, and to the response. Throughout Eastertide, Alleluia is added to all Antiphons or 'Sentences' which do not already have it.

2 In R: from Easter Sunday MP to the EP of Low Sunday, before Benedictus and Magnificat, this antiphon is used: **This is the day which was made by the Lord: let us rejoice and be glad. Alleluia.**

3 Preface: In CW, the '*short* preface' is the ancient Western Easter preface, which comes down to us via BCP. According to ancient custom, R: orders this preface, *and no other*, to be used until Low Sunday inclusive. Your Compiler urges its exclusive use during the Octave instead of the CW 'extended Preface'.

NOTES FOR ALL EASTERTIDE

4 A **SOLEMNITY** falling on a Sunday in Eastertide is transferred to the Monday. (CW allows Dedications and Patronal Festivals.) A **Festum** falling on a Sunday in Eastertide is omitted (Roman rules) or *may* be transferred to the first available weekday (CW).

5 **According to the provisions of *The Liturgy of the Hours*, the Office Hymns for Eastertide begin on Easter Day. EH: MP 123 EP 125 (122 may be used optionally at MP on Ferias after Easter Week).**
NEH: Sundays: MP 100 EP 101; Ferias: MP 124 EP 101.

6 Prefaces: the CW provision is very austere. After Low Sunday (see note 3 above) your Compiler urges the use also of ASB 14 = R:4, and of ASB 15 and/or R: prefaces 2, 3, and 5. (Unlike CW, R: draws upon Prefaces in the ancient Western Sacramentaries.)

7 The Paschal Candle is lit at Mass and Evening Prayer on Easter Day and daily during the octave; and thereafter on Sundays and greater feasts until the evening of Pentecost. It may be lit at other liturgical services according to custom.

8 *Regina Coeli* is recited instead of *Angelus* until the evening of Pentecost.

9 R: and CW provide *all three* Sunday Eucharistic readings from the New Testament throughout Eastertide.

10 On weekdays from Low Sunday until Pentecost, propers at mass are taken *either* from the Daily Eucharistic Lectionary (Weekday Missal) which is R: = CW, *or* from the previous Sunday (Friday and Saturday after Ascension, from the Ascension).

11 During the Easter Season it is particularly suitable to use the Asperges (Sprinkling) for the Penitential Rite, to remind us of our Baptism (Introduction Paragraph 12). See Introduction Paragraph 17 for the Creed.

12 The 'Julian' (Eastern) Easter this year is April 19, our Low Sunday.

MONDAY			**MONDAY IN EASTER WEEK**		
13	W	MP	Ps: 111, 117, 146	Song of Sol 1:9 – 2:7	Exod 15:1–18
				Mk 16:1–8	Lk 24:1–12
		Mass	*of the day; Gl; (Seq ad lib) Pref (I) of Easter*		
			Acts 2:14 & 22–32; Ps: 16:1 & 6–end; Mt 28:8–15		
		EP		Exod 12:1–14	Isa 12
			Ps: 135	I Cor 15:1–11	Rev 7:9–end
TUESDAY			**TUESDAY IN EASTER WEEK**		
14	W	MP	Ps: 112, 147:1–12	Song of Sol 2:8–end	Isa 25:1–9
				Lk 24:1–12	I Pet 1:1–12
		Mass	*as Monday*		
			Acts 2:36–41; Ps: 33:4–5 & 18–end; Jn 20:11–18		
		EP		Exod 12:14–36	Isa 26:1–19
			Ps: 136	I Cor 15:12–19	Mt 28:1–15
WEDNESDAY			**WEDNESDAY IN EASTER WEEK**		
15	W	MP	Ps: 113, 147:13–end	Song of Sol 3	Isa 61
				Mt 28:16–end	I Pet 1:13–end
		Mass	*as Monday*		
			Acts 3:1–10; Ps: 105:1–9; Lk 24:13–35		
		EP		Exod 12:37–end	Song of Sol 2:8–end
			Ps: 105	I Cor 15:20–28	Mt 28:16–end
THURSDAY			**THURSDAY IN EASTER WEEK**		
16	W	MP	Ps: 114, 148	Song of Sol 5:2 – 6:3	Job 14:1–15
				Lk 7:11–17	I Thess 4:13–end
		Mass	*as Monday*		
			Acts 3:11–26; Ps: 8; Lk 24:35–48		
		EP		Exod 13:1–16	Dan 12
			Ps: 106	I Cor 15:29–34	Mk 16
FRIDAY			**FRIDAY IN EASTER WEEK**		
17	W	MP	Ps: 115, 149	Song of Sol 7:10 – 8:4	Zeph 3:14–end
				Lk 8:41–end	Acts 17:16–31
		Mass	*as Monday*		
			Acts 4:1–12; Ps: 118:1–4 & 22–26; Jn 21:1–14		
		EP		Exod 13:17 – 14:14	II Kgs 4:8–37
			Ps: 107	I Cor 15:35–50	Jn 21:1–14
SATURDAY			**SATURDAY IN EASTER WEEK**		
18	W	MP	Ps: 116, 150	Song of Sol 8:5–7	Jer 31:1–14
				Jn 11:17–44	Acts 26:1–23
		Mass	*as Monday*		
			Acts 4:13–21; Ps: 118:1–4 & 14–21; Mk 16:9–15		
	W	1 EP of foll		Exod 14:15–end	Mic 7:7–end
			Ps: 145	I Cor 15:51–end	Jn 21:15–end

Low Sunday, in Western Christendom, is 'Divine Mercy Sunday'. In an Hour of Mercy before the End Time, the believer, even if perplexed by doubt, is drawn by the Risen Lord to reach out with trusting Faith to His Sacred Heart, pierced source (for all Christians as well as for the Paschal neophytes) of the Waters of Regeneration and the Blood of Redemption. (Acts 17:30–31; Mt 28:17; Jn 20:27–8 & 19:34; cf the Gallican collect now used in R: for this Sunday, and the Byzantine Festival, around this time of *Zoodochos Pege*, which also visits themes of Healing Streams but has a greater Marian bias). The old English title 'Mother of Mercy,' beloved of S Richard of Chichester, Bishop Grandisson of Exeter, and so many other saintly Anglicans, seems particularly suitable.

✠ *SUNDAY*

DIVINE MERCY SUNDAY
LOW SUNDAY, OF THE OCTAVE OF EASTER
(ELECTION, IN 2005, of BENEDICT XVI)
2nd SUNDAY and WEEK within EASTERTIDE (BCP EASTER 1)

19   W   MP   Ps: 22:20–31   Isa 53:6–12   Isa 51:1–16
                               Rom 4:13–25   Lk 24:13–35
R: Ps II   Mass   *Gl; Cr; Pref of Easter*
                   CW: Acts 4:32–35; Ps 133; I Jn 1:1 – 2:2; Jn 20:19–31
                   R: Acts 4:32–35; Ps 118; I Jn 5:1–6; Jn 20:19–31 (The Victory of Faith)
         2 EP   Isa 26:1–9 & 19   Exod 15:1–18
                         Ps: 143:1–11   Lk 24:1–12   Jn 20:24–end

MONDAY   *Feria*

20   W   MP   Ps: 1, 2, 3   Deut 1:3–18   Deut 1:3–18
                                 Jn 20:1–10   Acts 1:1–14
         Mass   *as Wednesday*
                   Acts 4:23–31; Ps 2:1–9; Jn 3:1–8
         EP   Exod 15:1–21   Deut 1:19–end
                         Ps: 4, 7   Col 1:1–14   Acts 1:15–end

TUESDAY   *Feria (S Anselm, B, Dr)*

21   W   MP   Ps: 5, 6, 8   Deut 1:19–40   Deut 2:1–25
                                   Jn 20:11–18   Acts 2:1–21
         Mass   *as Wednesday (or of the Saint)*
                   Acts 4:32–end; Ps 93; Jn 3:7–15
         EP   Exod 15:22 – 16:10   Deut 2:26 – 3:5
                         Ps: 9, 10   Col 1:15–end   Acts 2:22–end

WEDNESDAY   *Feria)*

22   W   MP   Ps: 119:1–32   Deut 3:18–end   Deut 3:18–end
                                   Jn 20:19–end   Acts 3:1 – 4:4
         Mass   *no Gl or Cr; Pref of Easter*
                   Acts 5:17–26; Ps 34:1–8; Jn 3:16–21
                 S GEORGE M, PATRON OF ENGLAND
         R   1 EP   H: 185   Jer 15:15–21   ◁
                         Ps: 111,116   Heb 11:32 – 12:2   ◁

THURSDAY

23   R   MP   H: 180   Josh 1:1–9   ◁
                         Ps: 5, 146   Eph 6:10–20   ◁
         Mass   *Gl; Cr; Pref of Martyrs (or Patrons) (CW of Saints)*
                   CW: Rev 12:7–12; Ps: 126; II Tim 2:3–13; Jn 15:18–21 (R: permits)
         2 EP   H: 181   Isa 43:1–7   ◁
                         Ps: 3, 11   Jn 15:1–8   ◁

FRIDAY   *Feria (☐ S Adalbert, B, M; ☐ S Fidelis of Sigmaringen, Pr, M;*
                 S Mellitus, B) **(INAUGURATION, IN 2005, OF BENEDICT XVI)**

24   W   MP   Ps: 17, 19   Deut 4:15–31   Deut 5:22–end
   (or R)   Jn 21:15–19   Acts 6:1 – 7:16
         Mass   *as Wednesday (or of the Saint)*
                   Acts 5:34–42; Ps 27:1–5 & 16 & 17; Jn 6:1–15
         EP   Exod 18:1–12   Deut 6
                         Ps: 22   Col 3:12 – 4:1   Acts 7:17–34

SATURDAY   **S Mark Ev**

25   R   MP   Ps: 37:23–41, 148   Isa 62:6–10 or Ecclus 51:13–30   Ezek 1:1–14
                                   Acts 12:25 – 13:13 (R: Eph 4:1–16)   Acts 15:35–end
         Mass   *Gl; R: Pref of Apostles (II); CW, Pref of Saints*
                   CW: Acts 15:35–41; Ps 119:9–16; Eph 4:7–16; Mk 13:5–13
                   R: I Pet 5:5–14; Ps 89; Mk 16:15–20
         W   1 EP of foll   Exod 18:13–end   Deut 7:12–end
                         Ps: 24, 25   Col 4:2–end   Acts 8:4–25

THE MAY DEVOTION TO OUR LADY,

so long traditional, suits well the Paschal celebration of Humanity, restored and deified. In the words of the great Russian Orthodox lay theologian Vladimir Lossky, 'freed from the limitations of time, Mary can be the cause of that which is before her; can preside over that which comes after her. She obtains eternal benefits. It is through her that men and angels receive grace. No gift is received in the Church without the assistance of the Mother of God, who is herself the first-fruits of the glorified Church. Thus, having attained to the limits of becoming, she necessarily watches over the destinies of the Church and of the Universe.' One of the greatest of the Greek fathers, S. Gregory Palamas, wrote that the All-Holy Mother of God 'is herself alone the boundary of created and uncreated nature, and nobody could come to God except through her ... she is the Treasury and President of the Wealth of the Godhead ... she stewards and encompasses God's graces ...'. PPL comments that the May Devotion 'highlights the earthly role played by the glorified Queen of Heaven, here and now, in the celebration of Baptism, Confirmation, and Eucharist.' As well as the Rosary (especially on Saturdays), the Akathist hymn to Our Lady of Victories seems appropriate (see p. xxvi).

1. Many priests begin the May Devotion with a (Class 2 – see p. xxi) votive of Our Lady on the first free day. **May 3**, in ancient 'Celtic' Calendars, was her Conception (in Poland, Solemnity of our Lady Queen of Poland, and in Russia the Feast of her Icon in the great Pechersk Monastery, fountainhead of the cenobitic monastic life in that country).
2. On the **Friday in Easter Week*** Byzantium emphasises the role of the Mother of God in pouring Christ's healing streams upon us (Zoodochos Pege: originally the Dedication of the ancient Sanctuary of the Mother of God of the Living Fountain beside its miraculous stream at Constantinople; the panorthodox chapel in the shrine church at Walsingham has this dedication). Collection of Masses (Int P 26b ii) mass 31 visits this theme.
3. The **Visitation of Our Lady** was deliberately moved in 1969 to associate it with May 31, the day long connected with the celebration of Our Lady as Mediatrix of All Graces, as an appropriate conclusion to the May devotion. This year it collides with Pentecost and is either suppressed (R:) or transferred to Monday (CW:): BUT SEE PAGE 69.
4. Rome moved **Ss Philip and James** from May 1 to May 3 to accommodate S Joseph the Craftsmen on the Workers' festival. (EAD allows either date.) But he never caught on, least of all in England, and after Vatican II was reduced from a Solemnity to an Optional Memorial.

* April 24 in this year's Julian Calendar.

May 1 **S Joseph the Workman** (Optional Memorial) MP and EP as on March 19
Mass: Gen 1:26 – 2:3; or Col 3:14–15 & 17 & 23–24; Ps 90; Mt 13: 54–58

Ss Philip and James Aps MAY 1 (CW) (SUPRESSED ON MAY 3 BY R:)

R	MP	Ps: 139, 146	Prov 4:10–18	Isa 30:15–21
			James 1:1–12	Jn 6:1–14
	Mass	Gl; R: Pref of Apostles (II); CW, Pref of Saints		
		CW: Isa 30:15–21; Ps 119:1–8; Eph 1:3–10; Jn 14:1–14		
		R: I Cor 15:1–8; Ps 19; Jn 14:6–14		
	EP		Job 23:1–12	Job 23:1–12
		Ps: 149	Jn 1:43–51	Jn 1:43–end

COLLISIONS IN LATE MAY

MAY	R: Calendar for England	Common Worship
24 Sun	SUNDAY* (Aldhelm suppressed)	SUNDAY*
25 Mon	Bede*	Bede† Aldhelm†
26 Tues	Philip Neri*	Augustine† Philip† (Calvin†)
27 Wed	Augustine*	Feria†

* Compulsory. † Optional.

✠ SUNDAY
26   W   MP   Ps: 77:11–20   Isa 63:7–15   Exod 16:2–15
                                        I Cor 10:1–13   I Cor 15:1–26
R: Ps III   Mass   *Gl; Cr; Pref of Easter*
                   CW: Acts 3:12–19; Ps 4; I Jn 3:1–7; Lk 24:36b–48
                   R: Acts 3:13–15 & 17–19; Ps 4; I Jn 2:1–5; Lk 24:35–48 (Our Advocate with the Father)
            EP   Deut 7:7–13   Exod 24
                   Ps: 142   Rev 2:1–11   Jn 21:1–14

MONDAY   **Feria**
27   W   MP   Ps: 27, 30   Deut 5:1–22   Deut 8
                                        Eph 1:1–14   Acts 8:26–end
            Mass   *no Gl or Cr; Pref of Easter (**Christina Rossetti**)*
                   Acts 6:8–15; Ps 119:17–24; Jn 6:22–29
            EP   Exod 19   Deut 9:1–10
                   Ps: 26, 28, 29   Lk 1:1–25   Acts 9:1–31

TUESDAY   **Feria**
                              (S Peter Chanel, Pr, M; □ S Louis Marie Grignion de Montfort, Pr)
28   W   MP   Ps: 32, 36   Deut 5:22–end   Deut 9:11–end
     (or R)   Eph 1:15–end   Acts 9:32–end
            Mass   *as Monday (or of the Saint)*
                   Acts 7:51 – 8:1; Ps 31:1–5 & 16; Jn 6:30–35
            EP   Exod 20:1–21   Deut 10
                   Ps: 33   Lk 1:26–38   Acts 10:1–23

WEDNESDAY   **S Catherine of Siena, V, Dr, Patron of Europe**
29   W   MP   [Ps: 34]   [Deut 6]   [Deut 11:1–12]
                                        [Eph 2:1–10]   [Acts 10:24–end]
            Mass   *Office Readings from Appendix 3: Doctors*
                   Gl; no Cr; Pref of Patrons or (CW) Saints
                   R: I Jn 1:5 – 2:2; Ps 45:10–11 & 13b–16; Mt 25:1–13
                   CW: Prov 8:1 & 6–11; Ps 34:11–17; Mt 25:1–13 or Jn 17:12–26
                   [Acts 8:1–8; Ps 66:1–6; Jn 6:35–40]
            EP   [Exod 24]   [Deut 11:13–end]
                   [Ps: 119:33–56]   [Lk 1:39–56]   [Acts 11:1–18]

THURSDAY   **Feria (Rogation Day) (□ S Pius, V, Pp)**
30   W   MP   Ps: 37   Deut 7:1–11   Deut 12:1–14
                                        Eph 2:11–end   Acts 11:19–end
            Mass   *as Monday (or of the Saint) (**Pandita Mary Ramabai**)*
                   Acts 8:26–40; Ps 66:7–8 & 14–end; Jn 6:44–51
            EP   Exod 25:1–22   Deut 15:1–18
                   Ps: 39, 40   Lk 1:57–end   Acts 12:1–24

M A Y
FRIDAY   **Feria (SS P & J? S Joseph? see p. 31)**
1   W   MP   Ps: 31   Deut 7:12–end   Deut 16:1–20
     (or R)   Eph 3:1–13   Acts 12:25 – 13:12
            Mass   *as Monday (First Friday: Sacred Heart, p. 42)*
                   Acts 9:1–20; Ps 117; Jn 6:52–59
            EP   Exod 28:1–4a, 29–38   Deut 17:8–end
                   Ps: 35   Lk 2:1–20   Acts 13:13–43

SATURDAY   **S Athanasius, B, Dr**
2   W   MP   Ps: 41, 42, 43   Deut 8   Deut 18:9–end
                                        Eph 3:14–end   Acts 13:44 – 14:7
            Mass   *of the Saint (First Saturday: Immaculate Heart, p. 42)*
                   Acts 9:31–42; Ps 116:10–15; Jn 6:60–69
         W   1 EP of foll   Exod 29:1–9   Deut 19
                   Ps: 45, 46   Lk 2:21–40   Acts 14:8–end

✠ *SUNDAY*   **4th SUNDAY and WEEK within EASTERTIDE (BCP EASTER 3)**

3   W   MP   Ps: 119:89–96   Neh 7:73b – 8:12   Exod 32:1–14 & 30–end

R: Ps IV   Lk 24:25–32   I Cor 15:35–end

R: Ps IV   Mass   *Gl; Cr; Pref of Easter*
                  CW: Acts 4:5–12; Ps 23; I Jn 3:16–24; Jn 10:11–18
                  R: Acts 4:8–12; Ps 118; I Jn 3:1–2; Jn 10:11–18 (The Good Shepherd; Vocations Sunday)

       2 EP   Exod 16:4–15   Exod 33:7–end
            Ps: 81:8–16   Rev 2:12–17   Jn 21:15–end

MONDAY   **The English Martyrs**

4   R   MP   Ps: 44   Deut 9:1–21   Deut 21:22 – 22:8
                      Eph 4:1–16   Acts 15:1–21

       Mass   *of the Saints*
                  Acts 11:1–18; Ps 42:1 & 2 & 43:1–4; Jn 10:1–10

       EP   Exod 32:1–14   Deut 24:5–end
            Ps: 47, 49   Lk 2:41–end   Acts 15:22–35

TUESDAY   **Feria**

5   W   MP   Ps: 48, 52   Deut 9:23 – 10:5   Deut 26
                      Eph 4:17–end   Acts 15:36 – 16:5

       Mass   *no Gl or Cr; Pref of Easter*
                  Acts 11:19–26; Ps 87; Jn 10:22–30

       EP   Exod 32:15–34   Deut 28:58–end
            Ps: 50   Lk 3:1–14   Acts 16:6–end

WEDNESDAY   **Feria**

6   W   MP   Ps: 119:57–80   Deut 10:12–end   Deut 29:10–end
                      Eph 5:1–14   Acts 17:1–15

       Mass   *as Tuesday*
                  Acts 12:24 – 13:5; Ps 67; Jn 12:44–end

       EP   Exod 33   Deut 30
            Ps: 59, 60, 67   Lk 3:15–22   Acts 17:16–end

THURSDAY   **Feria**

7   W   MP   Ps: 56, 57, 63   Deut 11:8–end   Deut 31:1–13
                      Eph 5:15–end   Acts 18:1–23

       Mass   *as Tuesday*
                  Acts 13:13–25; Ps 89:1–2 & 20–26; Jn 13:16–20

       EP   Exod 34:1–10 & 27–end   Deut 31:14–29
            Ps: 61, 62, 64   Lk 4:1–13   Acts 18:24 – 19:7

FRIDAY   **Feria**

8   W   MP   Ps: 51, 54   Deut 12:1–14   Deut 31:30 – 32:14
                      Eph 6:1–9   Acts 19:8–20

       Mass   *as Tuesday (**Julian of Norwich**)*
            (Our Lady, Mediatrix of Grace, 30; Mother of Fairest Love, 36)
                  Acts 13:26–33; Ps 2; Jn 14:1–6

       EP   Exod 35:20 – 36:7   Deut 32:15–47
            Ps: 38   Lk 4:14–30   Acts 19:21–end

SATURDAY   **Feria**

9   W   MP   Ps: 68   Deut 15:1–18   Deut 33
                      Eph 6:10–end   Acts 20:1–16

       Mass   *as Tuesday*
                  Acts 13:44–52; Ps 98:1–5; Jn 14:7–14

       W   1 EP of foll   Exod 40:17–end   Deut 32:48–end & 34
            Ps: 65, 66   Lk 4:31–37   Acts 20:17–end

✠ *SUNDAY*
10   R   **5th SUNDAY and WEEK within EASTERTIDE (BCP EASTER 4)**

		MP	Ps: 44:16–27	Dan 3:16–28	Exod 34:1–10
R: Ps I				Heb 11:32 – 12:2	I Pet 3:8–end
		Mass	*Gl; Cr; Pref of Easter*		
			CW: Acts 8:26–40; Ps 22:25–31; Jn 4:7–21; Jn 15:1–8		
			R: Acts 9:26–31; Ps 22; I Jn 3:18–24; Jn 15:1–8 (Christ the True Vine)		
		2 EP		Isa 60:1–14	Exod 35:30 – 36:1
			Ps: 96	Rev 3:1–13	Lk 16:19–end

7th WEEK OF YEAR

MONDAY
11   W   **Feria**

		MP	Ps: 71	Deut 16:1–20	Josh 1
				I Pet 1:1–12	Acts 21:1–16
		Mass	*no Gl or Cr; Common Pref (or of the Saint)*		
			Acts 14:5–18; Ps 118:1–3 & 14 & 15; Jn 14:21–26		
		EP		Num 9:15–end & 10:33–end	Josh 2
			Ps: 72, 75	Lk 4:38–end	Acts 21:17–36

TUESDAY
12   W   **Feria (☐ Ss Nereus and Achilleus, Ms; ☐ S Pancras, M)**
     (or R)

		MP	Ps: 73	Deut 17:8–end	Josh 3
				I Pet 1:13–end	Acts 21:37 – 22:22
		Mass	*no Gl or Cr; Common Pref (or of the Saint)*		
			Acts 14:19–28; Ps 145:10–end; Jn 14:27–31		
		EP		Num 11:1–33	Josh 4:1 – 5:1
			Ps: 74	Lk 5:1–11	Acts 22:23 – 23:11

WEDNESDAY
13   W   **Feria (☐ Our Lady of Fatima)***

		MP	Ps: 77	Deut 18:9–end	Josh 5:13 – 6:20
				I Pet 2:1–10	Acts 23:12–end
		Mass	*as Tuesday (or of our Lady)*		
			Acts 15:1–6; Ps 122:1–5; Jn 15:1–8		
		EP		Num 12	Josh 7
			Ps: 119:81–104	Lk 5:12–26	Acts 24:1–23

THURSDAY
14   R   **S Matthias, Apostle**

		MP	Ps: 16, 147:1–12	I Sam 2:27–35	Isa 22:15–22
				Acts 2:37–47	Mt 7:15–27
		Mass	*Gl; R: Pref of Apostles (II); CW, Pref of Saints CRP*		
			CW: Acts 1:15–26; Ps 15; I Cor 4:1–7; Jn 15:9–17		
			R: Acts 1:15–17 & 20–26; Ps 113; Jn 15:9–17		
		EP		I Sam 16:1–13a	I Sam 16:1–13
			Ps: 80	Mt 7:15–27	I Cor 4:1–8

FRIDAY
15   W   **Feria**

		MP	Ps: 55	Deut 21:22 – 22:8	Josh 21:43 – 22:8
				I Pet 3:1–12	Acts 26
		Mass	*as Tuesday*		
			Acts 15:22–31; Ps 57:8–end; Jn 15:12–17		
		EP		Num 14:1–25	Josh 22:9–end
			Ps: 69	Lk 6:1–11	Acts 27

SATURDAY
16   W   **Feria**

		MP	Ps: 76, 79	Deut 24:5–end	Josh 23
				I Pet 3:13–end	Acts 28:1–15
		Mass	*as Tuesday (**Caroline Chisholm**)*		
			Acts 16:1–10; Ps 100; Jn 15:18–21		
	W	1 EP of foll		Num 14:26–end	Josh 24:1–28
			Ps: 81, 84	Lk 6:12–26	Acts 28:16–end

---

* The Fatima visionaries can hardly have known that 'the Lady' appeared to them on the ancient commemoration of *S. Maria ad Martyres*. The Fatima devotion is particularly linked with the cult of the Immaculate Heart (p. 42); in recent years the prayer *sub tuum praesidium*, now identified on a third century papyrus, has been increasingly associated with our Lady of Fatima.

ASCENSION AND PENTECOST

1. Modern liturgical reforms recovered a primitive concept of the fifty days of Eastertide as a unitary festival, a Week of Weeks, 'the One Day', 'the Great Sunday'. That is why the Paschal candle burns from Easter Night until Pentecost Evening, when it is removed (and placed near the font). **However**, recent Roman directions allow the BCP-style Whitmonday: Mass and Office 'as yesterday'.

2. *Rogations*, instituted in Gaul around 475 'to repel calamities', became spring processions to ask that God 'give and preserve to our use the kindly fruits of the earth.' They are Class 2 votives (page xxi); CLC pp 231 and 115. We have Synodical encouragement for processing the relics of Saints on these days; and Monday has been episcopally designated (EXETER) Feast of the Translation of the Relics.

3. Rome now provides a *Vigil* mass for Ascension (as well as Pentecost), the Collect of which is used at 1 EP (God, whose Son this day ascended into the heavens as his Apostles stood by; grant us we beseech/beg thee/you, that, according to his promise, he may ever be with us upon earth and that we may be worthy to live with him in heaven.) The Tridentine = BCP = CW collect for Ascension *day* is now restored by R: as an option!

4. ***Prefaces from Ascension to Pentecost (exclusively) (including Sunday)***
   CW: 'From the day after Ascension Day until the Day of Pentecost'. R: Either of the Ascension or of Easter [even on Memorials]. CW *Short* Preface *for Ascension* is the traditional one.

5. ***Weekday Masses after Pentecost Sunday***
   According to R:, any 'green' Sunday Collect may be used, and CW (p. 406) offers Roman Sunday Collect 10 (= BCP Easter 5) in its Cranmerian translation. Mass readings come from the Week of the Year.

6. ***Weekday Masses after Trinity Sunday***
   CW expects the Trinity collect to be used; Rome both provides a collect and allows optionally any Sunday collect to be used. Mass readings come from the Week of the Year.

7. ***Hymns from Ascension to Pentecost (exclusively) (including Sunday)***
   MP 141 (NEH 128) EP 154 (NEH 138) [or, optionally, on Memorials, of the Saint].

8. Between Ascension and Pentecost, Evening Prayer has the Holy Spirit as its theme in both the Office Hymn and the Readings.

9. For those observing the Ascension, with the English Roman Catholic Church, on the Sunday following, the CW office readings can be:

Wednesday	EP:	Num 17:1–11; Lk 7:1–10
Thursday	MP:	Deut 29:2–15; 1 Jn 1:1 – 2:6
	EP:	Num 20:1–13; Lk 7:11–17
Friday	MP:	Deut 30; I Jn 2:7–17
	EP:	Num 21:4–9; Lk 7:18–35
Saturday	MP:	Num 22:1–35; Lk 7:36–end
	EP:	of the Ascension, tomorrow, as in the ORDO for Wednesday evening.
Sunday	All	as in the ORDO for last Thursday.

(Tridentinists and Prayer Book enthusiasts will presumably not wish to make this transference.)

Mass in the Roman Rite provides *Acts 18:1–8; Ps 98; Jn 16:16–20* as the readings for Thursday if the Ascension is transferred to Sunday.

✠ *SUNDAY*   **6th SUNDAY and WEEK within EASTERTIDE (BCP EASTER 5)**

17 W   MP   Ps: 104:28–34   Ezek 47:1–12   Deut 34
                                        Jn 21:1–19   Acts 13:26–43

R: Ps II   Mass   *Gl; Cr; Pref of Easter*
                   CW: Acts 10:44–48; Ps 98; I Jn 5:1–6; Jn 15:9–17
                   R: Acts 10:25–26 & 34–35 & 44–48; Ps 98; I Jn 4:7–10; Jn 15:9–17
                   (The Spirit of God's Love)

            2 EP   H: 159   Song of Sol 4:16 – 5:2 & 8:6–7   Deut 6
                   Ps: 45   Rev 3:14–22   Lk 10:38 – 11:13

                                                                8th WEEK of YEAR

MONDAY   *Feria (Rogation) (☐ S John 1, Pp, M)*

18 W   MP   Ps: 80, 82   Deut 26   Deut 7:6–13
     (or R)   I Pet 4:1–11   Mt 6:5–18

            Mass   *as Tuesday (or of the Saint)*
                   Acts 16:11–15; Ps 149:1–5; Jn 15:26 – 16:4

            EP   Num 16:1–35   Deut 8
                   Ps: 85, 86   Lk 6:27–38   Mt 6:19–end

TUESDAY   *Feria (Rogation) (S Dunstan, B)*

19 W   MP   Ps: 87, 89:1–18   Deut 28:1–14   Deut 11:8–21
                                        I Pet 4:12–end   Lk 5:1–11

            Mass   *of Sunday; no Gl or Cr; Pref of Easter*
                   Acts 16:22–34; Ps 138; Jn 16:5–11

            EP   Num 16:36–end   I Kgs 8:22–43
                   Ps: 89:19–end   Lk 6:39–end   Jas 5:1–18

WEDNESDAY   *Feria (Rogation) (☐ S Bernardine of Sienna, Pr)*

20 W   MP   Ps: 119:105–128   Deut 28:58–end   Joel 2:21–27
                                        I Pet 5   Jn 6:22–40

            Mass   *as Tuesday (or of the Saint)* **(Alcuin, Abbot, Dcn)**
                   Acts 17:15 & 22–18:1; Ps 148:1 & 2 & 11–end; Jn 16:12–15

✠   **ASCENSION OF THE LORD** (see p. 35 for TRANSFERENCE)

            1 EP of foll   II Sam 23:1–5   Song of the Three 29–37
                   Ps: 15, 24   Col 2:20 – 3:4   Mt 28:16–end

THURSDAY

21 W   MP   H: 141 (NEH 128)   Isa 52:7–15   II Kgs 2:1–15
                   Ps: 110   Heb 7:(11–25) 26–28 (R: Eph 4:1–24)   Jn 17

            Mass   *Gl; Cr; Pref of the Ascension*
                   CW: Acts 1:1–11; Ps 47; Eph 1:15–23; Lk 24:44–53
                   R: Acts 1:1–11; Ps 47; Eph 1:17–23; Mk 16:15–20

            2 EP   H: 144 (NEH 129)   Song of the Three 29–37   II Sam 23:1–5
                                        or II Kgs 2:1–15
                   Ps: 8   Rev 5   Heb 1

FRIDAY   *Feria (☐ S Rita of Cascia, Rel) (Hymns see p. 35 (6))*

22 W   MP   Ps: 88, 95   Deut 29:2–15   Judg 2:6–end
                                        I Jn 1:1 – 2:6   Heb 2

            Mass   *no Gl or Cr; Pref see p. 35 (7) (or of the Saint)*
                   Acts 18:9–18a; Ps 47:1–6; Jn 16:20–23

            EP   Exod 35:30 – 36:1   Judg 4
                   Ps: 102   Gal 5:13–26   Heb 3

SATURDAY   *Feria*

23 W   MP   Ps: 96, 97, 100   Deut 30   Judg 5
                                        I Jn 2:7–17   Heb 4:1–13

            Mass   *as Friday* **(Our Lady Queen of Apostles)**
                   Acts 18:22–end; Ps 47:1–2 & 7–end; Jn 16:23–28

        W   1 EP of foll   Num 11:16–17, 24–29   Judg 6:1–24
                   Ps: 104   I Cor 2   Heb 4:14 – 5:10

✠ *SUNDAY*

7th SUNDAY and WEEK within EASTERTIDE
SUNDAY AFTER ASCENSION

24 W MP Ps: 76 | Isa 14:3–15 | Isa 65:17–end
 | | Rev 14:1–13 | Lk 24:36–end

R: Ps III Mass *Gl; Cr; Pref see p. 35*
CW: Acts 1:15–17 & 21–26; Ps 1; I Jn 5:9–13; Jn 17:6–19
R: Acts 1:15–17 & 20–26; Ps 103; I Jn 4:11–16; Jn 17:11–19

2 EP | Isa 61 | Jer 31:1–13
Ps: 147:1–12 | Lk 4:14–21 | Jn 14:1–14

MONDAY **See p. 31**

25 MP Ps: 98, 99, 101 | Deut 31:1–13 | Ezek 11:14–20
 | | I Jn 2:18–end | Acts 2:12–36

Mass

Acts 19:1–8; Ps 68:1–6; Jn 16:29–33

EP | Num 27:15–23 | Wisd 1:1–7
Ps: 103, 105 | I Cor 3 | Acts 2:37–end

TUESDAY **See p. 31**

26 MP Ps: 106 | Deut 31:14–29 | Ezek 37:1–14
 | | I Jn 3:1–10 | I Cor 12:1–13

Mass

Acts 20:17–27; Ps 68:9–10 & 18–19; Jn 17:1–11

EP | I Sam 10:1–10 | Wisd 7:15 – 8:1
Ps: 107 | I Cor 12:1–13 | I Cor 12:27–13 end

WEDNESDAY **See p. 31**

27 MP Ps: 110, 111, 112 | Deut 31:30 – 32:14 | I Kgs 19:1–18
 | | I Jn 3:11–end | I Cor 2

Mass

Acts 20:28–38; Ps 68:27–28 & 32–end; Jn 17:11–19

EP | I Kgs 18:1–18 | Wisd 9
Ps: 119:129–152 | Mt 3:13–end | I Cor 3

THURSDAY **Feria**

28 W MP Ps: 113, 115 | Deut 32:15–47 | II Sam 23:1–6
 | | I Jn 4:1–6 | Eph 6:10–20

Mass *no Gl or Cr; Common Pref (**Lanfranc, Rel**)*
Acts 22:30 & 23:6–11; Ps 16:1 & 2 & 5–end; Jn 17:20–26

EP | Ezek 11:14–20 | Exod 35:30 – 36:1
Ps: 114, 116, 117 | Mt 9:35 – 10:20 | Gal 5:13–end

FRIDAY **Feria**

29 W MP Ps: 139 | Deut 33 | Num 11:16–17 & 24–29
 | | I Jn 4:7–end | II Cor 5:14 – 6:10

Mass *as Thursday*
Acts 25:13–21; Ps 103:1 & 2 & 11 & 12 & 19 & 20; Jn 21:15–19

EP | Ezek 36:22–28 | Jer 31:31–34
Ps: 130, 131, 137 | Mt 12:22–32 | II Cor 3

SATURDAY **Feria (S Joan of Arc)**

30 W MP Ps: 120, 121, 122 | Deut 32:48–end & 34 | Num 27:15–end
 | | I Jn 5 | Mt 9:35 – 10:20

Mass *as Thursday (or of the Saint) (**Josephine Butler; Apolo Kivebulaya, Pr**)*
Acts 28:16–20 & 30 & 31; Ps 11:4–end; Jn 21:20–25

R 1 EP of Pentecost H: 154 (NEH 138) Deut 16:9–15 | Gen 11:1–9
Ps: 48 | Jn 7:37–39 | Acts 18:24 – 19:7
R: Vigil Mass: Gen 11:1–9 (or Exod 19:3–8a & 16–20b; or Ezek 37:1–14; or Joel 2:28–32);
Ps: 104; Rom 8:22–27; Jn 7:37–39). The Vigil Collect is used at 1 EP.

✠ *SUNDAY*
31   G

	MP	**PENTECOST**		**(Whitsunday)**
		H: 151 (NEH 136)	Isa 11:1–9 or Wisd 7:15–23 (24–27)	Joel 2:28–end
		Ps: 145	I Cor 12:4–13	Rom 8:1–17 (=R:)
	Mass	*Gl; (R: Seq ad lib: EH 155 NEH 520) Cr; Pref (18)*		
		CW: Acts 2:1–21; Ps 104:26–36 & 37b; Rom 8:22–27; Jn 15:26–27 & 16:4b–15		
		R: Acts 2:1–11; Ps 104; Gal 5:15–25 or I Cor 12:3–7 & 12–13; sequence;		
		Jn15:26–27 & 16:12–15 or 20:19–23		
	2 EP	H: 154 (NEH 138)	Ezek 36:22–28	Isa 11:1–9
		Ps: 139:1–11 (13–24)	Acts 2:22–38	Rom 8:18–end (=R:)

**'ORDINARY TIME' – 'PER ANNUM' – 'THE GREEN SEASON'
RESUMES**   **9th WEEK OF YEAR**

JUNE

MONDAY
1   R

		S Justin, M (Visitation? see pages 31 and 69)		
	MP	Ps: 123, 124, 125, 126	Job 1	Judg 6:25–end
			Rom 1:1–17	Heb 5:11–6 end
	Mass	*of the Saint*		
		Tob 1:1–2 & 2:1–8; Ps 15; Mk 12:1–12		
	EP		Josh 1	Judg 7
		Ps: 127, 128, 129	Lk 9:18–27	Heb 7

TUESDAY
2   G
(or R)

		Feria (☐ Ss Marcellinus and Peter, Ms)		
	MP	Ps: 132, 133	Job 2	Judg 10:17 – 11:28
			Rom 1:18–end	Heb 8
	Mass	*see p. 31; no Gl or Cr; Common Pref (or of the Saints)*		
		Tob 2:9–end; Ps 112; Mk 12:13–17		
	EP		Josh 2	Judg 11:29 – 12:7
		Ps: 134, 135	Lk 9:28–36	Heb 9:1–14

WEDNESDAY
3   R

		Ss Charles Lwanga, Comp, Ms*		
	MP	Ps: 119:153–end	Job 3	Judg 13
			Rom 2:1–16	Heb 9:15–end
	Mass	*of the Saints*		
		Tob 3:1–11 & 16–end; Ps 25:1–8; Mk 12:18–27		
	EP		Josh 3	Judg 14
		Ps: 136	Lk 9:37–50	Heb 10:1–18

THURSDAY
4   G

		Feria (Truro: Solemnity of S Petroc, Ab, Principal Patron)		
	MP	Ps: 143, 146	Job 4	Judg 16:4–end
			Rom 2:17–end	Heb 10:19–end
	Mass	*as Tuesday*		
		Tob 6:9–11 & 7:1–15 & 8:4–8; Ps 128; Mk 12:28–34		
	EP		Josh 4:1 – 5:1	Ruth 1
		Ps: 138, 140, 141	Lk 9:51–end	Heb 11

FRIDAY
5   R

		S Boniface, B, M (Solemnity in Truro and Exeter)*		
	MP	Ps: 142, 144	Job 5	Ruth 2
			Rom 3:1–20	Heb 12:1–13
	Mass	*of the Saint (First Friday: Sacred Heart, see p. 42)*		
		Tob 11:5–15; Ps 146; Mk 12:35–37		
	EP		Josh 5:2–end	Ruth 3
		Ps: 145	Lk 10:1–16	Heb 12:14–end

SATURDAY
6   W
(or G)

		Our Lady on Saturday (or the Feria) (☐ S Norbert, B)*		
	MP	Ps: 147	Job 6	Ruth 4:1–17
			Rom 3:21–end	Heb 13
	Mass	*Introduction Paragraph 26(b) (First Saturday: Immaculate Heart, see p. 42)* (**Ini Kopuria**)		
		Tob 12:1 & 5–15 & 20a; Ps 103:1 & 8–13; Mk 12:38–end		
	W 1 EP of foll		Isa 40:12–31	Isa 61
		Ps: 97, 98	Mk 1:1–13	II Tim 1:3–14

---

* Ember Days. See Introduction, paragraph 25.

CORPUS CHRISTI is now officially known in the Roman Church as The Body and Blood of Christ, and, where, as now in the English Roman Catholic Church, it is not regarded as a Day of Obligation, is to be observed on the following Sunday. (See Introduction Para 5C4.) CW says that 'the Thursday after Trinity Sunday may be observed as a day of Thanksgiving for the Holy Communion (sometimes known as Corpus Christi), and may be kept as a festival'; readings were authorised by CW. The CW **short** preface for Maundy Thursday is suitable. R: Preface of the Eucharist.

Since there will be clergy who will wish to follow the English RC transference of this Solemnity to the following Sunday, we give here the propers for insertion according to local decision.

THE BODY AND BLOOD OF CHRIST, CORPUS CHRISTI
Mass: Gl; Cr; Proper Pref; WHITE. The Sequence (EH 317; NEH 521) is traditionally sung before the Gospel.

	CW	R: YEAR A (2008)	R: YEAR B (2009)	R: YEAR C (2010)
1 EP	H: 326 (NEH 268) Ps: 110, 111	◁	◁	◁
	Exod 16:2–15	◁	◁	◁
	Jn 6:22–35	◁	◁	◁
MP	H: 330 (NEH 269) Ps: 147	◁	◁	◁
	Deut 8:2–16	Exod 24:1–11*	Deut 8:2–16*	◁
	I Cor 10:1–17	Heb 9:11–15*	I Cor 10:1–17*	◁
Mass	Gen 14:18–20	Deut 8:2–3 & 14–16	Exod 24:3–8	Gen 14:18–20
	Ps 116:10–17	Ps 147:12–end	Ps 116:12–end	Ps 110
	I Cor 11:23–26	I Cor 10:16–17	Heb 9:11–15	I Cor 11:23–26
	Jn 6:51–58	Jn 6:51–58	Mk 14:12–16 & 22–26	Lk 9:11–17
2 EP	H: 326 (NEH 268) Ps: 23, 42, 43	◁	◁	◁
	Prov 9:1–5	◁	◁	◁
	Lk 9:11–17	◁	◁	Mk 14:12–25*

*Those who use the R: 3 year cycle and use an Anglican Office can avoid duplicating the mass reading by using these alternatives, mostly from the 1961 Lectionary.

S BARNABAS: If Corpus Christi is observed on Thursday, the Roman rules suppress S Barnabas but CW transfers him to Friday.

BENEDICTION, PROCESSIONS, AND EXPOSITION OF THE BLESSED SACRAMENT
are services clearly lawful under Canon B.5.2 if 'the minister having the cure of souls' considers them 'suitable' and uses, or 'permits another minister, to use' them. (The requirement of Canon B.5.3 that such services shall be 'neither contrary to, nor indicative of any departure from, the doctrine of the Church of England in any *essential* matter' need create no anxiety since ARCIC 1979 endorsed by Lambeth 1988 held that 'differences of practice' in this area can 'coexist with real consensus on the *essentials*'. A form was offered in Celebrating Common Prayer as commended by the then Archbishop of Canterbury.) If a reading and the Our Father are incorporated, Benediction etc come within the umbrella of CW pp 21–24 A Service Of The Word.

The *Assistant Curates Society* publishes a small, cheap *Rite of Eucharistic Exposition and Benediction* giving many alternatives for these most flexible of services. The traditional '**V** Thou gavest/You gave them Bread from Heaven **R** Containing in itself all sweetness' no longer appears in Roman texts but (Elliot) 'is still widely used.'

JUNE/JULY CONFLICTS

	BCP	'Traditional' Roman Rite in England	CW	'Modern' Roman Rite in England
June 20	Translation of S Edmund, Km*	Feria	Feria	S Alban, M (displaced from the 22nd)
June 22	(BCP mistakenly moves him to June 17)	S Alban, M (day of his martyrdom)	S Alban, M* (day of his martyrdom)	Ss John Fisher (day of his martyrdom) & Thomas More
July 6	Feria	Octave Day of Ss Peter & Paul	Ss John Fisher & Thomas More (day of his martyrdom)	S Mary Goretti, V, M*
July 9	Feria	Ss John Fisher & Thomas More (displaced from the 6th)	Feria	Feria

Your Compiler, unusually, prefers the CW arrangement as the most 'Traditional'. * Optional.

✠ SUNDAY
7 G

R: Ps III

TRINITY SUNDAY

	MP	H: 632 (NEH 144)	Prov 8:1–4 &22–31	Isa 6:1–8
		Ps: 33:1–12	II Cor 13:(5–10) 11–13	Mk 1:1–13
	Mass	*Gl; Cr; Pref of the Trinity*		
		CW: Isa 6:1–8; Ps 29; Rom 8:12–17; Jn 3:1–17		
		R: Deut 4:32–34 & 39–40; Ps 33; Rom 8:14–17; Mt 28:16–20		
		(The Lord Demands Love And Mercy, Not Sacrifice)		
	2 EP	H: 159 (NEH 145)	Ezek 1:4–10 & 22–28a	Isa 40:12–end
		Ps: 104:1–10	Rev 4	I Pet 1:3–12

10th WEEK OF YEAR

MONDAY
8 G

Feria

	MP	Ps:1, 2, 3	Job 7	I Sam 1
			Rom 4:1–12	Jas 1
	Mass	*see p. 35; no Gl or Cr; Common Pref (**Thomas Ken, B**)*		
		II Cor 1:1–7; Ps 34:1–8; Mt 5:1–12		
	EP		Josh 7:1–15	I Sam 2:1–21
		Ps: 4, 7	Lk 10:25–37	Mk 1:14–31

TUESDAY
9 G
(or W)

Feria (S Ephraim, Dcn, Dr; S Columba, Ab; FESTUM in IRELAND)

	MP	Ps: 5, 6, 8	Job 8	I Sam 2:22–end
			Rom 4:13–end	Jas 2:1–13
	Mass	*as Monday (or of the Saint) (**Our Lady of Grace**)*		
		II Cor 1:18–22; Ps 119:129–136; Mt 5:13–16		
	EP		Josh 7:16–end	I Sam 3
		Ps: 9, 10	Lk 10:38–end	Mk 1:32–end

WEDNESDAY
10 G

Feria

	MP	Ps: 119:1–32	Job 9	I Sam 4
			Rom 5:1–11	Jas 2:14–end
	Mass	*as Monday*		
		II Cor 3:4–11; Ps 78:1–4; Mt 8:17–19		
	EP	*of the Feria*	Josh 8:1–29	I Sam 7
	OR	*of **Corpus Christi?** (see p. 39)*		
		Ps: 11, 12, 13	Lk 11:1–13	Mk 2:1–22

THURSDAY
11

Feria or S Barnabas or Corpus Christi *(see p.39)*

	MP	Ps: 14, 15, 16	Job 10	I Sam 8
			Rom 5:12–end	Jas 3
	Mass	*as Monday*		
		II Cor 3:15 – 4:1 & 3–6; Ps 78:36–40; Mt 5:20–26		
	EP		Josh 8:30–end	I Sam 9:1–25
		Ps: 18	Lk 11:14–28	Mk 2:23 – 3:12

FRIDAY
12 G

Feria (S Barnabas? see p. 39)

	MP	Ps: 17, 19	Job 11	I Sam 9:26 – 10:16
			Rom 6:1–14	Jas 4
	Mass	*as Monday*		
		II Cor 4:7–15; Ps 99; Mt 5:27–32		
	EP		Josh 9:3–26	I Sam 10:17–end
		Ps: 22	Lk 11:29–36	Mk 3:13–end

SATURDAY
13 W

☐ S Anthony of Padua, Pr, Dr

	MP	Ps: 20, 21, 23	Job 12	I Sam 11
			Rom 6:15–end	Jas 5
	Mass	*of the Saint*		
		II Cor 5:14–end; Ps 103:1–12; Mt 5:33–37		
G	1 EP of foll		Josh 10:1–15	I Sam 12
		Ps: 24, 25	Lk 11:37–end	Mk 4:1–34

* In R: S Barnabas is only a Memoria.

✠ SUNDAY 14

			11th SUNDAY and WEEK of YEAR	TRINITY 1
G	MP	Ps: 42, 43	Deut 10:12 – 11:1	Josh 1:1–9
			Acts 23:12–35	Mk 1:21–34
	Mass	*Gl; Cr; Sunday Pref (PROPER 6)*		
		CW: Ezek 17:22–24; Ps 92:1–4 & 12–15; II Cor 5:6–10 (11–13) 14–17; Mk 4:26–34		
		R: Ezek 17:22–24; Ps 92; II Cor 5:6–10; Mk 4:26–34		
	2 EP		Jer 7:1–16	Hos 6:1–6
		Ps: 39	Rom 9:14–26	Acts 1:1–14

11th WEEK OF YEAR

MONDAY 15

Feria

G	MP	Ps: 27, 30	Job 13	I Sam 13
			Rom 7:1–6	I Pet 1:1–21
	Mass	*of Sunday; no Gl or Cr; Common Pref (**Evelyn Underhill**)*		
		II Cor 6:1–10; Ps 98; Mt 5:38–42		
	EP		Josh 14	I Sam 14:1–23
		Ps: 26, 28, 29	Lk 12:1–12	Mk 4:35 – 5:20

TUESDAY 16

Feria (S Richard, B: SOLEMNITY in Chichester)

G (or W)	MP	Ps: 32, 36	Job 14	I Sam 14:28–48
			Rom 7:7–end	I Pet 1:22 – 2:10
	Mass	*of Monday (or of the Saint) (**Joseph Butler, B**)*		
		II Cor 8:1–9; Ps 146; Mt 5:43–48		
	EP		Josh 21:43 – 22:8	I Sam 15
		Ps: 33	Lk 12:13–21	Mk 5:21–end

WEDNESDAY 17

Feria

G	MP	Ps: 34	Job 15	I Sam 16
			Rom 8:1–11	I Pet 2:11 – 3:7
	Mass	*as Monday (**Samuel and Henrietta Barnett**)*		
		II Cor 9:6–11; Ps 112; Mt 6:1–6 & 16–18		
	EP		Josh 22:9–end	I Sam 17:1–30
		Ps: 119:33–56	Lk 12:22–31	Mk 6:1–29

THURSDAY 18

Feria

G	MP	Ps: 37	Job 16:1 – 17:2	I Sam 17:31–54
			Rom 8:12–17	I Pet 3:8 – 4:6
	Mass	*as Monday (**Bernard Mizeki, M**)*		
		II Cor 11:1–11; Ps 111; Mt 6:7–15		

HEARTS OF JESUS & MARY? See p.42

	EP		Josh 23	I Sam 17:55 – 18:16
		Ps: 39, 40	Lk 12:32–40	Mk 6:30–end

FRIDAY 19

Feria (☐ S Romuald, Ab)

G (or W)	MP	Ps: 31	Job 17:3–end	I Sam 19
			Rom 8:18–30	I Pet 4:7–end
	Mass	*as Monday (or of the Saint) (**Sundar Singh**)*		
		II Cor 11:18 & 21a–30; Ps 34:1–6; Mt 6:19–23		
	EP		Josh 24:1–28	I Sam 20:1–17
		Ps: 35	Lk 12:41–48	Mk 7:1–23

SATURDAY 20

See p. 39

	MP	Ps: 41, 42, 43	Job 18	I Sam 20:18–end
			Rom 8:31–end	I Pet 5
	Mass	*(**Our Lady Mother of Consolation**)*		
		II Cor 12:1–10; Ps 89:20–33; Mt 6:24–34		
G	1 EP of foll		Josh 24:29–end	I Sam 21:1 – 22:5
		Ps: 45, 46	Lk 12:49–end	Mk 7:24 – 8:10

SACRED HEART. One of the most popular English devotions before 1559 and one of the most commonly used votive masses was the Five Wounds. This devotion to the Suffering Humanity of our loving Saviour received a broader Biblical and doctrinal form in the Western Church as the Sacred Heart of Jesus came to be celebrated on the second Friday after Trinity Sunday. (It is also common to say a public Class 2 votive of the Sacred Heart [as long as there is no solemnity or festum] on the first Friday of each month, except during Lent. White vestments.)

'In Biblical language, the Heart (Leb) indicates the centre of human life, the point where reason, will, temperament and sensitivity converge, where the person finds his unity and his interior orientation.'* It is because the loving Heart of Jesus the consubstantial Word is intimately at one with His Father that He feels our transgressions as a wound.

The following lectionary provision, to supplement CW, draws upon Roman materials. Other hymns: see especially NEH 89; EH 71 & 413 (=NEH 63 & 382); AMR 211.

THE SACRED HEART of JESUS *Mass: Gl; Cr; Proper Pref.* WHITE.			
	YEAR A (2011)	YEAR B (2009)	YEAR C (2010)
1 EP (Thursday)	H: 419 pt 1 (NEH 385) Ps: 113; 146	◁	◁
	Hos 11:1–9	Ezek 34:11–16	Deut 7:6–11
	Lk 15:3–7	Jn 7:37–39	Mt 11:25–30
MP (Friday)	H: 419 pt 2 (NEH 386) Ps: 36; 61	◁	◁
	Jer 31:1–11 & 31–4	◁	◁
	Rom 8:28–end (=R:)	◁	◁
Mass	Deut 7:6–11	Hos 11:1 & 3–4 & 8c–9	Ezek 34:11–16
	Ps 103:1–2 & 3–4 & 6–7 & 8 & 10	Ps Isa 12:2–3 & 4bcd & 5–6	Ps 23:1–3a & 3b–4 & 5–6
	I Jn 4:7–16	Eph 3:8–12 & 14–19	Rom 5:5b–11
	Mt 11:25–30	Jn 19:31–37	Lk 15:3–7
2 EP (Friday)	H: 419 pt 3 (NEH 385) Ps: 110; 111	◁	◁
	Ezek 34:11–16	Deut 7:6–11	Hos 11:1–9
	Rom 5:5b–11	Jn 20:26–29	Eph 3:8–19

The Immaculate Heart of Mary is kept on the Saturday after the Sacred Heart except when, as this year, it is displaced by a superior celebration. Mary kept and pondered in her heart all the great deeds of God. 'According to Mt 5:8, the Immaculate Heart is a heart which, with God's grace, has come to a perfect interior unity and therefore "sees God".'* Because her Immaculate (Ps 119: 80: *Tamin, amomos*: perfectly fitted to be a sacrifice to the Lord) Heart is attuned to Him (Luke 1:49, 2:19, 2:51) and to the needs of others (John 2:3), even before the Hour of the Lord's Glory (John 2:4) the intercession of her heart mediates through shared obedience (John 2:5) the first Sign of the fullness of His Kingdom (John 2:11). 'To be "devoted" to the Immaculate Heart of Mary means therefore to embrace this attitude of heart, which makes the *fiat* – "your will be done" – the defining centre of one's whole life,'* that the Kingdom may come.

There is a custom of saying a public Class 2 votive of the Immaculate Heart of Mary [as long as there is no solemnity or festum] on the first Saturday of each month, except during Lent (and MP may be a votive of the observance). The **Fatima** visionaries believed that our Lady called for communions of reparation on first Saturdays.

CW (p. 307), Presentation, Extended Preface, lines 1–3 and 11–end, is suitable.

The Roman Collection of Masses (Int Para 26b ii) gives variety for the celebration (Mass 26).

* Pope Benedict XVI.

THE IMMACULATE HEART OF MARY *Mass: no Gl or Cr; Pref of our Lady*
Mass readings: Isa 61:9–11; Ps I Sam 2:1 & 4–8; Lk 2:41–51

✠ SUNDAY
21 G   MP

R: Ps IV   Mass

   2 EP

			12th SUNDAY and WEEK of YEAR	TRINITY 2

✠ SUNDAY 21 G — R: Ps IV

12th SUNDAY and WEEK of YEAR   **TRINITY 2**

MP   Ps: 48   Deut 11:1–15   Josh 2
               Acts 27:1–12   Mk 2:23 – 3:19

Mass   *Gl; Cr; Sunday Pref (PROPER 7) (S John Baptist? see Int Para 5(A)*
       CW: Job 38:1–11; Ps 107:1–3 & 23–32; II Cor 6:1–13; Mk 4:35–41
       R: Job 38:1 & 8–11; Ps 107; II Cor 5:14–17; Mk 4:35–41 (The Lord of the Storm)

2 EP   Jer 10:1–16   Hos 11:1–9a
       Ps: 49   Rom 11:25–36   Acts 2:1–21

MONDAY
22   See p. 39

MP   Ps: 44   Job 19   I Sam 22:6–end
          Rom 9:1–18   II Pet 1

Mass   *(Our Lady Mother of Mercy)*
       Gen 12:1–9; Ps 33:12–21; Mt 7:1–5

EP   Judg 2   I Sam 23
       Ps: 47, 49   Lk 13:1–9   Mk 8:11 – 9:1

TUESDAY
23 G (or W)   Feria (S Etheldreda, Ab)

MP   Ps: 48, 52   Job 21   I Sam 24
          Rom 9:19–end   II Pet 2

Mass   *of Sunday; no Gl or Cr; Common Pref (or of the Saint)*
       Gen 13:2 & 5–end; Ps 15; Mt 7:6 & 12–14

BIRTH OF S JOHN BAPTIST
R: Vigil Mass: Jer 1:4–10; Ps 71; I Pet 1:8–12; Lk 1:5–17 (Vigil Collect; Gl; Cr)

W   1 EP   H: 223 (NEH 168)   Judg 13:2–7 & 24–25   Mal 3:1–6
          Ps: 71   Lk 1:5–25 (Vigil Collect)   Lk 3:1–20

WEDNESDAY
24 W

MP   H: 224   Mal 3:1–6 or Ecclus 48:1–10   Judg 13:1–7
       Ps: 50, 149   Lk 3:1–17   Lk 1:5–25

Mass   *Gl; Cr; R; Proper Pref; CW, of Saints CRP*
       CW: Isa 40:1–11; Ps 85:7–13; Acts 13:14b–26; Lk 1:57–66 & 80
       R: Isa 49:1–6; Ps 139; Acts 13:22–26; Lk 1:57–66 & 80

2 EP   H: 223 (NEH 168   Mal 4 (R: Jer 1:4–10 & 17–19)   Mal 4
       Ps: 80, 82   Mt 11:2–19   Mt 11:2–19

THURSDAY
25 G   Feria

MP   Ps: 56, 57, 63   Job 23   I Sam 31
          Rom 10:11–end   Jude

Mass   *as Tuesday*
       Gen 16:1–12 & 15 & 16; Ps 106:1–5; Mt 7:21–end

HEARTS OF JESUS AND MARY: see p. 42. If they are not observed, Friday is
a Feria (Ember*) and Saturday is optionally S Cyril of Alexandria, B, Dr (Ember*)
FERIAL readings are in the following box.

EP   Judg 6:1–24   II Sam 1
       Ps: 61, 62, 64   Lk 14:1–11   Mk 10:1–31

FRIDAY
26

MP   Ps: 51, 54   Job 24   II Sam 2:1 – 3:1
          Rom 11:1–12   I Jn 1:1 – 2:6

Mass   *(Our Lady of Tichwin)*
       Gen 17:1 & 9 & 10 & 15–22; Ps 128; Mt 8:1–4

EP   Judg 6:25–end   II Sam 3:17–end
       Ps: 38   Lk 14:12–24   Mk 10:32–end

SATURDAY
27 R

MP   Ps: 68   Job 25–26   II Sam 5:1–12
          Rom 11:13–24   I Jn 2:7–end

Mass   *(Our Lady of Perpetual Succour) (Our Lady Mother of Mercy)*
       Gen 18:1–15; Magnificat; Mt 8:5–17

✠
   R   1 EP of foll; **SS PETER & PAUL, APOSTLES**

1 EP of foll; H: 226 (NEH 171)   Ezek 3:4–11   ◁
       Ps: 66, 67   Gal 1:13 – 2:8 (=R:) (Vigil Collect)   ◁
       R: Vigil Mass; Acts 3:1–10; Ps 19; Gal 1:11–20; Jn 21:15–19 (Vigil Collect; Gl; Cr)

---

* If the Ember Week is desired before the Solemnity of SS Peter and Paul instead of in the week after Pentecost, as traditionally.

✠ *SUNDAY*
28   R   MP

SS PETER & PAUL, APOSTLES

MP	Ps: 71, 113	Isa 49:1–6	◁
		Acts 11:1–18	◁
Mass	*Gl; Cr; R: Pref of Ss Peter and Paul; CW, of Saints*		
	CW: = R: Acts 12:1–11; Ps 125 (R: 34); II Tim 4:6–8 & 17–18; Mt 16:13–19		
2 EP	H: 226 (NEH 171)	Ezek 34:11–16	◁
	Ps: 124, 138	Jn 21:15–22	◁

13th WEEK OF YEAR

MONDAY
29   G
R: Ps I

Feria

MP	Ps: 71	Job 27	II Sam 7
		Rom 11:25–end	I Jn 3:1–12
Mass	*of Trinity 3 or the 13th Sunday of the year; no Gl or Cr; Common Pref*		
	Gen 18:16–end; Ps 103:6–17; Mt 8:18–22		
EP		Judg 8:22–end	II Sam 9
	Ps: 72, 75	Lk 15:1–10	Mk 11:27 – 12:12

TUESDAY
30   G
(or R)

Feria (☐ First Martyrs of the Church in Rome)

MP	Ps: 73	Job 28	II Sam 11
		Rom 12:1–8	I Jn 3:13 – 4:6
Mass	*as Monday (or of the Saint)*		
	Gen 19:15–29; Ps 26; Mt 8:23–27		
EP		Judg 9:1–21	II Sam 12:1–23
	Ps: 74	Lk 15:11–end	Mk 12:13–34

J U L Y *

WEDNESDAY
1   G
(or R)

Feria (☐ S Oliver Plunket, B, M: FESTUM IN IRELAND)

MP	Ps: 77	Job 29	II Sam 13:38 – 14:24
		Rom 12:9–end	I Jn 4:7–end
Mass	*as Monday (or of the Saint)* (**John and Henry Venn, Prs**)		
	Gen 21:5 & 8–20; Ps 34:1–12; Mt 8:28–end		
EP		Judg 9:22–end	II Sam 14:25 – 15:12
	Ps: 119:81–104	Lk 16:1–18	Mk 12:35 – 13:13

THURSDAY
2   G

Feria (see p. 69: the Visitation?)

MP	Ps: 78:1–39	Job 30	II Sam 15:13–end
		Rom 13:1–7	I Jn 5
Mass	*as Monday*		
	Gen 22:1–19; Ps 116:1–7; Mt 9:1–8		
EP		Judg 11:1–11	II Sam 16:1–19
	Ps: 78:40–end	Lk 16:19–end	Mk 13:14–end

FRIDAY
3   R

S Thomas, Apostle

MP	Ps: 92, 146	II Sam 15:17–21 or Ecclus 2	II Sam 15:17–21
		Jn 11:1–16	Jn 11:1–16
Mass	*Gl; R: Pref of the Apostles; CW, of the Saint CRP*		
	CW: Hab 2:1–4; Ps 31:1–6; Eph 2:19–22; Jn 20:24–29		
	R: Eph 2:19–22; Ps 117; Jn 20:24–29		
EP		Job 42:1–6	Gen 12:1–5a
	Ps: 139	I Pet 1:3–12	I Pet 1:3–9

SATURDAY
4   W
(or G)

G

Our Lady on Saturday (or the Feria or ☐ S Elizabeth of Portugal)

MP	Ps: 76, 79	Job 32	II Sam 18:19–end
		Rom 14:1–12	III Jn
Mass	*Introduction Paragraph 26(b) (First Saturday: Immaculate Heart, see p. 42)*		
	Gen 27:1–5a & 15–29; Ps 135:1–6; Mt 9:14–17		
1 EP of foll		Judg 12:1–7	II Sam 19:1–23
	Ps: 81, 84	Lk 17:11–19	Mk 14:27–52

* A Votive Mass of the Most Precious Blood is traditional on the first free day.

✠ *SUNDAY*		**14th SUNDAY and WEEK of YEAR***			**TRINITY 4**
5	G	MP	Ps: 57	Deut 24:10–22	Josh 5:13 – 6:20
				Acts 28:1–16	Mk 4:21–end
R: Ps II		Mass	*Gl; Cr; Sunday Pref (PROPER 9)*		
			CW: Ezek 2:1–5; Ps 123; II Cor 12:2–10; Mk 6:1–13		
			R: Ezek 2:2–5; Ps 123; II Cor 12:7–10; Mk 6:1–6 (I send you as a prophet)		
		2 EP		Jer 20:1–11a	Joel 2:1–14
			Ps: 63, 64	Rom 14:1–17	Acts 3:1–16 (17–end)
MONDAY			**See p. 39**		
6		MP	Ps: 80, 82	Job 33	II Sam 19:24–end
				Rom 14:13–end	Rom 1
		Mass			
			Gen 28:10–end; Ps 91:1–10; Mt 9:18–26		
		EP		Judg 13:1–24	II Sam 23:1–17
			Ps: 85, 86	Lk 17:20–end	Mk 14:53–end
TUESDAY			**Feria (☐ Translation of S Thomas, B, M)**		
7	G	MP	Ps: 87, 89:1–18	Job 38	II Sam 24
	(or R)			Rom 15:1–13	Rom 2:1–16
		Mass	*of Sunday; no Gl or Cr; Common Pref (or of the Saint)*		
			Gen 32:22–end; Ps 17:1–8; Mt 9:32–end		
		EP		Judg 14	I Kgs 1:5–31
			Ps: 89:19–end	Lk 18:1–14	Mk 15:1–41
WEDNESDAY			**Feria**		
8	G	MP	Ps: 119:105–128	Job 39	I Kgs 1:32–end
				Rom 15:14–21	Rom 2:17–end
		Mass	*as Tuesday (**Our Lady of Kazan**)*		
			Gen 41:55–end & 42:5–7 & 17–end; Ps 33:1–4 & 18–end; Mt 10:1–7		
		EP		Judg 15:1 – 16:3	I Chron 22:2–end
			Ps: 91, 93	Lk 18:15–30	Mk 15:42–16 end
THURSDAY			**Feria (☐ S Augustine Zhao Rong, Pr, Comp, Ms)**		
9	G	MP	Ps: 90, 92	Job 40	I Chron 28:1–10
	(or R)			Rom 15:22–end	Rom 3
		Mass	*as Tuesday (or of the Saints) (**Our Lady Mother of Divine Hope (37)**)*		
			Gen 44:18–21 & 23–29 & 45:1–5; Ps 105:11–17; Mt 10:7–15		
		EP		Judg 16:4–end	I Chron 28:20 – 29:9
			Ps: 94	Lk 18:31–end	Lk 1:1–23
FRIDAY			**Feria**		
10	W	MP	Ps: 88, 95	Job 41	I Chron 29:10–end
				Rom 16:1–16	Rom 4
		Mass	*as Tuesday (**Our Lady of Koniev**)*		
			Gen 46:1–7 & 28–30; Ps 37:3–6 & 27–28; Mt 10:16–23		
		EP		Judg 17	I Kgs 3
			Ps: 102	Lk 19:1–10	Lk 1:24–56
SATURDAY			**S Benedict, Abbot, Patron of Europe**		
11	W	MP	Ps: [96, 97, 100]	[Job 42]	[I Kgs 4:21–end]
				[Rom 16:17–end]	[Rom 5]
		Mass	*Office Readings from Appendix 3: Religious*		
			of the Saint; Gl; no Cr; Pref (R:) of Patrons, (CW) of Saints		
			R: Prov 2:1–9; Ps 34:1–10; Mt 19:27–29		
			CW: I Cor 3:10–11; Ps 34:1–8; Mt 19:23–30		
			[Gen 49:29–end & 50:15–25; Ps 105:1–7; Mt 10:24–33]		
	G	1 EP of foll		Judg 18:1–20, 27–end	I Kgs 5
			Ps: 104	Lk 19:11–27	Lk 1:57–end

* In churches dedicated to S Thomas Becket, External Solemnity may be kept today of the Festival of his Translation (July 7).

✠ *SUNDAY*
12   G   MP   **15th SUNDAY and WEEK of YEAR**   **TRINITY 5**

✠ *SUNDAY*	G	MP	Ps: 65	Deut 28:1–14	Josh 24:1–5 & 13–25
12				Acts 28:17–31	Mk 6:7–32
R: Ps III		Mass	*Gl; Cr; Sunday Pref (PROPER 10)*		
			CW: Amos 7:7–15; Ps 85:8–13; Eph 1:3–14; Mk 6:14–29		
			R: Amos 7:12–15; Ps 85; Eph 1:3–10 (11–14); Mk 6:7–13 (The Missionary church)		
		2 EP		Job 4:1 & 5:6–27 or Ecclus 4:11–31	Joel 2:15–27
			Ps: 66	Rom 15:14–29	Acts 4:1–22 (23–31)

MONDAY	G	MP	*Feria (☐ S Henry)*		
13	(or W)		Ps: 98, 99, 101	Ezek 1:1–14	I Kgs 6:1–14
				II Cor 1:1–14	Rom 6
		Mass	*of Sunday; no Gl or Cr; Common Pref (or of the Saint)*		
			Exod 1:8–14 & 22; Ps 124; Mt 10:34 – 11:1		
		EP		I Sam 1:1–20	I Kgs 8:1–21
			Ps: 103, 105	Lk 19:28–40	Lk 2:1–21

TUESDAY	G	MP	*Feria (☐ S Camillus de Lelli, Pr)*		
14	(or W)		Ps: 106	Ezek 1:15 – 2:2	I Kgs 8:22–53
				II Cor 1:15 – 2:4	Rom 7
		Mass	*as Monday (or of the Saint) (**John Keble, Pr**)*		
			Exod 2:1–15; Ps 69:1 & 2 & 31–end; Mt 11:20–24		
		EP		I Sam 1:21 – 2:11	I Kgs 8:54 – 9:6
			Ps: 107	Lk 19:41–end	Lk 2:22–end

WEDNESDAY	W	MP	*S Bonaventura, B, Dr*		
15			Ps: 110, 111, 112	Ezek 2:3 – 3:11	I Kgs 10
				II Cor 2:5–end	Rom 8:1–17
		Mass	*of the Saint (**S Swithun, B**)*		
			Exod 3:1–6 & 9–12; Ps 103:1–7; Mt 11:25–27		
		EP		I Sam 2:12–26	I Kgs 11:1–13
			Ps: 119:129–152	Lk 20:1–8	Lk 3:1–22

THURSDAY			*Feria (☐ Our Lady of Mount Carmel; S Osmund, B; EAD*		
			Compulsory; FESTUM in Salisbury)		
16	G	MP	Ps: 113, 115	Ezek 3:12–end	I Kgs 11:26–end
	(or W)			II Cor 3	Rom 8:18–end
		Mass	*as Monday (or of Our Lady: Zec 2:10–end; Ps = Lk 1:46–55; Mt 12:46–50) (or of the Saint)*		
			Exod 3:13–20; Ps 105:1 & 2 & 23; Mt 11:28–end		
		EP		I Sam 2:27–end	I Kgs 12:1–24
			Ps: 114, 116, 117	Lk 20:9–19	Lk 4:1–30

FRIDAY	G	MP	*Feria*		
17			Ps: 139	Ezek 8	I Kgs 12:25 – 13:10
				II Cor 4	Rom 9
		Mass	*as Monday (**The Humility of Our Lady**)*		
			Exod 11:10 – 12:14; Ps 116:10–end; Mt 12:1–8		
		EP		I Sam 3:1 – 4:1a	I Kgs 13:11–end
			Ps: 130, 131, 137	Lk 20:20–26	Lk 4:31–end

SATURDAY	W	MP	*Our Lady on Saturday (or the Feria)*		
18	(or G)		Ps: 120, 121, 122	Ezek 9	I Kgs 14:1–20
				II Cor 5	Rom 10
		Mass	*Introduction Paragraph 26(b) (**Elizabeth Ferard**)*		
			Exod 12:37–42; Ps 136:1–4 & 10–15; Mt 12:14–21		
	G	1 EP of foll		I Sam 4:1b–end	II Chron 12
			Ps: 118	Lk 20:27–40	Lk 5:1–16

✠ *SUNDAY*   **16th SUNDAY and WEEK of YEAR**   **TRINITY 6**

19 G	MP	Ps: 67, 70	Deut 30:1–10	Judg 5
			Pet 3:8–18	Mk 6:53 – 7:23
R: Ps IV	Mass	*Gl; Cr; Sunday Pref (PROPER 11)*		
		CW: Jer 23:1–6; Ps 23; Eph 2:11–22; Mk 6:30–34 & 53–56		
		R: Jer 23:1–6; Ps 23; Eph 2:13–18; Mk 6:30–34 (Christ the Shepherd)		
	2 EP		Job 13:13 – 14:6 or Ecclus 18:1–14	Zech 2
		Ps: 73	Heb 2:5–18	Acts 6

MONDAY   **Feria (☐ S Apollinaris, B; S Margaret, M)**

20 G (or W)	MP	Ps: 123, 124, 125, 126	Ezek 10:1–19	II Chron 13
			II Cor 6:1 – 7:1	Rom 11:1–24
(or R)	Mass	*of Sunday; no Gl or Cr; Common Pref (or of the Saint)* (**Bartolomé de las Casas, B**)		
		Exod 14:5–18; Ps Exod 15:1–6; Mt 12:38–42		
	EP		I Sam 5	II Chron 14
		Ps: 127, 128, 129	Lk 20:41 – 21:4	Lk 5:17–end

TUESDAY   **Feria (☐ S Lawrence of Brindisi, Pr, Dr)**

21 G (or W)	MP	Ps: 132, 133	Ezek 11:14–end	II Chron 15
			II Cor 7:2–end	Rom 11:25–end
	Mass	*as Monday (or of the Saint)*		
		Exod 14:21 – 15:1; Ps Exod 15:8–10 & 12 & 17; Mt 12:46–end		
	EP		I Sam 6:1–16	II Chron 16
		Ps: 134, 135	Lk 21:5–19	Lk 6:1–19

WEDNESDAY   **S Mary Magdalene***

22 W	MP	H: 231 (NEH 174)*	I Sam 16:14–23	◁
		Ps: 30, 32, 150	Lk 8:1–3	◁
	Mass	*Gl*; no Cr; Pref of Saints*		
		CW = R: Song S 3:1–4; Ps 42:1–10 (R: 63); II Cor 5:14–17; Jn 20:1–2 & 11–18		
	EP		Zeph 3:14–20	Isa 25:1–9
		Ps: 63	Mk 15:40 – 16:7	◁

THURSDAY   **S Bridget, Religious, Patron of Europe**

23 W	MP	Ps: [143, 146]	[Ezek 12:17–end]	[I Kgs 18:1–16]
			[II Cor 8:16 – 9:5]	[Rom 13]
	Mass	*Office Reading from Appendix 3: Religious*		
		of the Saint; Gl; no Cr: Pref (R:) of Patrons; (CW) of Saints		
		R: Judith 8:2–8 or I Tim 5:3–10; Ps 10:1–2 & 10–15; Lk 2:36–38 or Mt 5:13–16		
		[Exod 19:1–2 & 9–11 & 16–20; Bless the Lord; Mt 13:10–17]		
	EP		[I Sam 8]	[I Kgs 18:17–end]
		Ps: [138, 140, 141]	[Lk 21:29–end]	[Lk 6:39 – 7:10]

FRIDAY   **Feria (☐ S Sharbel Makhluf, Pr)**

24 G (or W)	MP	Ps: 142, 144	Ezek 13:1–16	I Kgs 19
			II Cor 9:6–end	Rom 14
	Mass	*as Monday (or of the Saint)*		
		Exod 20:1–17; Ps 19:7–11; Mt 13:18–23		
	EP		I Sam 9:1–14	I Kgs 21
		Ps: 145	Lk 22:1–13	Lk 7:11–35

SATURDAY   **S James Apostle**

25 R	MP	Ps: 7, 29, 117	II Kgs 1:9–15	Jer 26:1–15
			Lk 9:46–56	Lk 9:46–56
	Mass	*Gl; R: Pref of Apostles; CW, of Saints CRP*		
		CW: Jer 45:1–5 or Acts 11:27 – 12:2; II Cor 4:7–15; Ps 126; Mt 20:20–28		
		R: II Cor 4:7–15; Ps 126; Mt 20:20–28		
G	1 EP of foll		I Sam 9:15 – 10:1	II Chron 20:1–30
		Ps: 148, 149, 150	Lk 22:14–23	Lk 7:36–end

---

* Like Byzantium, Rome, CW now disentangles S Mary M from Mary of Bethany and the Sinful Woman. In the Hymn, verse 5, correct 'feet' to 'limbs'. (In R: she is only a Memorial; no Gl.)

✠ SUNDAY			**17th SUNDAY and WEEK of YEAR**		**TRINITY 7**
26	G	MP	Ps: 75	Song of Sol 2	Judg 7:1–23
				I Pet 4:7–14	MK 9:14–29
R: Ps I		Mass	*Gl; Cr; Sunday Pref (PROPER 12)*		
			CW: II Kgs 4:42–44; Ps 145:10–19; Eph 3:14–21;. Jn 6:1–21		
			R: II Kgs 4:42–44; Ps 145; Eph 4:1–6; Jn 6:1–15 (Christ Feeds Us)		
		2 EP		Job 19:1–27a or Ecclus 38:24–34	Zech 8:1–17
			Ps: 74	Heb 8	Acts 8:4–17
MONDAY			**Feria**		
27	G	MP	Ps: 1, 2, 3	Ezek 14:12–end	II Kgs 1
				II Cor 11:1–15	Rom 15:14–end
		Mass	*of Sunday; no Gl or Cr; Common Pref (B. F. Westcott, B) (Our Lady Mother of Mercy)*		
			Exod 32:15–24 & 30–34; Ps 106:18–22; Mt 13:31–35		
		EP		I Sam 10:1–16	II Kgs 2:1–22
			Ps: 4, 7	Lk 22:24–30	Lk 8:1–21
TUESDAY			**Feria**		
28	G	MP	Ps: 5, 6, 8	Ezek 18:1–20	II Kgs 4:1–37
				II Cor 11:16–end	Rom 16
		Mass	*as Monday (Our Lady of Smolensk)*		
			Exod 33:7–11 & 34:5–9 & 28; Ps 103:8–12; Mt 13:36–43		
		EP		I Sam 10:17–end	II Kgs 5
			Ps: 9, 10	Lk 22:31–38	Lk 8:22–end
WEDNESDAY			**S Martha (CW: and Mary and Lazarus)**		
29	W	MP	Ps: 119:1–32	Ezek 18:21–32	II Kgs 6:1–23
				˙ II Cor 12	I Cor 1:1–25
		Mass	*of the Saint*		
			CW: Isa 25:6–9; Ps 49:5–10 & 16; Heb 2:10–15; Jn 12:1–8		
			R: I Jn 4:7–16; Ps 34; Jn 11:19–27 or Lk 10:38–42		
			[Exod 34:29–end; Ps 99; Mt 13:44–46]		
		EP		I Sam 11	II Kgs 6:24 – 7:2
			Ps: 11, 12, 13	Lk 22:39–46	Lk 9:1–17
THURSDAY			**Feria (□ S Peter Chrysologus, B, Dr)**		
30	G	MP	Ps: 14, 15, 16	Ezek 20:1–20	II Kgs 7:3–end
	(or W)			II Cor 13	I Cor 1:26–2 end
		Mass	*as Monday (or of the Saint) (William Wilberforce)*		
			Exod 40:16–21 & 34–end; Ps 84:1–6; Mt 13:47–53		
		EP		I Sam 12	II Kgs 8:1–15
			Ps: 18	Lk 22:47–62	Lk 9:18–50
FRIDAY			**S Ignatius of Loyola, Pr**		
31	W	MP	Ps: 17, 19	Ezek 20:21–38	II Kgs 9
				James 1:1–11	I Cor 3
		Mass	*of the Saint*		
			Lev 23:1 & 4–11 & 15–16 & 27 & 34–37; Ps 81:1–8; Mt 13:54–end		
		EP		I Sam 13:5–18	II Kgs 11:1–20
			Ps: 22	Lk 22:63–end	Lk 9:51–end

A U G U S T

SATURDAY			**□ S Alfonso Maria de'Liguori, B, Dr**		
1	W	MP	Ps: 20, 21, 23	Ezek 24:15–end	II Kgs 11:21–12 end
				James 1:12–end	II Cor 4:1–17
		Mass	*of the Saint (First Saturday: Immaculate Heart, p. 42)*		
			Lev 25:1 & 8–17; Ps 67; Mt 14:1–12		
	G	1 EP of foll		I Sam 13:19 – 14:15	II Kgs 13
			Ps: 24, 25	Lk 23:1–12	Lk 10:1–24

✠ *SUNDAY*
2 G MP

R: Ps II Mass

2 EP

18th SUNDAY and WEEK of YEAR **TRINITY 8**

Ps: 86	Song of Sol 5:2–16	Judg 16:4–end
	II Pet 1:1–15	Mk 9:30–end

Gl; Cr; Sunday Pref (PROPER 13) (TRANSFIGURATION? See Int Para 5A)
CW: Exod 16:2–4 & 9–15; Ps 78:23–29; Eph 4:1–16; Jn 6:24–35
R: Exod 16:2–4 & 12–15; Ps 78; Eph 4:17 & 20–24; Jn 6:24–35 (Bread from Heaven)

	Job 28 or Ecclus 42:15–25	Jonah 1 & 2
Ps: 88	Heb 11:17–31	Acts 8:26–39

MONDAY
3 G MP

Mass

EP

Feria

Ps: 27, 30	Ezek 28:1–19	II Kgs 14
	James 2:1–13	I Cor 4:18–5 end

as Wednesday
Num 11:4–15; Ps 81:11–end; Mt 14:13–21

	I Sam 14:24–46	II Chron 26
Ps: 26, 28, 29	Lk 23:13–25	Lk 10:25–end

TUESDAY
4 W MP

Mass

EP

S John Mary Vianney, Pr

Ps: 32, 36	Ezek 33:1–20	II Kgs 15:17–end
	James 2:14–end	I Cor 6

of the Saint
Num 12:1–13; Ps 51:1–8; Mt 14:22–end

	I Sam 15:1–23	II Kgs 16
Ps: 33	Lk 23:26–43	Lk 11:1–28

WEDNESDAY
5 G (or MP
  W or R)

Mass

EP

Feria (☐ Dedication of S Mary Major*; S Oswald, K, M)

Ps: 34	Ezek 33:21–end	Isa 7:1–17
	James 3	I Cor 7

of Sunday; no Gl or Cr; Common Pref (or of our Lady or the Saint)
R: for our Lady: Rev 21:1–5a; Ps Judith 13:18–19; Lk 11:27–8
Num 13:1–2 & 10–14 & 25–14:1 & 26–35; Ps 106:14–24; Mt 15:21–28

	I Sam 16	Isa 8:1–18
Ps: 119:33–56	Lk 23:44–56a	Lk 11:29–end

THURSDAY
6 W MP

Mass

EP

Transfiguration of the Lord

H: 233 or 238:1, 2, 4, 7, 8	Ecclus 48:1–10 or I Kgs 19:1–16	Exod 34:29–end
Ps: 27, 150	I Jn 3:1–3	II Cor 3 (=R:)

Gl; R: Pref of Transfiguration; CW, Common Pref
CW = R: Dan 7:9–10 & 13–14; Ps 97; II Pet 1:16–19; Lk 9:28–36 (R: Mk 9:2–10)

H: 234 (NEH 176)	Exod 34:29–35	I Kgs 19:1–16
Ps: 72	II Cor 3	II Pet 1:12–end

FRIDAY
7 G (or MP
  R or W)

Mass

EP

Feria (☐ Ss Xystus II, Pp, Comp, Ms; ☐ S Cajetan, Pr)

Ps: 31	Ezek 34:17–end	II Kgs 18:1–8
	James 4:13 – 5:6	I Cor 9

as Tuesday (or of a Saint) (Sarum & BCP: the Holy Name of Jesus: see p. 7)
*(First Friday: Sacred Heart, p. 42) (**John Mason Neale, Pr**) CPR*
Deut 4:32–40; Ps 77:11–end; Mt 16:24–end

	I Sam 17:31–54	II Chron 30
Ps: 35	Lk 24:13–35	Lk 12:35–53

SATURDAY
8 W MP

Mass

G 1 EP of foll

S Dominic, Pr

Ps: 41, 42, 43	Ezek 36:16–36	II Kgs 18:13–end
	James 5:7–end	I Cor 10:1 – 11:1

of the Saint
Deut 6:4–13; Ps 18:1–2 & 48–end; Mt 17:14–20

	I Sam 17:55 – 18:16	II Kgs 19
Ps: 45, 46	Lk 24:36–end	Lk 12:54 – 13:9

---

* Today's commemoration is of the Council of Ephesus, 431, which proclaimed our Lady *Theotokos* and was celebrated by the consecration of Great S Mary's in Rome – the first Western church dedicated to our Lady. Novenas in preparation for the Assumption may begin.

ASSUMPTION OF THE BVM

The Assumption is transferred to Sunday (see Introduction 5B).

1. August 15 was the Festival of Our Lady in Jerusalem by the fourth Century. (The word 'Assumption' in early Christian Latin antedates by many centuries the definition of 1950.) PPL: 'In many places the feast is synonymous with the person of our Lady. It is simply referred to as "Lady Day" or as "The Immacolada" in Spain and Latin America.' CW follows this Hispanic baroque instinct.

2. 'We affirm together the teaching that God has taken the Blessed Virgin Mary in the fullness of her person into his glory as consonant with Scripture, and only to be understood in the light of Scripture.' (ARCIC 2005).

3. The EVE: the Assumption has been called the Easter of the Mother of God (and preceded, in the Byzantine rite, by a Lent of fourteen days; in the west Novenas are kept). R: provides a separate collect for 1 EP and the Vigil mass. In some places the Eve is marked with some solemnity – texts from the compiler:–

- the lit Paschal Candle may be processed to our Lady's statue or icon, and incense offered to both;
- a form of *Exsultet;* then the Vigil mass *or* 1 EP *or* a Liturgy of the Word, including:
- Gospel (Ceremonies as at mass; Lk 10:38–42 & 11:27b–28 – cf Byzantium and Rome before 1950);
- Te Deum;
- Collect from the Vigil mass;
- Blessing or Benediction.

4. The *Office Hymns*, Eleventh Century and later, now used are not in EH or NEH but may be obtained from the Compiler. The Common Hymns are 213, 214, 215 (NEH 180, 181, 183). The Assumption is mentioned in EH 215 and 217, and NEH 182, 183, 184, and 185. For the Akathist Hymn see p. xxvi.

   EH 218 (NEH 188) – Fr V.S.S. Coles' hymn *Ye Who Own The Faith Of Jesus* – contains verses omitted in the hymnbooks (except in the good old English Catholic Hymn Book, which we still use in S Thomas's). Since the hymn thus (except as a Processional) becomes rather long, it could be divided and treated as two separate hymns: (A) 1, 2, 3, 4, 5, 7; (B) 1, 2a, 2b, 2c, 6, 7.

   2a Thus prepared, and thus exalted,
   Lowly still, and still unknown,
   Mary waited till the fullness
   Of her destiny was shown,
   Till the maid became God's Mother,
   And her nursing arms his throne: *Hail Mary . . .*

   2b For the King of men and angels
   Chose her out of all He made,
   And in robes of grace and glory

   Her humility arrayed,
   With the radiant sun He clothed her,
   At her feet the moon He laid: *Hail Mary . . .*

   2c As we sing, her prayer is rising,
   For her Heart with us is one;
   We with confidence will ask it
   That the Mother from her Son
   May obtain the full perfection
   Of His work in us begun: *Hail Mary . . .*

5. *Readings* prefixed * are those customarily offered in this ORDO, based upon Western Catholic tradition. Their use is covered by CLC p. 36 paragraph 6. Those prefixed † are now offered by CW.

6. August 22, Our Lady, Queen, is the old octave day.

✠ *SUNDAY*   **19th SUNDAY and WEEK of YEAR**   **TRINITY 9**

9   G   MP   Ps: 90   Song of Sol 8:5–7   I Sam 1:1–20

R: Ps III   II Pet 3:8–13   Mk 10:17–31

          Mass   *Gl; Cr; Sunday Pref (PROPER 14) (ASSUMPTION? See p. 50(1))*
                CW: I Kgs 19:4–8; Ps 34:1–8; Eph 4:25 – 5:2; Jn 6:35 & 41–51
                R: I Kgs 19:4–8; Ps 34; Eph 4:30 – 5:2; Jn 6:41–51 (The Strength of That Food)

          2 EP   Job 39:1 – 40:4 or Ecclus 43:13–33   Jonah 3 & 4
                Ps: 91   Heb 12:1–17   Acts 11:1–8

MONDAY   **S Lawrence, Dcn, M**

10   R   MP   Ps: [44]   [Ezek 37:1–14]   II Kgs 20
                        [Mk 1:1–13]   I Cor 11:2–end

          Mass   *of the Saint; Gl; no Cr; Pref of Ms*
                [Deut 10:12–end; Ps 147:13–end; Mt 17:22–end]

          EP   [I Sam 19:1–18]   II Chron 33
                Ps: [47, 49]   [Acts 1:1–14]   Lk 13:10–end

TUESDAY   **S Clare, V**

11   W   MP   Ps: 48, 52   Ezek 37:15–end   II Kgs 22
                        Mk 1:14–20   I Cor 12:1–27

          Mass   *of the Saint (**John Henry Newman, Pr**)**
                Deut 31:1–8; Ps 107:1–3 & 42–3; Mt 18:1–5 & 10 & 12–14

          EP   I Sam 20:1–17   II Kgs 23:1–20
                Ps: 50   Acts 1:15–end   Lk 14:1–24

WEDNESDAY   **Feria (☐ S Jane Frances de Chantal, Rel)**

12   G   MP   Ps: 119:57–80   Ezek 39:21–end   II Kgs 23:21–35
   (or W)   Mk 1:21–28   I Cor 12:27–13 end

          Mass   *as Sunday; no Gl or Cr; Common Pref (or of the Saint)*
                Deut 34; Ps 66:14–end; Mt 18:15–20

          EP   I Sam 20:18–end   II Kgs 23:36 – 24:17
                Ps: 59, 60, 67   Acts 2:1–21   Lk 14:25 – 15:10

THURSDAY   **Feria (☐ Ss Pontianus, Pp and Hippolytus, Pr, M)**

13   G   MP   Ps: 56, 57, 63   Ezek 43:1–12   II Kgs 24:18 – 25:7
   (or R)   Mk 1:29–end   I Cor 14:1–19

          Mass   *as Wednesday (or of the Saints) (**Jeremy Taylor, B; Florence Nightingale;***
                ***Octavia Hill**) (**Our Lady Refuge of Sinners; of Paletz**)*
                Josh 3:7–11 & 13–17; Ps 114; Mt 18:21 – 19:1

          EP   I Sam 21:1 – 22:5   II Kgs 25:8–end
                Ps: 61, 62, 64   Acts 2:22–36   Lk 15:11–end

FRIDAY   **S Maximilian Kolbe, Pr, M**

14   R   MP   Ps: 51, 54   Ezek 44:4–16   Jer 19
                        Mk 2:1–12   I Cor 14:20–end

          Mass   *of the Saint*
                Josh 24:1–13; Ps 136:1–3 & 16–22; Mt 19:3–12

          EP   I Sam 22:6–end   Jer 21:1–10
                Ps: 38   Acts 2:37–end   Lk 16

SATURDAY   **Our Lady on Saturday (or the Feria)**

15   W   MP   Ps: 68   Ezek 47:1–12   Jer 22:20 – 23:8
                        Mk 2:13–22   1 Cor 15:1–34

          Mass   *Introduction Paragraph 26(b)*
                Josh 24:14–29; Ps 16:1 & 5–end; Mt 19:13–15

✠   W   **ASSUMPTION OF THE BVM (see p. 50)**
                R: Vigil Mass: I Chron 15:3–4 & 15–16 & 16:1–2; Ps 132; I Cor 15:54b–57
                Lk 11:27–28 (Collect of Vigil; Gl; Cr)

          1 EP of foll   * Song of Sol 4:7–12 } or from the   †Prov 8:22–31
                Ps: 72   * Lk 1:26–38 } Vigil Mass   †Jn 19:23–27

---

* Will he have been beatified before this ORDO is on sale?

✠ *SUNDAY*   **ASSUMPTION OF THE BVM**   **TRINITY 10**

16 W   MP   Ps: 98, 138, 147:1–12   *Gen 3:1–15   †Isa 7:10–15
                                          *Eph 1:16 – 2:10 (=R:)   †Lk 11:27–28

R: Ps IV   Mass   *Gl; Cr; R: Proper Pref; CW, of the Annunciation; or ASB 6 CRP*
                   R: Rev 11:19a & 12:1–6a & 10ab; Ps 45; I Cor 15:20–26; Lk 1:39–56
                   CW: Rev 11:19 – 12:6 & 10; Ps 45:10–17; Gal 4:4–7; Lk 1:46–55

            2 EP   *Song of Sol 6:3–10   †Song of Sol 2:1–7
                   Ps: 132   * I Cor 15:37–44 & 49–54 (55–7)   †Acts 1:6–14

MONDAY   **Feria**

17 G   MP   Ps: 71   Prov 1:1–19   Jer 25:1–14
                           Mk 2:23 – 3:6   I Cor 15:35–end

            Mass   *of Sunday; no Gl or Cr; Common Pref*
                   Judg 2:11–19; Ps 106:34–42; Mt 19:16–22

            EP   I Sam 24   Jer 27:2–end
                   Ps: 72, 75   Acts 3:11–end   Lk 17:20–end

TUESDAY   **Feria**

18 G   MP   Ps: 73   Prov 1:20–end   Jer 28
                           Mk 3:7–19a   I Cor 16

            Mass   *as Monday*
                   Judg 6:11–24; Ps 85:8–end; Mt 19:23–end

            EP   1 Sam 26   Jer 29:1–20
                   Ps: 74   Acts 4:1–12   Lk 18:1–30

WEDNESDAY   **Feria (☐ S John Eudes, Pr)**

19 G   MP   Ps: 77   Prov 2   Jer 32:1–25
     (or W)   Mk 3:19b–end   II Cor 1:1–22

            Mass   *Feria (or of the Saint)*
                   Judg 9:6–15; Ps 21:1–6; Mt 20:1–16

            EP   I Sam 28:3–end   Jer 32:26–end
                   Ps: 119:81–104   Acts 4:13–31   Lk 18:31 – 19:10

THURSDAY   **S Bernard, Ab, Dr**

20 W   MP   Ps: 78:1–39   Prov 3:1–26   Jer 33
                                Mk 4:1–20   II Cor 1:23–2 end

            Mass   *of the Saint (**William and Catherine Booth**)*
                   Judg 11:29–end; Ps 40:4–11; Mt 22:1–14

            EP   I Sam 31   Jer 34:8–end
                   Ps: 78:40–end   Acts 4:32 – 5:11   Lk 19:11–28

FRIDAY   **☐ S Pius X, Pp***

21 W   MP   Ps: 55   Prov 3:27 – 4:19   Jer 37
                           Mk 4:21–34   II Cor 3

            Mass   *of the Saint*
                   Ruth 1:1 & 3–6 & 14–16 & 22; Ps 146; Mt 22:34–40

            EP   II Sam 1   Jer 38:1–13
                   Ps: 69   Acts 5:12–26   Lk 19:29–end

SATURDAY   **☐ BVM, Queen (EXETER & TRURO: FESTUM)**

22 W   MP   Ps: 76, 79   Prov 6:1–19   Jer 38:14–end
                               Mk 4:35–end   II Cor 4

            Mass   *of our Lady (Isa 9:2–4 & 6–7; Ps 113; Lk 1:26–38)*
                   [Ruth 2:1–3 & 8–11 & 4:13–17; Ps 128; Mt 23:1–12]

        G   1 EP of foll   II Sam 2:1–11   Jer 39
                           Ps: 81, 84   Acts 5:27–end   Lk 20:1–26

---

* The Society of S Pius X, of course, keeps the old date, September 3, which now collides with S Gregory the Great.

✠ SUNDAY 23 — G — 21st SUNDAY and WEEK of YEAR — TRINITY 11

MP	Ps: 115	Jonah 2	I Sam 9:1 – 10:11
		Rev 1	Rom 1:1–25 (26–end)

R: Ps I — Mass — *Gl; Cr; Sunday Pref (PROPER 16)*
CW: Josh 24:1–2a & 14–18; Ps 34:15–22; Eph 6:10–20; Jn 6:56–69
R: Josh 24:1–2 & 15–18; Ps 34; Eph 5:21–32; Jn 6:60–69 (How can we desert Him?)

2 EP		Exod 4:27 – 5:1	Prov 8:1–17
	Ps: 116	Heb 13:16–21	Mt 4:23 – 5:20

MONDAY 24 — R — S Bartholomew, Apostle

MP	Ps: 86, 117	Gen 28:10–17	Deut 18:15–19
		Jn 1:43–51	Mt 10:1–15

Mass — *Gl; R: Pref of Apostles; CW: of Saints*
CW: (Isa 43:8–13); Ps 145:1–7; Acts 5:12–16 (I Cor 4:9–15); Lk 22:24–30
R: Rev 21:9–14; Ps 145; Jn 1:45–51

EP		Ecclus 39:1–10 or Deut 18:15–19	Isa 49:1–13
	Ps: 91, 116	Mt 10:1–22	Mt 10:16–22

TUESDAY 25 — G (or W) — Feria (□ S Louis; □ S Joseph Calasanz, Pr)

MP	Ps: 87, 89:1–18	Prov 8:22–end	Jer 42
		Mk 5:21–34	II Cor 5:20 – 7:1

Mass — *of Sunday; no Gl or Cr; Common Pref (or of a Saint)*
I Thess 2:1–8; Ps 139:1–9; Mt 23:23–26

EP		II Sam 5:1–12	Jer 43
	Ps: 89:19–end	Acts 7:1–16	Lk 21:5–end

WEDNESDAY 26 — G (or W) — Feria (S Ninian?, see p. 54. □ Bl Dominic Barberi, Pr, Rel, Miss)

MP	Ps: 119:105–128	Prov 9	Jer 44:1–14
		Mk 5:35–end	II Cor 7:2–end

Mass — *as Tuesday*
I Thess 2:9–13; Ps 126; Mt 23:27–32

EP		II Sam 6:1–19	Jer 44:15–end
	Ps: 91, 93	Acts 7:17–43	Lk 22:1–38

THURSDAY 27 — W — S Monica

MP	Ps: 90, 92	Prov 10:1–12	Ezek 1:1–14
		Mk 6:1–13	II Cor 8

Mass — *of the Saint*
I Thess 3:7–end; Ps 90:13–end; Mt 24:42–end

EP		II Sam 7:1–17	Ezek 2:1 – 3:3
	Ps: 94	Acts 7:44–53	Lk 22:39–53

FRIDAY 28 — W — S Augustine, B, Dr

MP	Ps: 88, 95	Prov 11:1–12	Ezek 3:4–end
		Mk 6:14–29	II Cor 9

Mass — *of the Saint*
I Thess 4:1–8; Ps 97; Mt 25:1–13

2 EP		II Sam 7:18–end	Ezek 8
	Ps: 102	Acts 7:54 – 8:3	Lk 22:54–end

SATURDAY 29 — R — Beheading of S John Baptist, M

MP	Ps: 96, 97, 100	Prov 12:10–end	Ezek 11:14–end
		Mk 6:30–44	II Cor 10

Mass — *of the Saint (**Our Lady Help of the Sick; of Consolation**)*
CW: Jer 1:4–10; Ps 11; Heb 11:32 – 12:2; Mt 14:1–12
R: Jer 1:17–19; Ps 71; Mk 6:17–29
[I Thess 4:9–12; Ps 98:1–2 & 8–end; Mt 25:14–30]

G — 1 EP of foll		II Sam 9	Ezek 12:17–end
	Ps: 104	Acts 8:4–25	Lk 23:1–25

SEPTEMBER FESTIVALS

1. On **September 3** the Ebbsfleet Apostolic District celebrates S Gregory, who sent S Augustine (Ebbsfleet his landing place), as its Patron with the rank of Solemnity. Gl and Cr at mass; 1 EP on Saturday; Office from the Commons (p. xxx; a R: reading is Titus 1:7–11 & 2:1–8). Ebbsfleet propers: *Ecclus 47:8–11; Ps 36:1–3 & 7–8 & 10; Response verse 3; I Thess 2:2–8; Alleluia, Alleluia! The Lord sent me to bring the good news to the poor, and liberty to captives. Alleluia! Mt 16:13–19.*

2. **September 8** began in Jerusalem as a festival of the (5th Century) Basilica of Holy Mary's Birthplace; such tend to be the origins of early feasts of those who left no bodily relics (cf. September 29 and November 21). **September 14** also began in Jerusalem when, on the day after the Dedication of the Basilica of the Resurrection, the Wood of the Holy Cross was exposed for veneration.

3. Since CW provides no Office for **September 8**, we offer: *middle column* the ASB provision; *right hand column* a typological provision based upon Orthodox provisions, which your Compiler owes to Bishop Wilkinson of the Canadian TAC.

4. In Churches where August 15 is not observed, CW suggests **September 8** as the principal solemnity of our Lady. In such churches it will have a 1 EP. The Propers of August 14–15 are used.

5. The memorial of the Holy Name of Mary, which originally occupied the Sunday after her Nativity, has now been restored, as an optional memorial, to **September 12**. The mass propers may be had from your Compiler (see *PRAENOTANDA*) and remind us that, as well, as *Mary*, the Lord's Mother is 'named' *Mother of God* and *Ever-Virgin*. Rome urges those compiling local calendars who need a place for 'Our Lady of N' to consider September 12.

6. The old Octave day of the Nativity, **September 15**, which is also the day after Holy Cross Day, is, very neatly, the memorial of our Lady *Perdolentis*. (It was David Silk who had the happy notion of Englishing this as *Mary at the Cross*.) [The Stabat Mater, EH 115 (NEH 97) is optionally used as a Sequence at Mass. Divided, it is used for the Office Hymn.] But when CW put S John Chrysostom back onto its R: date of September 13, S Cyprian was evicted onto September 15, leaving our Lady out in the cold. This ORDO lets her back in and follows the significant tradition of associating S Cyprian with S Cornelius on their R: date of the 16th.

7. **September 16.** S Ninian, observed on the 16th in CW and other Anglican Calendars, is on August 26 in Roman Calendars.

8. **September 24** Our Lady of Walsingham is observed at Walsingham as a Solemnity, and as a Festum in the Diocese. Outside England, it is 'Our Lady of Ransom'.

9. **September 29** (originally the Dedication of the Roman Basilica of S Michael) had 'and All Angels' added by Dr Cranmer; 'and Ss Gabriel and Raphael' by the Roman revisers of 1969.

OCTOBER has traditionally been marked by the saying of the Rosary, followed by the Litany of our Lady. October 1, among Byzantines, commemorates the Protecting Veil of the Mother of God – ie., Our Lady, Mother of Mercy.

10. **October 7**, originally the feast of Our Lady of Victories, commemorated the victory of Christian arms at the Battle of Lepanto. The politically incorrect will be particularly attracted to this lovely commemoration. Our Lady's military prowess down the ages has led the Orthodox to call her the *hypermachos strategos*, 'Our Protecting Fieldmarshal' or possibly 'The general who is always on top of the battle'.

✠ **SUNDAY**   **22nd SUNDAY and WEEK of YEAR**   **TRINITY 12**

30   G   MP   Ps: 119:17–40   Jonah 3:1–9   I Sam 16:1–13
                                          Rev 3:14–22   Rom 5:1–11
R: Ps II   Mass   *Gl; Cr; Sunday Pref (PROPER 17)*
                        CW: Deut 4:1–2 & 6–9; Ps 15; Jas 1:17–27; Mk 7:1–8 & 14–15 & 21–23
                        R: Deut 4:1–2 & 6–8; Ps 15; Jas 1:17–18 & 21–22 & 27; Mk 7:1–8 & 14–15 & 21–23
                        (The Commandments of Life)
                2 EP   Exod 12:21–27   Prov 8:1 & 22–end
                        Ps: 119:1–6   Mt 4:23 – 5:20   Mt 5:21–end

MONDAY   **Feria (S Aidan, B)**

31   G   MP   Ps: 98, 99, 101   Prov 14:31 – 15:17   Ezek 13:1–16
      (or W)   Mk 6:45–end   II Cor 11
                Mass   *of Sunday; no Gl or Cr; Common Pref (or of the Saint)*
                        I Thess 4:13–end; Ps 96; Lk 4:16–30
                EP   II Sam 11   Ezek 14:1–11
                        Ps: 103, 105   Acts 8:26–end   Lk 23:26–49

SEPTEMBER

TUESDAY   **Feria (S Giles, Rel)**

1   G   MP   Ps: 106   Prov 15:18–end   Ezek 14:12–end
     (or W)   Mk 7:1–13   II Cor 12:1–13
                Mass   *as Monday (or of the Saint)*
                        I Thess 5:1–6 & 9–11; Ps 27:1–8; Lk 4:31–37
                EP   II Sam 12:1–25   Ezek 20:1–20
                        Ps: 107   Acts 9:1–19a   Lk 23:50 – 24:12

WEDNESDAY   **Feria**

2   G   MP   Ps: 110, 111, 112   Prov 18:10–end   Ezek 20:27–44
                                          Mk 7:14–23   II Cor 12:14–13 end
                Mass   *as Monday (**The Martyrs of Papua New Guinea**)*
                        Col 1:1–8; Ps 34:11–18; Lk 4:38–end
                EP   II Sam 15:1–12   Ezek 33:21–end
                        Ps: 119:129–152   Acts 9:19b–31   Lk 24:13–end

THURSDAY   **S Gregory the Great, Pp, Dr (EAD SOLEMNITY see p. 54)**

3   W   MP   Ps: 113, 115   Prov 20:1–22   Ezek 34:1–16
                                          Mk 7:24–30   Gal 1
                Mass   *of the Saint (National Appendix in Missal) (**Our Lady Mother of the Good Shepherd**)*
                        Col 1:9–14; Ps 98:1–5; Lk 5:1–11
                EP   II Sam 15:13–end   Ezek 34:17–end
                        Ps: 114, 116, 117   Acts 9:32–end   Jn 1:1–28

FRIDAY   **Feria (S Cuthbert, B, Rel; S Birinus, B? – see p. 1)**

4   G   MP   Ps: 139   Prov 22:1–16   Ezek 36:22–36
     (or W)   Mk 7:31–end   Gal 2
                Mass   *as Monday (or of the Saint) (First Friday: Sacred Heart, see p. 42)*
                        Col 1:15–20; Ps 89:19b–28; Lk 5:33–end
                EP   II Sam 16:1–14   Ezek 37:1–14
                        Ps: 130, 131, 137   Acts 10:1–16   Jn 1:29–end

SATURDAY   **Our Lady on Saturday (or the Feria) (☐ Bl Teresa of Calcutta, V, Rel)**

5   W   MP   Ps: 120, 121, 122   Prov 24:23–end   Ezek 37:15–end
     (or G)   Mk 8:1–10   Gal 3
                Mass   *Introduction Paragraph 26(b) (**Allen Gardiner**) (First Saturday: Immaculate Heart, see p. 42)*
                        Col 1:21–23; Ps 117; Lk 6:1–5
         G   1 EP of foll   II Sam 17:1–23   Ezek 47:1–12
                        Ps: 118   Acts 10:17–33   Jn 2

✠ *SUNDAY*			**23rd SUNDAY and WEEK of YEAR**		**TRINITY 13**
6	G	MP	Ps: 119:57–72	Jonah 3:10 – 4:11	I Sam 17:1–11 & 32–51
				Rev 8:1–5	Rom 12
R: Ps IV		Mass	*Gl; Cr; Sunday Pref (PROPER 18)*		
			CW: Isa 35:4–7a; Ps 146; Jas 2:1–10 (11–13) 14–17; Mk 7:24–37		
			R: Isa 35:4–7; Ps 146; Jas 2:1–5; Mk 7:31–37 (Opening Mouths and Ears)		
		2 EP		Exod 14:5–31	Prov 14:31 – 15:17
			Ps: 119:41–56	Mt 6:1–18	Mt 6:1–18
MONDAY			**Feria**		
7	G	MP	Ps: 123, 124, 125, 126	Prov 25:1–14	Ezra 1
				Mk 8:11–21	Gal 4:1 – 5:1
		Mass	*of Sunday; no Gl or Cr; Common Pref*		
			Col 1:24 – 2:3; Ps 62:1–7; Lk 6:6–11		
		EP		II Sam 18:1–18	Ezra 3
			Ps: 127, 128, 129	Acts 10:34–end	Jn 3:1–21
TUESDAY			**Birth of the BVM** *(see p. 54)*		
8	W	MP	H: 214 or 215	Isa 61:10 – 62:3 (R: Gen 3:9–20)	Gen 28:10–17
			(NEH 181 or 183)		
			Ps: 72	Jn 2:1–12	Rev 12:1–6
		Mass	*Gl; Pref of BVM (R:); Annunciation (CW)*		
			CW: Micah 5:1–4; Ps 45:10–17; Rom 8:18–30; Lk 1:39–47		
			R: Micah 5:1–4 or Rom 8:28–30; Ps 13; Mt 1: (1–16) 18–23		
		EP	H: 213 (NEH 180)	Prov 8:22–31	Ezek 44:1–4
			Ps: 98, 138	Jn 19:23–27	Rev 7:9–12
WEDNESDAY			**Feria (▢ S Peter Claver)**		
9	G	MP	Ps: 119:153–end	Prov 26:12–end	Zech 1:1–17
				Mk 8:27 – 9:1	Gal 6
		Mass	*as Monday (or of the Saint)* (**Charles Fuge Lowder, Pr**)		
			Col 3:1–11; Ps 15; Lk 6:20–26		
		EP		II Sam 19:8b–23	Zech 1:18–2 end
			Ps: 136	Acts 11:19–end	Jn 4:1–26
THURSDAY			**Feria**		
10	G	MP	Ps: 143, 146	Prov 27:1–22	Zech 3
				Mk 9:2–13	Eph 1:1–14
		Mass	*as Monday*		
			Col 3:12–17; Ps 149:1–5; Lk 6:27–38		
		EP		II Sam 19:24–end	Zech 4
			Ps: 138, 140, 141	Acts 12:1–17	Jn 4:27–end
FRIDAY			**Feria**		
11	G	MP	Ps: 142, 144	Prov 30:1–9 & 24–31	Zech 6:9–end
				Mk 9:14–29	Eph 1:15–end
		Mass	*as Monday*		
			I Tim 1:1–2 & 12–14; Ps 16; Lk 6:39–42		
		EP		II Sam 23:1–7	Hag 2:10–end
			Ps: 145	Acts 12:18–end	Jn 5:1–23
SATURDAY			**▢ Most Holy Name of Mary (or Feria)** *(see p. 54)*		
12	W	MP	Ps: 147	Prov 31:10–end	Ezra 5
	(or G)			Mk 9:30–37	Eph 2:1–10
		Mass	*of our Lady*		
			I Tim 1:15–17; Ps 113; Lk 6:43–end		
	G	EP		II Sam 24	Ezra 6
			Ps: 148, 149, 150	Acts 13:1–12	Jn 5:24–end

✠ SUNDAY
13   G
R: Ps III

		24th SUNDAY and WEEK of YEAR	**TRINITY 14**
MP	Ps: 119:105–120	Isa 44:24 – 45:8	I Sam 18:1–16
		Rev 12:1–12	Rom 14:1 –15:3
Mass	*Gl; Cr; Sunday Pref (PROPER 19)*		
	CW: Isa 50:4–9a; Ps 116: 1–8; Jas 3:1–12; Mk 8:27–38		
	R: Isa 50:5–9; Ps 116; Jas 2:14–18; Mk 8:27–35		
EP		Exod 18:13–26	Prov 31:10–end
	Ps: 119:73–88	Mt 7:1–14	Mt 6:19–end

MONDAY
14   R

		Holy Cross Day (The Triumph of the Cross)*	
MP	H: 96 (NEH 78)	Gen 3:1–15	◁
	Ps: 2, 8, 146	Jn 12:27–36a	◁
Mass	*of the Feast; Gl; Pref of Cross (R:) or (CW) the Short Pref 'From the Fifth Sunday of Lent . . .'*		
	CW=R: Num 21:4–9; Ps 22:23–28 (R: 78); Phil 2:6–11; Jn 3:13–17		
2 EP	H: 94 (NEH 79)	Isa 63:1–16	◁
	Ps: 110, 150	I Cor 1:18–25	◁

TUESDAY
15   W

		☐ Our Lady at the Cross (see p. 54)	
MP	Ps: 5, 6, 8	Wisd 2	Ezra 7
		Mk 10:1–16	Eph 3
Mass	*of our Lady (Heb 5:7–9; Jn 19:25–7 or Lk 2:33–5)*		
	I Tim 3:1–13; Ps 101; Lk 7:11–17		
EP		I Kgs 1:32 – 2:4 & 2:10–12	Ezra 8:15–end
	Ps: 9, 10	Acts 13:44 – 14:7	Jn 6:22–40

WEDNESDAY
16   R

		Ss Cornelius, Pp and Cyprian, B, M (see p. 54)†	
MP	Ps: 119:1–32	Wisd 3:1–9	Ezra 9
		Mk 10:17–31	Eph 4:1–16
Mass	*of the Saints (**Edward Bouverie Pusey, Pr**)*		
	I Tim 3:14–end; Ps 111:1–5; Lk 7:31–35		
EP		I Kgs 3	Ezra 10:1–19
	Ps: 11, 12, 13	Acts 14:8–end	Jn 6:41–end

THURSDAY
17   G
(or W)

		Feria (☐ S Robert Bellarmine, B, Dr; S Hildegard, Ab)	
MP	Ps: 14, 15, 16	Wisd 4:7–end	Neh 1
		Mk 10:32–34	Eph 4:17–30
Mass	*of Sunday; no Gl or Cr; Common Pref (or of the Saint)*		
	I Tim 4:12–end; Ps 111:6–end; Lk 7:36–end		
EP		I Kgs 4:29 – 5:12	Neh 2
	Ps: 18	Acts 15:1–21	Jn 7:1–24

FRIDAY
18   G

		Feria†	
MP	Ps: 17, 19	Wisd 5:1–16	Neh 4
		Mk 10:35–45	Eph 4:31 – 5:21
Mass	*as Thursday*		
	I Tim 6:2–12; Ps 49:1–9; Lk 8:1–3		
EP		I Kgs 6:1 & 11–28	Neh 5
	Ps: 22	Acts 15:22–35	Jn 7:25 end

SATURDAY
19   W
(or G or R)
    G

		Our Lady on Saturday† (or the Feria)	
		(☐ S Januarius, B, M; S Theodore, B)	
MP	Ps: 20, 21, 23	Wisd 5:17 – 6:11	Neh 6:1 – 7:4
		Mk 10:46–end	Eph 5:22–end
Mass	*Introduction Paragraph 26(b)*		
	I Tim 6:13–16; Ps 100; Lk 8:4–15		
1 EP of foll		I Kgs 8:1–30	Neh 8
	Ps: 24, 25	Acts 15:36 – 16:5	Jn 8:1–30

---

* In medieval England, Crouchmas. For SSC members, should it be a Solemnity (1EP, p. xxx)?.
† Ember Days. See Introduction, Paragraph 25.

✠ *SUNDAY*
20   G   MP   **25th SUNDAY and WEEK of YEAR**   TRINITY 15

R: Ps I

		Ps: 119:153–176	Isa 45:9–22	I Sam 26
			Rev 14:1–5	I Pet 1:13–end
	Mass	*Gl; Cr; Sunday Pref (PROPER 20)*		
		CW: Wisd 1:16 – 2:1 & 12–22; Ps 54; Jas 3:13 – 4:3 & 7–8a; Mk 9:30–37		
		R: Wisd 2:12 & 17–20; Ps 54; Jas 3:16 – 4:3; Mk 9:30–37 (What They will Do to Him)		
	2 EP		Exod 19:10–25	Job 1
		Ps: 119:137–152	Mt 8:23–34	Mt 7:1–14

MONDAY
21   R   MP   **S Matthew, Apostle**

		Ps: 49, 117	I Kgs 19:15–21	Prov 3:1–17
			II Tim 3:14–17	Mt 19:16–end
	Mass	*Gl; R: Pref of Apostles; CW, of Saints*		
		CW: Prov 3:13–18; Ps 119:65–72; II Cor 4:1–6; Mt 9:9–13		
		R: Eph 4:1–7 & 11–13; Ps 19; Mt 9:9–13		
	EP		Eccles 5:4–12	I Chron 29:9–18
		Ps: 119:33–40 & 89–96	Mt 19:16–30	I Tim 6:6–19

TUESDAY
22   G   MP   **Feria**

		Ps: 32, 36	Wisd 7:1–14	Neh 13
			Mk 11:12–16	Eph 6:10–end
	Mass	*of Sunday; no Gl or Cr; Common Pref*		
		Ezra 6:7–8 & 12 & 14–20; Ps 124; Lk 8:19–21		
	EP		I Kgs 8:63 – 9:9	Dan 1
		Ps: 33	Acts 16:25–end	Jn 9

WEDNESDAY
23   W   MP   ☐ **S Pius of Pietralcina, Pr**

		Ps: 34	Wisd 7:15 – 8:4	Dan 2:1–24
			Mk 11:27–end	Phil 1:1–11
	Mass	*of the Saint (**'Padre Pio'**)*		
		Ezra 9:5–9; Ps Tobit 13:1–2 & 3b–4 & 6b; Lk 9:1–6		
	EP		I Kgs 10:1–25	Dan 2:25–end
		Ps: 119:33–56	Acts 17:1–15	Jn 10:1–21

THURSDAY
24   W   MP   ☐ *Our Lady of Walsingham*

		Ps: 37	Wisd 8:5–18	Dan 4:1–18
			Mk 12:1–12	Phil 1:12–end
	Mass	*of our Lady (National Appendix)*		
		Hag 1:1–8; Ps 149:1–5; Lk 9:7–9		
	EP		I Kgs 11:1–13	Dan 4:19–end
		Ps: 39, 40	Acts 17:16–end	Jn 10:22–end

FRIDAY
25   G   MP   **Feria (S Sergei of Radonezh, Rel)**
    (or W)

		Ps: 31	Wisd 8:21 – 9 end	Dan 7:9–end
			Mk 12:13–17	Phil 2:1–11
	Mass	*as Tuesday (or of the Saint) (**Lancelot Andrewes, B**)*		
		(Anniversary of the Episcopal Ordination, in 1996, of John, tenth Bishop of Fulham)		
		Hag 1:15b – 2:9; Ps 43; Lk 9:18–22		
	EP		I Kgs 11:26–end	Dan 9
		Ps: 35	Acts 18:1–21	Jn 11:1–44

SATURDAY   **Our Lady on Saturday (or the Feria)**
                (☐ Ss Cosmas and Damian, Ms)
26   W   MP
    (or G)

		Ps: 41, 42, 43	Wisd 10:15 – 11:10	Dan 10
			Mk 12:18–27	Phil 2:12–end
	Mass	*see Introduction Paragraph 26(b) (or the Saint) (**Wilson Carlile**)*		
		Zech 2:1–5 & 10–11; Ps 125; Lk 9:43–45		
	G	1 EP of foll	I Kgs 12:1–24	Dan 12
		Ps: 45, 46	Acts 18:22 – 19:7	Jn 11:45–end

✠ *SUNDAY*   **26th SUNDAY and WEEK of YEAR**   **TRINITY 16**

27   G   MP   Ps: 122   Isa 48:12–22   I Sam 28:3–end

                                         Lk 11:37–54   I Pet 2:1–17

R: Ps II   Mass   *Gl; Cr; Common Pref (PROPER 21)*

                         CW: Num 11:4–6 & 10–16 & 24–29; Ps 19:7–14; Jas 5:13–20; Mk 9:38–50

                         R: Num 11:25–29; Ps 19; Jas 5:1–6; Mk 9:38–43 & 47–48 (Who is with the Lord?)

               2 EP   Exod 24   Job 2

                        Ps: 120, 121   Mt 9:1–8   Mt 7:15–end

MONDAY   *Feria (☐ S Wenceslas, M)*

28   W   MP   Ps: 44   Wisd 11:21 – 12:2   Esther 1

    (or R)   Mk 12:28–34   Phil 3

              Mass   *of Sunday; no Gl or Cr; Common Pref (or of the Saint)*

                        Zech 8:1–18; Ps 102:12–22; Lk 9:46–50

              EP   I Kgs 12:25 – 13:10   Esther 2:5–11 & 15–end

                        Ps: 47, 49   Acts 19:8–20   Jn 12:1–19

TUESDAY   **Michaelmas (see p. 54)**

29   W   MP   H: 241   Tobit 12:6–22   II Kgs 6:8–17

                        Ps: 34, 150   Acts 12:1–11   ◁

              Mass   *Gl; R: Pref of Angels; CW Common Pref*

                        CW: Gen 28:10–17; Ps 103:19–22; Rev 12:7–12; Jn 1:47–51

                        R: Dan 7:9–10 & 13–14 or Rev 12:7–12; Ps 138; Jn 1:47–51

              EP   Dan 10:4–21 & 12:1–4   ◁

                        Ps: 138, 148   Rev 5   ◁

WEDNESDAY   *S Jerome, Pr, Dr*

30   W   MP   Ps: 119:57–80   Wisd 13:1–19   Esther 5

                                 Mk 13:1–13   Col 1:1–20

              Mass   *of the Saint*

                        Neh 2:1–8; Ps 137:1–6; Lk 9:57–end

              EP   I Kgs 17   Esther 6 & 7

                        Ps: 59, 60, 67   Acts 20:1–16   Jn 13

OCTOBER

THURSDAY   ☐ *S Teresa of the Child Jesus, V, Dr*

1   W   MP   Ps: 56, 57, 63   Wisd 16:15 – 17:1   I Macc 1:1–19

                                 Mk 13:14–23   Col 1:21 – 2:7

              Mass   *of the Saint (**S Remigius, B; A. A. Cooper**)*

                        Neh 8:1–12; Ps 19:7–11; Lk 10:1–12

              EP   I Kgs 18:1–20   I Macc 1:20–40

                        Ps: 61, 62, 64   Acts 20:17–end   Jn 14

FRIDAY   ☐ *The Holy Guardian Angels*

2   W   MP   Ps: 51, 54   Wisd 18:6–19   I Macc 1:41–end

                               Mk 13:24–31   Col 2:8–19

              Mass   *of the Angels (Exod 23:20–23a; Ps 90; Mt 18:1–5 & 10) (First Friday: Sacred Heart, see p. 42)*

                        Bar 1:15–end; Ps 79:1–9; Lk 10:13–16

              EP   I Kgs 18:21–end   I Macc 2:1–28

                        Ps: 38   Acts 21:1–16   Jn 15

SATURDAY   *Our Lady on Saturday (or the Feria)*

3   W   MP   Ps: 68   Wisd 19   I Macc 2:29–48

    (or G)   Mk 13:32–end   Col 2:20 – 3:11

              Mass   *Introduction Paragraph 26(b) (First Saturday: Immaculate Heart, see p. 42)*

                        Bar 4:5–12 & 27–29; Ps 69:33–37; Lk 10:17–24

          G   1 EP of foll   I Kgs 19   I Macc 2:49–end

                        Ps: 65, 66   Acts 21:17–36   Jn 16

✠ **SUNDAY**			**27th SUNDAY and WEEK of YEAR**		**TRINITY 17***
4	G	MP	Ps: 123, 124	Isa 49:13–23	II Sam 1
				Lk 12:1–12	I Pet 4
R: Ps III		Mass	*Gl; Cr; Sunday Pref (PROPER 22)**		
			CW: Gen 2:18–24; Ps 8; Heb 1:1–4 & 2:5–12; Mk 10:2–16		
			R: Gen 2:18–24; Ps 128; Heb 2:9–11; Mk 10:2–12 (13–16) (One Flesh)		
		2 EP		Josh 3:7–17	Job 4:1 & 5:6–end
			Ps: 125, 26	Mt 10:1–22	Mt 11:2–19
MONDAY			**Feria**		
5	G	MP	Ps: 71	I Macc 1:1–19	I Macc 3:1–26
				Mk 14:1–11	Col 3:12 –4:1
		Mass	*of Sunday; no Gl or Cr; Common Pref*		
			Jonah 1:1 – 2:1–2 & 10; Ps Jonah 2:2–4 & 7; Lk 10:25–37		
		EP		I Kgs 21	I Macc 3:27–41
			Ps: 72, 75	Acts 21:37 – 22:31	Jn 17
TUESDAY			**Feria (☐ S Bruno, Pr)**		
6	G	MP	Ps: 73	I Macc 1:20–40	I Macc 3:42–end
	(or W)			Mk 14:12–25	Col 4:2–end
		Mass	*as Monday (or of the Saint)* **(William Tyndale Ref M)**		
			Jonah 3; Ps 130; Lk 10:38–end		
		EP		I Kgs 22:1–28	I Macc 4:1–25
			Ps: 74	Acts 22:22 – 23:11	Jn 18:1–27
WEDNESDAY			**☐ Our Lady of the Rosary**		
7	W	MP	Ps: 77	I Macc 1:41–end	I Macc 4:26–35
				Mk 14:26–42	Philemon
		Mass	*of our Lady (Acts 1:12–14; Magnificat; Lk 1:26–38)*		
			Jonah 4; Ps 86:1–9; Lk 11:1–4		
		EP		I Kgs 22:29–45	I Macc 4:36–end
			Ps: 119:81–104	Acts 23:12–end	Jn 18:28–end
THURSDAY			**Feria**		
8	G	MP	Ps: 78:1–39	I Macc 2:1–28	I Macc 6:1–17
				Mk 14:43–52	I Thess 1
		Mass	*as Monday*		
			Mal 3:13 – 4:2a; Ps 1; Lk 11:5–13		
		EP		II Kgs 1:2–17	I Macc 6:18–47
			Ps: 78:40–end	Acts 24:1–23	Jn 19:1–30
FRIDAY			**Feria (Ss Denys, B, Comp, Ms; ☐ S John Leonard, Pr)**		
9	G (or	MP	Ps: 55	I Macc 2:29–48	I Macc 7:1–20
	R or			Mk 14:53–65	I Thess 2:1–16
	W)	Mass	*as Monday (or of the Saint)* **(Robert Grosseteste, B)**		
			Joel 1:13–15 & 2:1–2; Ps 9:1–7; Lk 11:15–26		
		EP		II Kgs 2:1–18	I Macc 7:21–end
			Ps: 69	Acts 24:24 – 25:12	Jn 19:31–end
SATURDAY			**Our Lady on Saturday (or the Feria; or S Paulinus, B)**		
10	W	MP	Ps: 76, 79	I Macc 2:49–end	I Macc 9:1–22
	(or G)			Mk 14:66–end	I Thess 2:17–3 end
		Mass	*Introduction Paragraph 26(b)* **(Thomas Traherne)**		
			Joel 3:12–21; Ps 97:1 & 8–end; Lk 11:27–28		
	G	1 EP of foll		II Kgs 4:1–37	I Macc 13:41–end & 14:4–15
			Ps: 81, 84	Acts 25:13–end	Jn 20

* Dedication? Appendix 1.

✠ *SUNDAY*   **28th SUNDAY and WEEK of YEAR**   **TRINITY 18**

11   G

R: Ps IV

	MP	Ps: 129, 130	Isa 50:4–10	II Sam 7
			Lk 13:22–30	I Pet 5:1–11
	Mass	*Gl; Cr; Sunday Pref (PROPER 23)*		
		CW: Amos 5:6–7 & 10–15; Ps 90:12–17; Heb 4:12–16; Mk 10:17–31		
		R: Wisd 7:7–11; Ps 90; Heb 4:12–13; Mk 10:17–27 (28–30) (True Riches)		
	2 EP		Josh 5:13 – 6:20	Job 19:1–27a
		Ps: 127, 128	Mt 11:20–30	Mt 11:20–end

MONDAY   **Feria (S Wilfrid, B)**

12   G (or W)

	MP	Ps: 80, 82	I Macc 3:1–26	Job 1
			Mk 15:1–15	I Thess 4:1–12
	Mass	*of Sunday; no Gl or Cr; Common Pref (or of the Saint)* (**Elizabeth Fry; Edith Cavell**)		
		Rom 1:1–7; Ps 98; Lk 11:29–32		
	EP		II Kgs 5	Job 2
		Ps: 85, 86	Acts 26:1–23	Jn 21

TUESDAY   **Feria (S Edward the Confessor)**

13   G (or W)

	MP	Ps: 87, 89:1–18	I Macc 3:27–41	Job 3
			Mk 15:16–32	I Thess 4:13 – 5:11
	Mass	*as Monday (or of the Saint)* (**Our Lady of Iverskia**)		
		Rom 1:16–25; Ps 19:1–4; Lk 11:37–41		
	EP		II Kgs 6:1–23	Job 4
		Ps: 89:19–end	Acts 26:24–end	Heb 1

WEDNESDAY   **Feria (☐ S Callistus I, Pp, M)**

14   G (or R)

	MP	Ps: 119:105–128	I Macc 3:42–end	Job 5
			Mk 15:33–41	I Thess 5:12–end
	Mass	*as Monday (or of the Saint)*		
		Rom 2:1–11; Ps 62:1–8; Lk 11:42–46		
	EP		II Kgs 9:1–16	Job 6
		Ps: 91, 93	Acts 27:1–26	Heb 2

THURSDAY   **S Teresa of Jesus, V, Dr**

15   W

	MP	Ps: 90, 92	I Macc 4:1–25	Job 7
			Mk 15:42–end	II Thess 1
	Mass	*of the Saint*		
		Rom 3:21–30; Ps 130; Lk 11:47–end		
	EP		II Kgs 9:17–end	Job 8
		Ps: 94	Acts 27:27–end	Heb 3

FRIDAY   **Feria (☐ S Hedwig, Rel; ☐ S Margaret Mary Alacoque, V)**

16   G (or W)

	MP	Ps: 88, 95	I Macc 4:26–35	Job 9
			Mk 16:1–8	II Thess 2
	Mass	*as Monday (or of the Saint)* (**Nicolas Ridley & Hugh Latimer, Bs, Ref Ms**)		
		(**The Purity of Our Lady**)		
		Rom 4:1–8; Ps 32; Lk 12:1–7		
	EP		II Kgs 12:1–19	Job 10
		Ps: 102	Acts 28:1–16	Heb 4:1–13

SATURDAY   **S Ignatius of Antioch, B, M**

17   R

	MP	Ps: 96, 97, 100	I Macc 4:36–end	Job 11
			Mk 16:9–end	II Thess 3
	Mass	*of the Saint*		
		Rom 4:13 & 16–18; Ps 105:6–10 & 41–44; Lk 12:8–12		
G	1 EP of foll		II Kgs 17:1–23	Job 12
		Ps: 104	Acts 28:17–end	Heb 4:14 – 5:10

✠ SUNDAY   **29th SUNDAY and WEEK of YEAR***   **TRINITY 19**

18   G   MP   Ps: 133, 134, 137:1–6   Isa 54:1–14   II Sam 12:1–23

                                      Lk 13:31–35   Col 1:21 – 2:7

R: Ps I   Mass   *Gl; Cr; Sunday Pref (PROPER 24)*

                  CW: Isa 53:4–12; Ps 91:9–16; Heb 5:1–10; Mk 10:35–45

                  R: Isa 53:10–11; Ps 33; Heb 4:14–16; Mk 10:(35–41) 42–45 (Servant of All)

           2 EP   Josh 14:6–14   Job 28

                  Ps: 141   Mt 12:1–12   Mt 12:22–45

MONDAY   *Feria (☐ Ss John de Brebeuf & Isaac Jogues, Pr, Comp, Ms;*

                  *☐ S Paul of the Cross, Pr)**

19   G (or   MP   Ps: 98, 99, 101   I Macc 6:1–17   Job 13

      R or   Jn 13:1–11   I Tim 1:1–17

      W)   Mass   *of Sunday; no Gl or Cr; Common Pref (or of the Saints)* (**Henry Martyn**)

                  Rom 4:20–end; Benedictus 1–6; Lk 12:13–21

           EP   II Kgs 17:24–end   Job 14

                  Ps: 103, 105   Phil 1:1–11   Heb 5:11–6 end

TUESDAY   *Feria*

20   G   MP   Ps: 106   I Macc 6:18–47   Job 15:1–16

                           Jn 13:12–20   I Tim 1:18–2 end

           Mass   *as Monday*

                  Rom 5:12 & 15 & 17–end; Ps 40:7–12; Lk 12:35–38

           EP   II Kgs 18:1–12   Job 16:1 – 17:2

                  Ps: 107   Phil 1:12–end   Heb 7

WEDNESDAY   *Feria*

21   G   MP   Ps: 110, 111, 112   I Macc 7:1–20   Job 17:3–end

                             Jn 13:21–30   I Tim 3

           Mass   *as Monday*

                  Rom 6:12–18; Ps 124; Lk 12:39–48

           EP   II Kgs 18:13–end   Job 18

                  Ps: 119:129–152   Phil 2:1–13   Heb 8

THURSDAY   *Feria*

22   G   MP   Ps: 113, 115   I Macc 7:21–end   Job 19

                         Jn 13:31–end   I Tim 4

           Mass   *as Monday* (**Our Lady of Kazan**)

                  Rom 6:19–end; Ps 1; Lk 12:49–53

           EP   II Kgs 19:1–19   Job 21

                  Ps: 114, 116, 117   Phil 2:14–end   Heb 9:1–14

FRIDAY   *Feria (☐ S John of Capistrano, Pr)†*

23   G   MP   Ps: 139   I Macc 9:1–22   Job 22

   (or W)   Jn 14:1–14   I Tim 5

           Mass   *as Monday (or of the Saint)*

                  Rom 7:18–end; Ps 119:33–40; Lk 12:54–end

          EP   II Kgs 19:20–36   Job 23

                  Ps: 130, 131, 137   Phil 3:1 – 4:1   Heb 9:15–end

SATURDAY   *Our Lady on Saturday (or the Feria or ☐ S Antony Mary Claret, B)*

24   W   MP   Ps: 120, 121, 122   I Macc 13:41–end & 14:4–15   Job 24

   (or G)   Jn 14:15–end   I Tim 6

           Mass   *Introduction Paragraph 26(b)* (**Our Lady Joy of the Afflicted**)

                  Rom 8:1–11; Ps 24:1–6; Lk 13:1–9

         G   1 EP of foll   II Kgs 20   Job 25 & 26

                  Ps: 118   Phil 4:2–end.   Heb 10:1–18

---

* S Luke? See Praenotanda.

† In the Church of Ireland and in the East: S James, Brother of God.

✠ *SUNDAY* | **30th SUNDAY and WEEK of YEAR (CW: LAST AFTER TRINITY; BCP: TRINITY 20)**

25	G	MP	Ps: 119:89–104	Isa 59:9–20	II Sam 18
				Lk 14:1–14	Col 3:12 – 4:6
R: Ps II		Mass	Gl; Cr; Sunday Pref (PROPER 25)		
			CW: Jer 31:7–9; Ps 126; Heb 7:23–28; Mk 10:46–52		
			R: Jer 31:7–9; Ps 126; Heb 5:1–6; Mk 10:46–52 (Joy for the Blind))		
		EP		Eccles 11 & 12	Job 38 & 42:1–6
			Ps: 119:121–136	II Tim 2:1–7	Mt 13:44–end

MONDAY | **Feria (Ss Chad and/or Cedd, Bs)**

26	G (or W)	MP	Ps: 123, 124, 125, 126	II Macc 4:7–17	Job 27
				Jn 15:1–11	Titus 1:1 – 2:8
		Mass	of Sunday; no Gl or Cr; Common Pref (or of the Saint) (**Alfred the Great**)*		
			Rom 8:12–17; Ps 68:1–6 & 19; Lk 13:10–17		
		EP		II Kgs 21:1–18	Job 28
			Ps: 127, 128, 129	I Tim 1:1–17	Heb 10:19–end

TUESDAY | **Feria**

27	G	MP	Ps: 132, 133	II Macc 6:12–end	Job 29:1 – 30:1
				Jn 15:12–17	Titus 2:9–3 end
		Mass	as Monday		
			Rom 8:18–25; Ps 126; Lk 13:18–21		
		EP		II Kgs 22:1 – 23:3	Job 31:13–end
			Ps: 134, 135	I Tim 1:18–2 end	Heb 11:1–16

WEDNESDAY | **Ss Simon & Jude, Apostles**

28	R	MP	Ps: 116, 117	Wisd 5:1–16 or Isa 45:18–26	Isa 45:18–end
				Lk 6:12–16	Lk 6:12–19
		Mass	Gl; R: Pref of Apostles; CW, of Saints		
			CW: Isa 28:14–16; Ps 119:89–96; Eph 2:19–22; Jn 15:17–27		
			R: Eph 2:19–22; Ps 19; Lk 6:12–16 (17–19)		
		EP		I Macc 2:42–66	Jer 3:11–18
			Ps: 119:1–16	or Jer 3:11–18	
				Jude 1–4 & 17–25	Eph 2:11–end

THURSDAY | **Feria**

29	G	MP	Ps: 143, 146	II Macc 7:20–41	Job 38:1–21
				Jn 16:1–15	II Tim 2
		Mass	as Monday (**James Hannington, B, M**)		
			Rom 8:31–end; Ps 109:20–21; Lk 13:31–end		
		EP		II Kgs 23:36 – 24:17	Job 38:22–end
			Ps: 138, 140, 141	I Tim 4	Heb 12:1–13

FRIDAY | **Feria**

30	G	MP	Ps: 142, 144	Tob 1	Job 39
				Jn 16:16–22	II Tim 3
		Mass	as Monday		
			Rom 9:1–5; Ps 147:13–end; Lk 14:1–6		
		EP		II Kgs 24:18 – 25:12	Job 40
			Ps: 145	I Tim 5:1–16	Heb 12:14–end

SATURDAY | **Our Lady on Saturday (or the Feria)**

31	W (or G)	MP	Ps: 147	Tob 2	Job 41
				Jn 16:23–end	II Tim 4
		Mass	Introduction Paragraph 26(b) (**Martin Luther, Pr**)		
			Rom 11:1–2 & 11–12 & 25–29; Ps 94:14–19; Lk 14:1 & 7–11		
		ALL SAINTS			
	W	1 EP of foll; H: 249 (NEH 196)		Ecclus 44:1–15 or Isa 40:27–31	Isa 65:17–end
		Ps: 1, 5		Rev 19:6–10 (R: 5:1–14)	Heb 11:32 – 12:2

---

* 'S Alfred the Great' is given an optional memorial in the diocesan calendar of the RC diocese of Northampton!

NOVEMBER FESTIVALS

1. **November 2**: ALL SOULS DAY. Rome retains the custom that arose (1915) during the carnage of the First World War, of allowing every priest to say three masses, for these intentions: (1) the priest's own; (2) for all the Departed; (3) to make up for testamentary masses neglected or forgotten, and for the souls of all, especially youth, who fall victim to the appalling carnage of war. The Missal provides three sets of texts; CW 'Pastoral Services' could be drawn upon. (The three masses should be said at different times.) PHG provides the Office.

2. **November 9**: Dedication of the Lateran Basilica, the papal Cathedral in Rome, dedicated to Christ (replicated by S Augustine in the dedication of Canterbury Cathedral), is a Festum of the Lord. Office and Mass readings from Appendix 2. *Gl and Cr; Dedication Pref.* In creating a 'Little Rome' at Canterbury, the Augustinian Mission there also perpetuated the Roman dedications to Ss Peter and Paul and S Mary (see August 5).

3. **November 11**: Where the great patriarch of Western Monasticism, S Martin of Tours, is Patron, PHG suggests:1EP Isa 58:6–12 & Acts 20:28–35 MP Ezek 34:11–16 & 11 Cor 4:1–10 2EP Mal 2:5–7 & Phil 4:4–9 (Psalms 1, 15, 112). Forward in Faith celebrates this day as its foundation day.

4. **November 17, 18, and 19**:

	R:	CW
November 17 18 19	Ss Hilda†, Hugh†, Elizabeth†, or BVM on Saturday Dedication of SS Peter and Paul†*	S Hugh† Elizabeth† S Hilda† or S Mechtild†

† Optional – all of them, in both Calendars.
* Mass: Acts 28:11–16 & 30–31; Ps 98; Mt 14:22–33. Propers of Apostles NOT of Dedication; the mass theme is Rome as the place of their linked martyrdoms.

5. **November 21**: Presentation of our Lady: *not* a mistaken duplication of February 2! Originally (543) the Dedication of New S Mary's By The Temple in Jerusalem, it is one of the year's Twelve Great Festivals among the Orthodox, from whom it reached Saxon England (it was not grudgingly accepted by Rome until 1585). FESTUM in Ebbsfleet.

Your Compiler tentatively suggests that those for whom their Cathedral is no longer their Mother Church because they doubt the orders of its Eucharistic celebrants might treat this as a substitute for the Solemnity of the Dedication of the Cathedral.

The *mythos* that, aged three, Mary was lodged as a contemplative in the Temple and fed by angels with fruit as from the Tree of Life in Eden, highlights her immaculate sanctity and anticipates her bodily Assumption.

✠ SUNDAY
1   W   MP   **ALL SAINTS (see p. 64)**

✠ SUNDAY	W	MP	Ps: 15, 84, 149	Isa 35:1–9	Wisd 3:1–9
1				Lk 9:18–27	Rev 19:6–10

           Mass   *Gl; Cr; R: and CW: Proper Pref CRP*
                  CW: Wisd 3:1–9 or Isa 25:6–9; Ps 24:1–6; Rev 21:1–6a; Jn 11:32–44
                  R: Rev 7:2–4 & 9–14; Ps 24:1–6; I Jn 3:1–3; Mt 5:1–12

	2 EP*		H: 249 (NEH 196)	Isa 65:17–25	Ecclus 44:1–15
			Ps: 148, 150	Heb 11:32 – 12:2	Heb 12:18–24

MONDAY
2   B or P   MP   **ALL SOULS DAY (see p. 64)**

MONDAY	B or P	MP	Ps: 90	Job 19:21–27a	◁
2				II Cor 4:16 – 5:10	I Cor 15:51–end

           Mass   *of the day; no Gl or Cr; Seq ad lib (EH 351 NEH 524); ASB Pref (16) is the traditional Pref for*
                  the Departed. R: additionally offers four more Prefaces of Christian Death.
                  CW: Lam 3:17–26 & 31–33 or Wisd 3:1–9; Ps 23 or 27:1–6 & 16–17; Rom 5:5–11 or
                  I Pet 1:3–9; Jn 5:19–25 or Jn 6:37–40
                  R: (others allowed) Isa 25:6–9; Ps 23; Rom 5:5–11; Jn 6:37–40 (three Masses may be said)

	B or P	EP of the day: H: 350 (NEH 327)	Dan 12:1–3		Isa 43:1–7
			Ps: 121, 130	I Thess 4:13–end	Rev 1:9–18

                                                                     31st WEEK OF YEAR

TUESDAY
3   G (or W)   Feria (S Martin Porres, Rel; ☐ S Winefride, V)

TUESDAY	G	MP	Ps: 5, 6, 8	Isa 1:21–end	Prov 2
3	(or W)			Mt 2:1–15	Jas 2:1–13

           Mass   *of Trinity 21 or the 31st of the year or the 4th before Advent; no Gl or Cr; Common Pref (or of the*
                  Saint) (**Richard Hooker, Pr**)
                  Rom 12:5–16; Ps 131; Lk 14:15–24

		EP		Dan 2:1–24	Prov 3:1–26
			Ps: 9, 10	Rev 2:1–11	Jas 2:14–end

WEDNESDAY
4   W   ☐ S Charles Borromeo, B

WEDNESDAY	W	MP	Ps: 119:1–32	Isa 1:2–11	Prov 3:27 – 4:19
4				Mt 2:16–end	Jas 3

           Mass   *of the Saint*
                  Rom 13:8–10; Ps 112; Lk 14:25–33

		EP		Dan 2:25–end	Prov 4:20 – 5:14
			Ps: 11, 12, 13	Rev 2:12–end	Jas 4

THURSDAY
5   G   Feria

THURSDAY	G	MP	Ps: 14, 15, 16	Isa 2:12–end	Prov 6:1–19
5				Mt 3	Jas 5

           Mass   *as Tuesday*
                  Rom 14:7–12; Ps 27:14–end; Lk 15:1–10

		EP		Dan 3:1–18	Prov 8
			Ps: 18	Rev 3:1–13	I Pet 1:1–12

FRIDAY
6   G   Feria (S Leonard, Rel; ☐ All Saints of Ireland)

FRIDAY	G	MP	Ps: 17, 19	Isa 3:1–15	Prov 9
6				Mt 4:1–11	I Pet 1:13–end

           Mass   *as Tuesday (First Friday: Sacred Heart, see p. 42) (or of the Saint)* (**William Temple, B**)
                  Rom 15:14–21; Ps 98; Lk 16:1–8

		EP		Dan 3:19–end	Prov 10:1–22
			Ps: 22	Rev 3:14–end	I Pet 2:1–10

SATURDAY
7   W (or G)   Our Lady on Saturday (or the Feria or S Willibrord, B)

SATURDAY	W	MP	Ps: 20, 21, 23	Isa 4:2 – 5:7	Prov 11:1–23
7	(or G)			Mt 4:12–22	I Pet 2:11 – 3:7

           Mass   *Introduction Paragraph 26(b) (First Saturday: Immaculate Heart, p. 42)*
                  Rom 16:3–9 & 16 & 22–end; Ps 145:1–7; Lk 16:9–15

	G	1 EP of foll		Dan 4:1–18	Prov 12:10–end
			Ps: 24, 25	Rev 4	I Pet 3:8–end

---

* May be followed by another EP, for the Departed.

✠ *SUNDAY*

8   G   MP

32nd SUNDAY and WEEK of YEAR (CW: 3rd BEFORE ADVENT; BCP: TRINITY 22)

MP	Ps: 136	Micah 4:1–5	Wisd 4:7–17
		Phil 4:6–9	Jas 1:1–18 (19–end)

R: Ps III   Mass   *Gl; Cr; Sunday Pref (**Remembrance Sunday, p. xxii; Lateran Basilica, see p. 64**)*
CW: *Jonah 3:1–5 & 10; Ps 62:5–12; Heb 9:24–28; Mk 1:14–20*
R: *I Kgs 17:10–16; Ps 146; Heb 9:24–28; Mk 12: (38–40) 41–44 (The Widow's Poverty)*

2 EP		Isa 10:33 – 11:9	Baruch 4:36–5 end
	Ps: 46, 82	Jn 14:1 (1–22) 23–29	Mt 16:13–end

MONDAY

9   W   MP

☐ **Dedication of the Lateran Basilica, see p. 64, note 2**

MP	Ps: 27, 30	Isa 5:8–24	Prov 14:9–27
		Mt 4:23 – 5:12	I Pet 4:1–11

Mass   *of the Dedication; Gl; Pref Proper readings from the Common (Introd Appendix 2) (**Margery Kempe**) (Obit, in 2003, of John, First Bishop of Ebbsfleet)*
[Wisd 1:1–7; Ps 139:1–9; Lk 17:1–6]

EP		Dan 4:19–end	Prov 15:18–end
	Ps: 26, 28, 29	Rev 5	I Pet 4:12–end

TUESDAY

10   W   MP

S Leo the Great, Pp, Dr

MP	Ps: 32, 36	Isa 5:25–end	Prov 16:31 – 17:17
		Mt 5:13–20	I Pet 5

Mass   *of the Saint*
Wisd 2:23 – 3:9; Ps 34:1–6; Lk 17:7–10

EP		Dan 5:1–12	Prov 18:10–end
	Ps: 33	Rev 6	I Jn 1:1 – 2:6

WEDNESDAY

11   W   MP

S Martin of Tours, B (see p. 64)

MP	Ps: 34	Isa 6	Prov 20:1–22
		Mt 5:21–37	I Jn 2:7–17

Mass   *of the Saint*
Wisd 6:1–11; Ps 82; Lk 17:11–19

EP		Dan 5:13–end	Prov 22:1–16
	Ps: 119:33–56	Rev 7:1–4 & 9–end	I Jn 2:18–end

THURSDAY

12   R   MP

☐ *S Josaphat, B, M*

MP	Ps: 37	Isa 7:1–17	Prov 24:23–end
		Mt 5:38–end	I Jn 3:1–18

Mass   *of the Saint*
Wisd 7:22 – 8:1; Ps 119:89–96; Lk 17:20–25

EP		Dan 6	Prov 25
	Ps: 39, 40	Rev 8	I Jn 3:19 – 4:6

FRIDAY

13   G   MP

Feria

MP	Ps: 31	Isa 8:1–15	Prov 26:12–end
		Mt 6:1–18	I Jn 4:7–end

Mass   *of Sunday; no Gl or Cr; Common Pref (**Charles Simeon, Pr**)*
Wisd 13:1–9; Ps 19:1–4; Lk 17:26–end

EP		Dan 7:1–14	Prov 27:1–22
	Ps: 35	Rev 9:1–12	I Jn 5

SATURDAY

14   W   MP
   (or G)
   (or R)

Our Lady on Saturday (or the Feria) (☐ The Reading Martyrs, FESTUM in the Reading Vicariate)

MP	Ps: 41, 42, 43	Isa 8:16 – 9:7	Prov 30:1–16
		Mt 6:19–end	2 Jn

Mass   *Introduction Paragraph 26(b) (**Samuel Seabury, B**)*
*(**Our Lady Mother of Divine Providence**)*
Wisd 18:14–16 & 19:6–9; Ps 105; 1–5 & 35–42; Lk 18:1–8

G 1 EP of foll		Dan 7:15–end	Prov 31:10–end
	Ps: 45, 46	Rev 9:13–end	3 Jn

✠ SUNDAY

33rd SUNDAY and WEEK of YEAR (CW: 2nd BEFORE ADVENT; BCP: TRINITY 23)

15   G   MP   Ps: 96   I Sam 9:27 – 10:2a & 10:17–26   Wisd 6:1–21

R: Ps IV   Mt 13:31–35   James 2:1–13 (14–end)

     Mass   *Gl; Cr; Sunday Pref*
           CW: Dan 12:1–3; Ps 16; Heb 10:11–14 (15–18) 19–25; Mk 13:1–8
           R: Dan 12:1–3; Ps 16; Heb 10:11–14 & 18; Mk 13:24–32 (It will be soon)

     2 EP   Dan 3: (1–12) 13–30   Jer 11:1–14

                Ps: 95   Mt 13:24–30 & 36–43   Mt 18:1–20

MONDAY   *Feria (S Margaret of Scotland; ☐ S Gertrude V; S Edmund Rich)*

16   G   MP   Ps: 44   Isa 9:8 – 10:4   Eccles 1
    (or W)   Mt 7:1–12   Acts 1

     Mass   *as Friday (or of the Saint) (**Our Lady Mother of Divine Providence**)*
           I Macc 1:10–15 & 41–43 & 54–57 & 62–64; Ps 79:1–5; Lk 18:35–end

     EP   Dan 8:1–14   Eccles 2:1–23
                Ps: 47. 49   Rev 10   Acts 2:1–21

TUESDAY   *See p. 64*

17   G   MP   Ps: 48, 52   Isa 10:5–19   Eccles 3:1–15
    (or W)   Mt 7:13–end   Acts 2:22–end

     Mass   *II Macc 6:18–end; Ps 11; Lk 19:1–10*

     EP   Dan 8:15–end   Eccles 3:16 – 4:6
                Ps: 50   Rev 11:1–14   Acts 3:1 – 4:4

WEDNESDAY   *See p. 64*

18   G   MP   Ps: 119:57–80   Isa 10:20–32   Eccles 4:7–end
    (or W)   Mt 8:1–13   Acts 4:5–31

     Mass   *II Macc 7:1 & 20–31; Ps 116:10–end; Lk 19:11–28*

     EP   Dan 9:1–19   Eccles 5
                Ps: 59, 60, 67   Rev 11:15–end   Acts 4:32 – 5:11

THURSDAY   *See p. 64*

19   G   MP   Ps: 56, 57, 63   Isa 10:33 – 11:9   Eccles 6
    (or W)   Mt 8:14–22   Acts 5:12–end

     Mass   *I Macc 2:15–29; Ps 129; Lk 19:41–44*

     EP   Dan 9:20–end   Eccles 7:1–14
                Ps: 61, 62, 64   Rev 12   Acts 6:1 – 7:16

FRIDAY   *Feria (S Edmund, K, M)*

20   G   MP   Ps: 51, 54   Isa 11:10–12 end   Eccles 7:15–end
    (or R)   Mt 8:23–end   Acts 7:17–34

     Mass   *of Sunday; no Gl or Cr; Common Pref (or of the Saint) (**Priscilla Lydia Sellon, Rel**)*
           I Macc 4:36–37 & 52–59; Ps 122; Lk 19:45–end

     EP   Dan 10:1 – 11:1   Eccles 8
                Ps: 38   Rev 13:1–10   Acts 7:35 – 8:4

SATURDAY   *☐ The Presentation of the BVM (see p. 64)*

21   W   MP   Ps: 68   Isa 13:1–13   Eccles 9
              Mt 9:1–17   Acts 8:4–25

     Mass   *of our Lady (Zech 2:14–17; Ps Mag; Mt 12:46–50)*
           I Macc 6:1–13; Ps 124; Lk 20:27–34

     W   1 EP of foll   Isa 10:33 – 11:9   [Eccles 10:5–18]
                Ps: 99, 100   I Tim 6:11–16   [Acts 8:2–end]

✠ *SUNDAY* **CHRIST THE KING 34th SUNDAY and WEEK of YEAR**
(BCP: LAST AFTER TRINITY; PROPERS OF 25th)

22 W MP H: 142 (NEH 129) Isa 32:1–8 [Eccles 11 & 12]
Ps: 29, 110 Rev 3:7–22 [Heb 11:1–16]
R: Ps II Mass Gl; Cr; Proper Pref (CW page 327 = R:)
CW: Dan 7:9–10 & 13–14; Ps 93; Rev 1:4b–8; Jn 18:33–37
R: Dan 7:13–14; Ps 93; Rev 1:5–8; Jn 18:33–37
2 EP H: 419 pt 2 (NEH 386) Dan 5 [Mal 3:1–6 & 4]
Ps: 72 Jn 6:1–15 [Heb 11:17 – 12:2]

MONDAY **Feria (S Clement I, P, M; S Columbanus, Ab; IRELAND Festum)**
23 G MP Ps: 71 Isa 14:3–20 Wisd 1
(or R Mt 9:18–34 Mt 5:1–16
or W) Mass of the 5th before Christmas or the last week of the year. No Gl or Cr; Common Pref (or of the Saint)
Dan 1:1–6 & 8–20; Bless the Lord; Lk 21:1–4
EP Isa 40:1–11 Wisd 2
Ps: 72, 75 Rev 14:1–13 Rev 1

TUESDAY ☐ **S Andrew Dung Lac, Pr, Comp, Ms***
24 R MP Ps: 73 Isa 17 Wisd 3:1–9
Mt 9:35 – 10:15 Mt 5:17–end
Mass of the Saints (**Isaac Watts**)
Dan 2:31–45; Benedicite 1–3; Lk 21:5–11
EP Isa 40:12–26 Wisd 4:7–end
Ps: 74 Rev 14:14–15 end Rev 2:1–17

WEDNESDAY **Feria (S Catherine, M)***
25 G MP Ps: 77 Isa 19 Wisd 5:1–16
(or R) Mt 10:16–33 Mt 6:1–18
Mass as Monday (or of the Saint) (**Isaac Watts**)
Dan 5:1–6 & 13–14 & 16–17 & 23–28; Benedicite 4–5; Lk 21:12–19
EP Isa 40:27 – 41:7 Wisd 6:1–21
Ps: 119:81–104 Rev 16:1–11 Rev 2:18 – 3:6

THURSDAY **Feria***
26 G MP Ps: 78:1–39 Isa 21:1–12 Wisd 7:15 – 8:4
Mt 10:34 – 11:1 Mt 6:19–end
Mass as Monday
Dan 6:12–end; Benedicite 6–8a; Lk 21:20–28
EP Isa 41:8–20 Wisd 8:5–18
Ps: 78:40–end Rev 16:12–end Rev 3:7–end

FRIDAY **Feria***
27 G MP Ps: 55 Isa 22:1–14 Wisd 8:21–9 end
Mt 11:2–19 Mt 7:1–14
Mass as Monday (**Our Lady of the Miraculous Medal; of Novgorod**)
Dan 7:2–14; Benedicite 8b–10a; Lk 21:29–33
EP Isa 41:21 – 42:9 Wisd 10:15 – 11:10
Ps: 69 Rev 17 Rev 4

SATURDAY **Our Lady on Saturday (or the Feria)***
28 W MP Ps: 76, 79 Isa 24 Wisd 11:21 – 12:2
(or G) Mt 11:20–end Mt 7:15–end
Mass Introduction Paragraph 26(b)
Dan 7:15–27; Benedicite 10b–end; Lk 21:34–36
P 1 EP of Advent 1; H: 1 Isa 42:10–17 Wisd 12:12–21
Ps: 81, 84 Rev 18 Rev 5

---

* Ferial (or Sanctoral) Office Hymns, as before: BUT, during this week optionally Dies Irae: EH 351 (NEH 524). MP vv 1–8;
EP vv 9–18.

2009

NOVEMBER

29	SUNDAY	ADVENT 1
30	Monday	S Andrew

DECEMBER

1	Tuesday	Feria
2	Wednesday	Feria
3	Thursday	S Francis
4	Friday	(S John)
5	Saturday	Feria
6	SUNDAY	ADVENT 2
7	Monday	Feria
8	Tuesday	MARY
9	Wednesday	(S John)
10	Thursday	Feria
11	Friday	(S Damasus)
12	Saturday	(BVM)
13	SUNDAY	ADVENT 3
14	Monday	S John
15	Tuesday	Feria
16	Wednesday	Feria
17	Thursday	Feria
18	Friday	Feria
19	Saturday	Feria

20	SUNDAY	ADVENT 4
21	Monday	Feria
22	Tuesday	Feria
23	Wednesday	Feria
24	Thursday	Christmas Eve
25	Friday	CHRISTMAS
26	Saturday	S Stephen
27	SUNDAY	HOLY FAMILY
28	Monday	Holy Innocents
29	Tuesday	In the Octave
30	Wednesday	In the Octave
31	Thursday	In the Octave

2010

JANUARY

1	Friday	MARY
2	Saturday	Ss Basil & Gregory
3	SUNDAY	EPIPHANY transferred
4	Monday	Feria
5	Tuesday	Feria
6	Wednesday	[EPIPHANY]
7	Thursday	(S Raymund)
8	Friday	Feria
9	Saturday	Feria
10	SUNDAY	BAPTISM

HOW TO BE ECUMENICAL

JULY 2

Among Byzantines, July 2 is the Festival of the Deposition of the Protecting Robe (homo-phorion) of the Mother of God in the Basilica of Blachernae at Constantinople. In the early medieval West, the theme of the Visitation of Mary to Elizabeth suggested itself as a natural idea, in several liturgical texts, immediately after the Octave Day of SJB (July 1). In 1389 Urban VI instituted the Feast of the Visitation of the BVM for July 2, to pray for the end of the breach between East and West.

It seems to your compiler a shame that this spendidly ecumenical idea should now be ignored. Since, this year, the Visitation is suppressed on May 31 because it collides with Pentecost, might it not be a beautiful ecumenical gesture to use a votive of our Lady, or even the old Visitation Mass, on July 2? As a mark of respect to the Orthodox and to the Prayer Book Society and to the Society of S Pius X? And to show enthusiasm for the *Motu proprio* Summorum Pontificum?

S ANDREW

is a problem. Since Christ the King was transferred to the Sunday next before Advent, there has never been a possibility, where Andrew is patron, of observing him, or an external solemnity of him, on the Sundays before or after his festival.

But he is a significant ecumenical Saint. He is patron of the Ecumenical Patriarchate in Constantinople; patron of the Monastery on the Caelian Hill from which the Augustinian mission set out; so a disproportionately large number of English churches are accordingly dedicated to him. And it was on S Andrew's day 1554 that Cardinal Pole formally reconciled the Provinces of Canterbury and York to full communion with the rest of the Western Church! Unity Day!

2010 (C2)

JANUARY

	E	B	2	3	4
Sun	3	10	17	24	31
Mon	4	11	18	25	
Tue	5	12	19	26	
Wed	**6**	13	20	27	
Thu	7	14	21	28	
Fri	1	8	15	22	29
Sat	2	9	16	23	30

FEBRUARY

	5	6	1	2
Sun	7	14	21	28
Mon	1	8	15	22
Tue	2	9	16	23
Wed	3	10	**17**	24
Thu	4	11	18	25
Fri	5	12	19	26
Sat	6	13	20	27

MARCH

	3	4	5	P
Sun	7	14	21	28
Mon	1	8	15	22	29
Tue	2	9	16	23	30
Wed	3	10	17	24	31
Thu	4	11	18	25
Fri	5	12	19	26
Sat	6	13	20	27

APRIL

	E	2	3	4
Sun	**4**	11	18	25
Mon	5	12	19	26
Tue	6	13	20	27
Wed	7	14	21	28
Thu	1	8	15	22	29
Fri	2	9	16	23	30
Sat	3	10	17	24

MAY

	5	6	7	P	T
Sun	2	9	16	**23**	30
Mon	3	10	17	24	31
Tue	4	11	18	25	
Wed	5	12	19	26	
Thu	6	**13**	20	27	
Fri	7	14	21	28	
Sat	1	8	15	22	29

JUNE

	10	11	12	13
Sun	6	13	20	27
Mon	7	14	21	28
Tue	1	8	15	22	**29**
Wed	2	9	16	23	30
Thu	**3**	10	17	24
Fri	4	11	18	25
Sat	5	12	19	26

JULY

	14	15	16	17
Sun	4	11	18	25
Mon	5	12	19	26
Tue	6	13	20	27
Wed	7	14	21	28
Thu	1	8	15	22	29
Fri	2	9	16	23	30
Sat	3	10	17	24	31

AUGUST

	18	19	A	21	22
Sun	1	8	**15**	22	29
Mon	2	9	16	23	30
Tue	3	10	17	24	31
Wed	4	11	18	25	
Thu	5	12	19	26	
Fri	6	13	20	27	
Sat	7	14	21	28	

SEPTEMBER

	23	24	25	26
Sun	5	12	19	26
Mon	6	13	20	27
Tue	7	14	21	28
Wed	1	8	15	22	29
Thu	2	9	16	23	30
Fri	3	10	17	24
Sat	4	11	18	25

OCTOBER

	27	28	29	30	31
Sun	3	10	17	24	31
Mon	4	11	18	25	
Tue	5	12	19	26	
Wed	6	13	20	27	
Thu	7	14	21	28	
Fri	1	8	15	22	29
Sat	2	9	16	23	30

NOVEMBER

	32	33	CK	1
Sun	7	14	21	28
Mon	1	8	15	22	29
Tue	2	9	16	23	30
Wed	3	10	17	24
Thu	4	11	18	25
Fri	5	12	19	26
Sat	6	13	20	27

DECEMBER

	2	3	4	HF
Sun	5	12	19	26
Mon	6	13	20	27
Tue	7	14	21	28
Wed	1	8	15	22	29
Thu	2	9	16	23	30
Fri	3	10	17	24	31
Sat	4	11	18	**25**

Sundays are numbered 'of the Year' or 'in Advent' or 'of Lent' or 'of Easter.'